TELL the TRUTH

The Whole Gospel
to the Whole Person
by Whole People

A TRAINING MANUAL ON THE MESSAGE AND
METHOD OF GOD-CENTERED WITNESSING
TO A GRACE-CENTERED GOSPEL

WILL METZGER

REVISED AND EXPANDED　•　STUDY GUIDE INCLUDED

IVP Books

An imprint of InterVarsity Press
Downers Grove, Illinois

InterVarsity Press
P.O. Box 1400, Downers Grove, IL 60515-1426
World Wide Web: www.ivpress.com
E-mail: email@ivpress.com

InterVarsity Press® is the book-publishing division of InterVarsity Christian Fellowship/USA®, a student movement active on campus at hundreds of universities, colleges and schools of nursing in the United States of America, and a member movement of the International Fellowship of Evangelical Students. For information about local and regional activities, write Public Relations Dept., InterVarsity Christian Fellowship/USA, 6400 Schroeder Rd., P.O. Box 7895, Madison, WI 53707-7895, or visit the IVCF website at <www.intervarsity.org>.

Cover illustration: Jane Yeomans/Photonica

ISBN-10: 0-8308-2322-0
ISBN-13: 978-0-8308-2322-2

Printed in the United States of America ∞

Library of Congress Cataloging-in-Publication Data

Metzger, Will, 1940-
  Tell the truth: the whole Gospel to the whole person by whole people
: a training manual on the message and method of God-centered witnessing
/Will Metzger.—Rev. and expanded ed.
      p. cm.
Includes bibliographical references.
  ISBN 0-8308-2322-0 (pbk.: alk. paper)
  1. Witness bearing (Christianity) 2. Evangelistic work. I. Title.
  BV4520 .M48 2002
  248'.5—dc21

                                                                    2002009251

P	24	23	22	21	20	19	18	17	16	15	14	13	12	11	10
Y	21	20	19	18	17	16	15	14	13	12	11	10	09	08	

Acknowledgments

What follows is motivated by
a desire to help others and
a sense of debt owed to

GOD
for his glorious, gracious
and free salvation;

MY TEACHERS
for the rich heritage of Christian truth
they have passed on to me through
their words and writings;

MY FAMILY AND FRIENDS
for helping me see that truth
is not theoretical.

CONTENTS

Our Fears
Wholeness in Attitudes and Motivation
Prayer and the Spirit

No Perfect Methods, but Help for Starting
Different People, Different Places
Getting Started
Conversation Turners
Conversation with a Direction
The Uninterested
Using a Summary of the Gospel
Bloom Where You Are Planted
Practical Effects of Grace-Centered Evangelism
Our Goal: Disciples
Plans to Obey

APPENDIXES

Training Materials for Learning God-Centered Evangelism

I. The Kind of Person God Uses in Evangelism

II. Preparing Your Testimony

III. Learning to Say What You Mean

IV. Being a Good Listener

V. How to Ask Good Questions

VI. Friendship Evangelism

VII. Language Barriers

VIII. Four Role Plays for Learning to Witness

IX. Evaluating the Content of a Gospel Presentation

X. Questions Non-Christians Ask

XI. Guidelines for Organizing Contact Evangelism

XII. Spiritual Interest Questionnaire

XIII. Schedule for a God-Centered
Evangelism Training Seminar Weekend

Learning the Gospel Diagram "Come Home"

Preface to the Revised and Expanded Edition

Picture this: a runner in ancient Greece arrives exhausted before the emperor. Gasping, he blurts out, "My lord, I was given an urgent message, but . . . I'm afraid I have forgotten what it was!"

This book, originally published in 1981, was written to address a concern that many Christians, entrusted with the gospel message, had forgotten the message and their responsibility to accurately convey it. I wish I could now say that the message has been remembered. The recovery of a God/grace-centered gospel, or, as James Boice has put it, a "rediscovery of the doctrines that shook the world," is imperative.

This revision includes an expansion of two of the topics: grace and worship. In addition, I desired to offer a new outline of a God-centered gospel for training Christians to share their faith with non-Christians.

GRACE

As my passion for God-centered evangelism grew, I longed to emphasize the centrality of sovereign, saving grace. Why? Because the quickening grace of God in salvation completely exalts God. Grace is God-honoring and humanity-humbling. A clear understanding that success in evangelism is a result of God's initiating grace frees the evangelist from fear of rejection by others. Indeed evangelism is impossible without grace, for grace is what frees nonbelievers from their enslavement to sin.

Grace continues its effect beyond our initial liberation from unbelief and continues to energize Christians. After nonbelievers become Christians, the gracious power of the Holy Spirit upholds them throughout their Christian journey. Saved under God-centered and grace-oriented evangelism, they have a wonderful framework for a Christian life of God-centered, grace-oriented sanctification. The majesty of grace in salvation brings honor to the Father who designed it, prestige to the Son who accomplished it and fame to the Holy Spirit who effects it.

I quickly came to realize that I couldn't develop the marvel of grace without explaining the horror of sin. Grace only functions as grace when it comes to people who have absolutely nothing to recommend them as a candidate for God's favor. People deserve the very opposite—his disfavor in this life and for eternity. Grace is magnified when I see myself as undeserving. I have no right to and no claim on God's mercy. God is not obligated to love me. He does not exist just to make me happy. Grace is highlighted by my inability to keep from sinning. Salvation by my efforts is unattainable, no matter how hard I try to improve myself.

I didn't want to write more about sin, but it couldn't be helped. There is a type of love that arises in response to the beauty, value and other commendable qualities of its recipient. Grace is a different kind of love, one that exists although there is nothing commendable in the recipient. Grace only functions as such if its objects are the undeserving and the unable. As I wrestled with touching nonbelievers with love by my actions and attitudes, it was this doctrine of grace that inspired me to witness and connected me with both their minds and hearts. Fantastic grace.

WORSHIP

My entry into teachings on grace brought me into deeper worship. Instead of theology being cold, intellectual, academic and impractical, the doctrine of grace was warm, personal, inspiring and satisfying. It was functional, shaping the God-honoring methods to fit with the God-honoring gospel I was proclaiming. Worshiping an autonomous and graceful Creator-Redeemer freed me to initiate personal evangelism and sustain evangelistic zeal—two major issues that need to be addressed when helping people witness. Reprogramming Christians to experience a macro God through worship led to a recognition that much evangelism training focuses on me-centered techniques and a reshaped gospel emphasizing only "what's in it for me." God-centeredness is the basis for the grace that saves people. Without grace-full God-centeredness, evangelism will evolve into nice people being nice to other people in hopes that they will be nice to God, a compromised gospel with a mild God who exists to benefit me. This results in nice "Christians" who are unconverted, not knowing the joy of forgiving and empowering grace, and unready to meet God on that final day.

COME HOME

I have decided to revamp an outline of a God-centered gospel to have a theme that unifies the points, a diagram to illustrate our road in life, a Bible story and illustration from life, and more personalizing of the objective truths of the gospel. There are two versions: the Amplified version for training Christians and the Simplified version for telling non-Christians. The extensiveness of this gospel summary may surprise you. I do not apologize for this. I am convinced that God purposes our speaking the *truth* in love as the predestined means of salvation. If all Christians learned these truths, their witness would be more God-honoring and their spiritual growth enhanced as they daily reexperience a gospel of grace. The gospel is for *Christians*. God may use a minimal amount of truth to quicken someone; that's his prerogative. Our privilege is to enter into the depths of the whole gospel, sinking roots into that life-giving water. I hope that "Come Home" will help Christians to be thoroughly knowledgeable of the life-giving truth content of the gospel. Then, not speaking misleading half-truths but the whole truth in love, they can lift up the living Jesus and let him draw many to himself for salvation.

This is a book about the scandal of sovereign salvation. In it, I blame God for salvation, in the sense that he is totally responsible. He organized a rescue operation within the Trinity—designing, supplying, accomplishing and restoring those who were in peril. Our triune God is the Author and Fulfiller, the Originator and Consummator, the Creator and the Redeemer. It's all God's fault—a grace that gives response-ability to the spiritually dead.

The Lord of the universe is a *lover* who woos spiritual adulterers like you and me, providing everything needed to reconstitute a relationship.

"Therefore I am now going to allure her;
I will lead her into the desert
and speak tenderly to her.
There I will . . .
make the valley of Achor [trouble] a door of hope.
There she will sing. . . .

"In that day," declares the LORD,
"you will call me 'my husband.' . . .
I will betroth you to me forever
. . . in righteousness and justice,
in love and compassion.
I will betroth you in faithfulness,
and you will acknowledge the LORD. . . .

I will show my love to the one I called 'Not my loved one.'
I will say to those called 'Not my people,' 'You are my people';
and they will say, 'You are my God.'" (Hos 2:14-16, 19-20, 23)

I want to express my deep appreciation to Mrs. Kathy Wargo whose ability to translate my handwriting and whose efficiency in computer skill made it possible to bring this revision to you, and to Jim Hoover and Allison Rieck for editing. The prayers of friends, family and especially students at the University of Delaware undergirded my writing.

Together, let us make God's name famous.

Sola Gracia Dei
By God's Grace Alone

Introduction

The Whole Gospel to the Whole Person Wholly by Grace by Whole People: Our Task in Evangelism

H̲ave you ever been stymied by evangelism? Do you feel you are tossed between two unacceptable alternatives and can't find your niche? On the one side you see Christians who have great rapport with others but don't say much about Jesus Christ. On the other side are those who are always "giving out the gospel" but seem to know nothing about genuine friendship. The frustration of bumping into these two extremes in Christian circles is very real.

This book is designed to help you "show and tell" the gospel in a way honoring to God, helpful to others and liberating for you. It is neither a plan for buttonholing people nor a plea for being just a nice person who lets others come to you if and when they want to talk religion. Rather, its goal is to help you recover the theological content of the gospel because *only as your view of God's active grace in salvation is changed can you find the confidence, joy and gratitude to undergird a new evangelistic lifestyle.*

WHAT IS THE BIBLICAL MODEL?

I was one of those Christians who believed in friendship evangelism, but for me it turned out to be all friendship and little evangelism. Motivation was not a problem for me. I had gone through a life-changing conversion to Christ during my high school years, and Jesus Christ was very real to me. I had a strong desire to tell others about him, yet most of my models for doing so tended toward one or the other of the extremes I mentioned above. I had other liabilities: my own lack of Bible knowledge, my personal immaturity, my tendency to view God as existing only for my benefit and a fear of being rejected. With those drawbacks I began my personal pilgrimage to find out what it meant to be a witness for Christ.

At first, witnessing seemed so simple. I knew the message and I knew who needed it. What could be so confusing or difficult about that? I found out all too soon. I didn't have a clear grasp of the *content* of the gospel. Therefore, my Christian life was stunted, and my ability to winsomely expose nonbelievers to Christ was handicapped.

I was soon beset by a barrage of advice. I was told I should witness by showing others a good time, bringing my high school acquaintances to fun gatherings at church or in the inoffensive setting of a home. The evening would end with a challenging talk. That sounded easy. Others would articulate the gospel for me.

In college I met Christians who emphasized a more direct approach: I should invite anyone and everyone to a small group Bible study or a talk by a layperson in a "neutral" setting. Nonbelievers should be confronted directly with the Scriptures. *Well,* I said to myself, *that sounds reasonable. Perhaps this is the approach to take.* Yet these seemed impersonal and manipulative. I hungered for an effective evangelistic method. Training seminars and booklets abounded.

Not too much later my confusion was intensified because I came in contact with still other Christians who exhorted me to evangelize by the apostolic pattern of preaching: I should bring my friends to hear gifted speakers at church or at special meetings. Still, I was relying on others to do the talking.

Then I had a grand awakening. I saw that *I* was to witness, not just bring people to others who would witness for me. Fearful, and yet convinced of my duty, I looked for help. Again, I met some Christians who were very zealous and explained to me an entirely new set of ideas and techniques for personal evangelism. I was motivated by an awesome sense of responsibility and increasing guilt because I was led to believe that I was unspiritual—or at least unfaithful—if I hadn't "led someone to Christ." So I uncritically grabbed onto various methods of witnessing. This approach did involve me in speaking the truth to others. Yet the criterion of success was a numbers game: counting those who prayed, raised a hand or filled out a card.

I was a failure. I had started out with misgivings about the appropriateness of the slick techniques advocated by various "successful" evangelists. I ended up with misgivings as to whether they fit in with Scripture. My concerns led me to some basic questions of theology.

Uncertainties whirled in my mind. Could a person be motivated to witness, yet actually dishonor God and misrepresent his message through ignorance or manipulation? Was I motivated by guilt or the expectations of others? Was I trying to make excuses for my lack of enthusiasm and success? How could I limit God's use of me to just "friends" and "invitations to meetings"? How could I deny that God's providence brought people into my life, even if for just a few minutes?

I began to feel like I was caught in a revolving door. Certain questions kept twirling me around. In what way could I lovingly speak to those (even strangers) God brings across my path? Why are the converts of different Christian groups often distinguished by certain personality types? Am I evangelizing only when I see conversions? What are the essential elements of our message? Do I unite with anyone in evangelism because of the great need of people to hear or because of a mutual commitment to gospel doctrines? Why is there such reticence to examine the biblical basis for methods of witness (especially if they are the ones our church uses)?

Why is there such disagreement, confusion and vagueness among those who witness, even on some very basic elements of the gospel. For example, do we just present Christ as Savior or also as Lord to the unbeliever? Is repentance and teaching the law of God part of the gospel? Why is the new birth necessary? What actually happens in the new birth? What is our part in salvation, and what is God's? How can a person know he or she has been born again? The gospel—is it a set of doctrines or a person? If God has done all he can and now leaves the appropriation of salvation to our willpower, how can spiritually dead people respond?

It boggled my mind that once Christians passed beyond the common notion that everyone needs Christ for salvation, there was confusion and even contradiction on what triggered the new birth—our faith and repentance or God's enabling Spirit? These are haunting, important, fundamental questions. How could the majority of evangelicals be so oblivious to the need to research what is the biblical gospel? I could see there were many wrong methods, and I began to despair that I could ever find a way to witness that would take its shape from truth, not pragmatism or the sovereignty of our will in salvation.

All my questions could be boiled down to one: what was the way to witness that would be shaped by a high view of a Creator-Redeemer God who does not merely make salvation available but actually empowers a person to respond by repenting and receiving?

In spite of the unhelpfulness of the advice initially given to me about personal evangelism, I have to admit that the resurgent interest in this topic in evangelical circles is healthy. Who can deny that there has been an increased participation in evangelism? Who could find fault with the new evangelistic concern of many Christians? They have made great sacrifices in money, time and energy. People are using modern media creatively. I am truly thankful for these things. Yet something bothers me—and I believe others also have an uneasy conscience. Could some aspects of contemporary evangelism lack biblical integrity?

METHODOLOGY FLOWS FROM THEOLOGY

Before we can find an answer to this central question we must evaluate the current practices in evangelism. Let me paraphrase Francis Schaeffer's address before the World Congress on Evangelism in Berlin (1966): It is just because we are committed to evangelism that we must speak in antithesis at times. If we do not make clear by word and practice our position for truth and against false doctrine, we are building a wall between the next generation and the gospel. The unity of evangelicals should be on the basis of truth and not on evangelism as such. If this is not so, "success" in evangelism can result in weakening Christianity. Any consideration of methods is secondary to this central principle. Though we need to evaluate doctrine and methods, however, we are not to judge the motives of others.

In part one of this book I will pose pertinent questions concerning the theology underlying the methodology in modern evangelism. I do not pretend to give an exhaustive theology of evangelism. I speak as a family member to those within the family of God. May we look into our hearts and into the Bible to find how to be better change agents. I hope that my analysis will lead to constructive dialogue and modification for all of us. Should any tradition, technique or person be beyond our evaluation by scriptural standards? I think not.

If it is true that there are serious differences among evangelicals on the message and methods of evangelism, then we must ask, to what extent are these differences justified? If the differences are simply due to the different audience we are reaching or the variety of gifts God has given us, these differences are not bad. But if in evangelism we are just being loyal to our tradition, molding truth to our personality, diluting the gospel or manipulating people, we are wrong. If we are convinced there is a *theological* foundation for our methodology, we may be justified in evangelizing accordingly. Then our difference is a matter of our conscience bound by what we conceive Scripture teaches. A scriptural doctrine of evangelism should be the controlling element in any practice of evangelism.

Nevertheless, even when we can articulate a theological base for our evangelism, I do not believe our responsibility has ended until we compare our doctrinal interpretation with that of others and in humility be willing to rethink what the Holy Spirit is telling us in Scripture. Not to do so is to say that we cannot learn from each other. It is to deny that new light can break forth on our understanding of the Scripture. It is to limit the Holy Spirit in communicating to us through other Christians. It is to evangelize a certain way out of tradition and not out of conviction.

In short, to be unwilling to evaluate our evangelism in the light of the Bible is to not take Scripture seriously. We could end up being less than honest with each other, allowing unbelievers to be misled and frustrating those who wish to learn to witness. We could condemn our children and the church to untold problems. We could be dishonoring the God of the gospel. We must take a thorough look at current evangelistic practice to see if we who witness to Christ have a balanced and whole gospel.

In part two, then, I consider what the total effect of the gospel should be on our lives and on the lives of those we evangelize. Evaluation is again necessary and right in order to determine why there are so many "false" conversions. A commitment to Christ is not a mere prayer and that's it. Rather, it is a *conversion* in the true sense of the word; our whole lives are changed. Paul says we become new creations. I discuss how this change must affect our entire being—our minds, our wills and our emotions—the whole person.

Part three plumbs the depths of how the grace of God operates in salvation. Grace uproots three myths—my inalienable rights, my human goodness, my free will—that act as barriers, shielding people from the full impact of the gospel. These barriers are penetrated by the scandal of grace. Only a grace-centered gospel saves and gives *response*-ability, which solves the nonbeliever's main problem. This results in passionate worship, which is the goal of evangelism—not just decisions but fervent disciples.

But our responsibility does not end with correct understanding of the new birth. We must put that gospel into action. We are called to obedience in telling the truth to others. Therefore, part four is devoted to the practice of witnessing, plus some practical ideas on how to get started. We are to be whole (complete and real) people. Finally, in the appendixes are numerous worksheets that can be duplicated for training yourself and others, a God-centered diagram of the gospel, and a comment on healthy controversy.

EVANGELISM: WON BY ONE

I have intentionally confined my subject to personal witnessing. This is not because other forms are invalid but because, as the evangelical statesman Carl Henry contends, a one-to-one approach initiated by every believer still holds the best promise of evangelizing the earth in our century.[1] Renowned Yale historian Kenneth S. Latourette reinforces this concept when he reminds us that "the chief agents in the expansion of Christianity appear not to have been those who made it a profession . . . but men and women who carried on their livelihood in some purely secular manner and spoke of their faith to those they met in this natural fashion."[2]

Some may question the validity of stressing person-to-person evangelism. Perhaps their questions stem from the many abuses of this approach. But legitimate misgivings should not cause you to neglect the Scripture emphasis on speaking to others. An overreaction to extremes of individualism has made some people promote exclusively the corporate nature of Christian witness. "May they be brought to complete unity to let the world know that you sent me and have loved them even as you have loved me" (Jn 17:23).

The body of believers, united out of various economic and ethnic backgrounds while retaining individual personalities and interests, should be like a flashing neon sign to the world. The amazing unity in the diversity of Christ's body can convince unbelievers that Jesus Christ was sent by God. A dynamic group of vibrant Christians forms the base for ongoing evangelism, yet if individuals in the group are not verbalizing the gospel, the net result will still be weak evangelism. Although not readily admitted, reasons for downgrading personal initiatives in witnessing might be pride, a critical spirit or an unnecessary fear of offending, or even the well-meant attitude that "glorifying God in my vocation" is enough.

In Scripture we find many examples of the gospel being spread in a person-to-person fashion. Jesus himself constantly converses with people to whom he is providentially led. He brings the word of life to them in the midst of their daily life. Christ promises the disciples that they will become fishers of men and then twice sends his followers out in pairs to spread the glad tidings (Mk 6:7-13; Lk 10:1-24). In the early church the average Christian is found gossiping the gospel (Acts 8:1, 4). A leader in the church, Philip, is commanded by God to leave a successful ministry in order to speak to an individual who is searching (Acts 8:26-40). Paul emphasizes the responsibility of all believers to be Christ's ambassadors and says that the ministry of reconciliation has been given to them (2 Cor 5:17-20). God gives greater ability in evangelism to certain people not in order that they might do it all but in order to equip each believer in the body to do this ministry (Eph 4:11-12).

In our world probably 99.9 percent of all Christians are not in the ministry. Unless everyone engages in evangelism—praying, initiating and fervently speaking the gospel—not much will happen. New birth into God's kingdom usually involves people as spiritual midwives. Like little children, we "show and tell" the gospel. Inherent in every approach to evangelism (small group Bible study, preaching, use of various media and so on) is the need for personal encounter. More often than not, people must speak with non-Christians in order to clarify and urge them to believe. Aren't you a believer today because someone reached out personally to you? It is Jane and Joe Christian who are Christ's ambassadors; they are the ones whom God appoints to tell the gospel. Open your mouth. God will fill it with his words.

In conclusion, let me add a word of encouragement to those struggling with being faithful in evangelism. Nothing has the potential for producing more guilt among Christians than this subject (unless it's sex!). I can guarantee the reaction I will get when I speak on this topic: eyes lower, feet shuffle, hands fidget. There is usually some tension-releasing laughter. But all these reactions are unnecessary. There is hope, encouragement and liberation to be found when evangelism is built on a God-centered gospel. The doorway into a hopeful and joyful witness is found by focusing on God as Creator and Redeemer.

Throughout this book I will lay a theological foundation: The whole gospel . . . wholly by grace. The platform on which we can build a life of evangelism will be God's sovereignty. We shall see the skillful interweaving of each person of the Trinity working in harmony in salvation. The Father has planned salvation. Christ has accomplished it. The Spirit will inevitably apply it. Therefore, no seat will be empty at the banquet table in the kingdom. All are assigned, with name cards in place, for they heard the inner call of compelling love and came to feast. God always goes before us as we witness. As we learn and tell the truth, may we find our theology turning into doxology!

PART ONE

The Whole Gospel
Content of Our Message

1

Personal Witness as Planting and Watering

I waited expectantly as the speaker began his comments. His topic was evangelism. I was taken aback when he started using the phrase "soul winning" to describe his evangelistic practice. "Okay," I thought to myself, "so this impersonal phrase grates you. Let's see if the rest of the talk gets any better." It didn't. What followed was a string of success stories about people he had led to Christ. He reinforced his point by citing famous stars and athletes as victorious evangelists. Then came an emphasis on techniques and manipulation of people reminiscent of cults I had studied.

His crowning illustration of how to "get the gospel out to every person" was a detailed set of instructions on how to roll up a gospel tract in such a way that it could be accurately dropped from the window of a moving car. The object was for it to drift to the feet of a hitchhiker—as you passed him by! He justified this technique on the basis of the startling story of a young man who was converted by this sort of "gospel bomb." The speaker's conclusion, "It works," sounded to me like the unbiblical idea "the end justifies the means." As I left the church that night I wondered, *Instead of sending his Son, why didn't God just send a tract?*

Perhaps closer to your experience is the evangelistic approach of majoring on the conscious (felt) needs of people (loneliness, lack of love, hurt, stress, discouragement and so on) and molding Jesus into a supplier of their desires. Often the deep sinful nature of their selfishness is never addressed. Well-meaning Christians dilute the gospel into a bandage for surface wounds and medicine for selfish wishes. The deeper need of reconciliation with their Maker on his terms of unconditional surrender is omitted. Legitimate desires (to be loved, have health, not be lonely) can become idols.

WHAT IS WITNESSING?

We have good cause to wonder what kind of a gospel is being conveyed in our day. I am referring not only to individual speakers (this man was a professor of evangelism at a Christian school) but to seminars and books that purport to train Christians in evangelism. I'm embarrassed at the shoddy methods and anemic view of God prevalent among evangelicals. We need a growing concern for a God-honoring witness to his grand gospel. Before we can make any headway, however, we should define our terms. What do we mean by *evangelism* and *witness?*

In thinking of *witnessing,* we have to walk between a narrow and a broad definition. Narrowly defined, *witnessing* is confined to a rehearsal of a few gospel facts in the hearing of a nonbeliever. Broadly defined, it is whatever we do as Christians before the watching world. Neither of these definitions is satisfactory. The first narrows witness to only our lips; the second broadens it to just being nice. Both our words *and* our ways are inextricably bound together in witness. It is easy to excuse ourselves by saying either "Well, I told her the gospel!" or "I just live my life before others." These two extremes seem to have developed more in reaction to each other than on any biblical basis. What might be a more balanced view?

The main design for each man and woman is not "to be a super soul-winner night and day." As the Westminster Catechism says, it is "to glorify God and enjoy Him forever." This means that we, as whole people, are to enjoy God, starting now, and keep his honor in focus in all that we do. Clearly the way we live is a primary aspect of our witness. Yet our life is to be coupled with telling God's truth. People need to be told *who* makes our lives different. Our lives, then, will illuminate the truth we express to nonbelievers. The airplane of Christian witness has two wings: our lives (conduct) and our lips (conversation).

To remain silent and let others interpret our actions is wrong; God himself did not do this. The pivotal points of God's redemptive action in history are accompanied with verbal revelation. God wants us to understand the meaning of his actions. Likewise, we must speak—and speak of Christ—even if we sense our own inconsistency of life. We must speak even when we do not know much about the Bible. We must speak even when it is inconvenient. God is bigger than our sins, our ignorance, our pride. He will honor his word in our mouths.

Nevertheless, at times our actions do speak louder than our words. When John describes our commission to witness, he says that as the Father sent the Son, so we are sent to others (Jn 20:21). God didn't send a tract; he prepared a body. Likewise, God has prepared your life and personality to demonstrate him. We need to be creative and selfless in our love to others. We need to learn how to be friends as well as perceive the needs of others and *do* something for them. Much of Jesus' witness was in response to a question following an act of kindness or a miracle. But we need to make sure that we are not condescending. We should allow others to help us, let them minister to us. Jesus asked the Samaritan woman to give him some water. We need to learn to be human and treat others as God's image-bearers. If we are friendly only as long as someone is interested in discussing the gospel, we don't know much about friendship. We need to listen and seek to serve, not just talk.

How does the Bible define *witnessing?* In the Great Commission as expressed by Luke, we have central truths to which we are witnesses (Lk 24:48). At the ascension, Christ's last words command the disciples to witness about him, a person (Acts 1:8). In the Gospels we see the writers selecting incidents from the life of Christ to convey the gospel. The background for the word *witness* is the law court. To witness is to testify that Christ is who he said he is. Such testimony is a means to an end—to give an eyewitness account of the truth (1 Jn 1:1-3).

Studying in the Swiss Alps at L'Abri in the 1960s with Francis and Edith Schaeffer, my wife and I had little idea that God would use us to help someone find God's grace. A young man, Chris, arrived one afternoon when our community was working in the gardens and carpentry shop, cleaning and cooking. He was a student of religion at the University of Pennsylvania, touring Europe to learn about life. He eagerly joined in with those of us from every continent who had come to search for truth. He liked the intellectual stimulation, friendliness and high morals, and seemed confident in himself.

In this man's eyes, Jesus was intriguing but unnecessary to living the good life. One day I asked him to read Paul's account of why he had transferred his confidence from self-righteousness to a gift-righteousness. Pondering this question, Chris began to spend time alone, reading Scripture and asking God to make Christ real to him. Later that summer we parted with a promise to see each other back in Philadelphia.

At the same time that I was getting to know Chris, a young woman named Franny, whom I knew from Philadelphia, was also studying at L'Abri. Franny had been raised in a reputable New England family and had moved to Philadelphia two years previously. Following her religious upbringing was important to her, so she sought out a church with the refined atmosphere and high liturgy to which she was accustomed. It wasn't long before her cousin, who had become a Christian, contacted her and introduced her to his Christian friends. Providentially, one of them belonged to a group of students at Westminster Theological Seminary who had a burden for evangelism. Each Sunday these students would invite friends to church and then to the pastor's home that night for a discussion. Franny protested that if anyone was a Christian, she certainly was.

Slowly, however, realization of her unbelief began to dawn on her. In her own words, "I found myself confronted with my self-delusion at each church service as I said the Apostles' Creed. I got to a point where, after I began 'I believe in God the Father Almighty,' I became silent for the rest of the recitation. I admitted I didn't believe anything else in that creed. I had

come to realize that my supposed faith was nothing more than a
dition—a warm nostalgia."

She began to search in earnest. Again in God's providence, he brought a speaker and author to the city—and he was from her religious tradition! His name was J. I. Packer. Eagerly she attended his lectures on the epistle to the Ephesians. She was dumbfounded by the depth and richness of Scripture and by the fact that her own church (Episcopal) had once been united in teaching the importance of new birth. At the meetings she was introduced to a Baptist business executive who mailed her a copy of Bishop J. C. Ryle's book on the confessional statement of her church (The Thirty-Nine Articles), which she began to read. Several weeks later, Franny called me. "Could you come to my apartment as soon as possible? This is all making sense. I believe! I want to talk to you." This is the background that later led to her visit to L'Abri with two of her Christian girlfriends.

While at L'Abri, Franny caught Chris's eye, and they agreed to see each other back in Philadelphia. Since I was serving the students at the University of Pennsylvania through InterVarsity Christian Fellowship, Chris joined the group and started going to church. He and Franny, both new Christians, began to date and soon were married. As the years have passed, our friendship has continued. In a unique twist to this story of evangelism, Chris joined the staff of InterVarsity Christian Fellowship and is now my supervisor! How I long for those reading this book to be used by God in bringing others to Christ. Aside from worshiping God, there is nothing else in this world that is more deeply fulfilling.

THE DIFFERENCE BETWEEN THE GOSPEL AND OUR TESTIMONY

The content of our message is Christ and God, not our journey to faith. Our personal testimony may be included, but witnessing is more than reciting our spiritual autobiography. Specific truths about a specific person are the subject of our proclamation. A message has been committed to us—a word of reconciliation to the world (2 Cor 5:19).

Good evaluation questions to keep in mind after hearing a testimony are "How much did I learn about Christ? How much about the speaker? Which was more prominent?" When people are very much in love, you find them expressing many things about their loved one and not always focusing on themselves. I still remember the change that came over an especially shy girl every time she got the chance to talk about her boyfriend. You couldn't keep her quiet! It is the same with a healthy testimony about our lover Christ. (See appendix A.II.)

Why is it important to distinguish between gospel truths and testimony? In an age of religious pluralism, we find many who are testifying. I'll never forget the time when I had been speaking to a young man about the change Christ had made in my life. His sincere response was, "Listening to New Age music does the same for me." What would you have said in reply? Some people recommend faith in a guru or in a technique of meditation or in self or in relationships. Many cite experiences of a change in life. If our witness has no truth content, we can expect the typical response: "That's interesting. I'm glad for you, but what you have isn't for me." Can you imagine the apostle Paul saying, "I just have this warm feeling in my heart"?

Faith is not to be looked on as a separate entity ("I wish I had your faith") but as an ability given by God that is valid only because it connects us with Jesus Christ. "It is worth noting that the New Testament Christians never attempted to establish the truth of Christianity on their inward experiences. . . . To put it another way, never do we find Paul trying to prove the truth of Christianity to others 'because of the difference it has made in my life.' "[1]

Distinguishing Our Role from God's

The crucial thing to remember in evangelism is the distinction between our responsibility and God's. Our task is to faithfully present the gospel message by our lives and our lips.[2] Any definition of our task that includes results is confusing our responsibility with God's prerogative, which is regeneration. Picture a fragile, thin-stemmed wine glass. Now think of a rock the size of a basketball. Imagine lifting that rock and dropping it into that delicately constructed glass. Shattered. We too will be broken if we try to carry something that only God can carry. We plant and water; God gives the increase (1 Cor 3:5-9). We *may* reap—but only when God has brought the grain to maturity.

The question of whether or not we are evangelizing cannot be settled by counting the number of converts. In that case, many faithful missionaries who have seen no converts from years of labor would have to be rebuked for lack of witnessing. To define *evangelism* in terms of results is too broad. Then its essence becomes a quantitative measurement: if there are no results, then no evangelism has been done. I do not mean to suggest we should not evaluate both our results and nonresults, building a holy dissatisfaction with nonresults. We are not content with never catching any fish when fishing (Lk 5:4-11) or having empty seats at God's kingdom banquet (Lk 14:15-24). Have you ever pleaded for lost people with deep sorrow as did Jesus and Paul? Have you wept?

It is just as misleading to narrow our definition of *evangelism* to the type of meeting, literature, appeal or Bible passage used. If we did this, then we would be embarrassed to find little evangelism done in the New Testament times. Can you find a biblical example of the methods employed in today's typical evangelistic rally and appeal?[3] Rather, we need to evaluate all supposed evangelism by the question "What truth was taught?" If we think wrongly about our definition of *evangelism*, we are likely to act wrongly in our methods of evangelism. (See appendix A.IX.)

In the Bible we have many examples of witnessing from which we can draw numerous principles. Studying the way Jesus interacted with people and the way the apostles witnessed in the Spirit can help in our own witness. From these models of witnessing, however, I will mention only one. The passage is an account of Paul's witness before Agrippa (Acts 26:16-29), and it highlights the characteristic of bold, conscience-directed speech.

Paul describes himself as appointed by God as a servant and a witness (a good combination to keep in mind). In a series of striking contrasts, the goal of his mission is summarized as nothing less than conversion. Repentance and evidence of it are his major concerns. Paul centers on fulfillment of Scripture and Christ's death and resurrection. He speaks to Agrippa's conscience—an element often neglected in witnessing. Genuine witnessing involves persuading people to convert but stops short of evaluating the success only in terms of results.

There are two main ways that we can study the presentation of the gospel. First, we can study the Bible itself, especially the book of Acts, the Epistles and the life of Christ. Second, we can study the history of the Christian church. That is, we can look at the revivals and, in particular, the people whose preaching has been honored in the conversion of others. From such study, Martyn Lloyd-Jones has drawn the following foundational principles for evangelism:

1. The supreme object of the work of evangelism is to glorify God, not to save souls.

2. The only power that can do this work is the Holy Spirit, not our own strength.

3. The one and only medium through which the Spirit works is the Scriptures; therefore, we "reason out of the Scriptures" like Paul did.

4. These preceding principles give us the true motivation for evangelism—a zeal for God and a love for others.

5. There is a constant danger of heresy through a false zeal and employment of unscriptural methods.[4]

Understanding that God, not us, is the evangelizer (the one who brings results) is wonderfully liberating. This makes witnessing an adventure in which we merely ride along with God as he moves out. We don't force open any doors, just walk through the ones he opens! In *The Lion, the Witch, and the Wardrobe,* C. S. Lewis allegorically describes the sensation of riding on Christ (symbolized as the lion Aslan) over the wall into the enemy's territory, as he confronts the power of sin to bring rebirth.

> "And now," said Aslan presently . . . "we have a long journey to go. *You must ride on me.*" . . . And with a great heave he rose underneath [the children] and then shot off, faster than any horse could go, down hill and into the thick of the forest.
>
>   That ride was perhaps the most wonderful thing that happened to them in Narnia. Have you ever had a gallop on a horse? Think of that; and then take away the heavy noise of the hoofs and the jingle of the bits and imagine instead the almost noiseless padding of the great paws. Then imagine instead of the black or grey or chestnut back of the horse the soft roughness of golden fur, and the mane flying back in the wind. And then imagine you are going about twice as fast as the fastest racehorse. But this is a mount that doesn't need to be guided and never grows tired. He rushes on and on. . . .

It was nearly midday when they found themselves looking down a steep hillside at a castle. . . . No face looked over the battlements and the gates were fast shut. And Aslan, not at all slacking his pace, rushed straight as a bullet towards it. . . .

Next moment the whole world seemed to turn upside down, and the children felt as if they had left their insides behind them; for the Lion had gathered himself together for a greater leap than any he had yet made and jumped—or you may call it flying rather than jumping—right over the castle wall.[5]

Here's a story of how I rode on God's back (and the prayers of a Christian family). It all began with a father who was concerned about a college student who wanted to date his daughter. Since the young man was not a believer, the father and daughter agreed that the only "date" would be on Sunday mornings at church. They told him to come talk to me about the Lord—and he did!

I was skeptical as a lanky Colombian with a ponytail settled on the sofa in my office. One hour and forty minutes later, I had become hopeful and encouraged by his interest in spiritual things and the Bible. He had already been attending a good church for three months; God's Spirit was definitely working. As I told him the story of the conversion of two "religious" men— Paul and the rich, moral young man—a light seemed to come on. He too considered himself religious and moral, but now he saw his pride, hypocrisy and guilt before a holy and loving God. I repeatedly warned him not to play with God in order to win favor with this Christian young woman.

Two weeks later Pablo came to tell me his story. When he left my office after the first visit, he went to a park for several hours and read his Bible, thought, prayed and reviewed the Scriptures we had gone over, and eventually repented of his sin. He said:

The next day I was changed. I felt joy, peace, forgiveness. Before, I only saw religion as mental acceptance of certain historical facts: Jesus lived in the Middle East; Jesus rose from the dead, etc. Now I feel the meaning of those facts.

That night my friends were drinking and had rented a porno video. As soon as I realized what it was, I couldn't stay in the house. I got up and left. Jesus would not want me to watch this. They were shocked and worried about me. I didn't know how to explain to them. But they know I'm into God now and are suspicious, yet curious.

Later, I wrote a letter to a friend, who has a good job and money but is depressed and lonely, telling her what I had found: "Jesus is the Savior for our sins." She thinks I'm just young and have a Christian girlfriend, and I'll grow up someday.

Every day now I'm God-conscious. When I read the Bible, it's like I'm listening; it seems to be speaking to me and taking me somewhere. I am much more aware of my sin now, but also of my sorrow for sinning before God (Psalm 51), and have experienced release from guilt. As I face temptations daily, I'm surprised at how I can now resist some of them. I feel strangely stronger. God has become more important than my career plans and the girl that I like. I could never meet all her needs and vice versa. Each of us needs God to be number one. It seems that God has even arranged our summer so that we will see very little of each other for 2 months. This is good. I have a lot of reading and evaluating to do.

I love to ask new babes in Christ, "What's it like?" and just listen. Of course, I'm comparing it with Scripture—especially 1 John, which was written to give the marks of true salvation and assurance. I avoid telling them they are saved. The Holy Spirit gives assurances as they see the fruits of a changing life. How thankful I am for the prayers and wisdom of the Christian family who took Pablo to church and for a church that gives the gospel "straight." *Wow!* Will you pray and speak to someone today? Invite them to church?

I have begun this examination of evangelism by describing the idea of witness. Now let's shift to a scriptural study of what constitutes the "whole gospel." We'll do this both negatively (by way of contrast with a partial gospel) and positively (by way of presenting an outline and commentary on the central elements of the gospel).

The Gospel Reduced

What is the difference between these two statements?

"The minimum amount of truth to the maximum number of people."

"The maximum amount of truth to the maximum number of people."

Only two words: *minimum, maximum.* But those words constitute a difference as great as night and day. The first statement unfortunately seems to summarize the goal of much contemporary evangelism. The second describes the historic and biblical goal in evangelism.

PACKAGING THE GOSPEL

The first statement typifies how many look at our evangelistic task. The evangelism professor I described earlier exemplifies this approach. Yes, he is an extreme example. Nevertheless, he has merely taken to a logical conclusion the assumptions that undergird the majority of today's evangelistic training materials, seminars and speakers. So often we are told to think of the gospel content in terms of a simple plan of salvation with three or four basic facts. Yet the evangelistic mandate our Lord gave us was "teaching them to obey everything I have commanded you" (Mt 28:20). In another version of this command we find what we are witnesses to: Christ, the necessity of his suffering, the historical resurrection, repentance, forgiveness of sins (Lk 24:46-48). Precisely so, comments the modern evangelist; we are only to repeat a few central facts, for Paul himself summarizes the gospel ever so briefly (1 Cor 15:3-4) and explicitly tells us in the second chapter of the same book that he "resolved to know nothing while I was with you except Jesus Christ and him crucified" (v. 2). Likewise, many of today's evangelists continue trying to prove their case for stripping down the extensive theology of the gospel to a minimal amount of truth content. While they no doubt are sincerely seeking to help others toward salvation, they can end up dangerously misleading people by making the gospel simplistic.

Is this simplistic gospel approach adequate? Are we to reduce and package the gospel for easy distribution? Are we to imagine that Paul merely parroted the words "Jesus Christ crucified" up and down the streets of Corinth? No. Each of these words is like the tip of an iceberg rising above the water. Underneath is a large mass of assumptions and deep meanings. Only when we grapple with these can we begin to understand the nature and breadth of our evangelistic task. This is why in the book of Acts we see the apostles as *teachers*—reasoning, persuading, explaining—involved in all sorts of teaching activity in order to communicate as much truth as possible to nonbelievers.[1]

J. I. Packer in *Evangelism and the Sovereignty of God* has pointed out that the gospel was a message of some complexity, needing to be learned before it could be lived by and understood before it could be applied. It needed, therefore, to be taught. The first and fundamental job of Paul as a preacher of the gospel was to communicate knowledge, to get truth fixed in people's minds. Teaching the truth was the basic evangelistic activity.[2] Although the apostles as evangelists did keep certain themes in the forefront, these central doctrines could never be communicated in a vacuum. They must be related to the whole counsel of God. There must be a context given to the points of the gospel or else communication cannot take place. We must allow, however, for a great difference between what a Christian's understanding of the gospel should be and that of a non-Christian who is just beginning to learn it. For Paul, the only right method of evangelism was the teaching method. Therefore, scriptural evangelism has extensive—not minimal—instruction as its goal.

In place of this scriptural stance, since about 1900, a new method of packaging the gospel has now come into evangelicalism worldwide.[3] We are to make the gospel readily transferable so as to gain the mental assent of the hearer. This has led to the idea of "the simple gospel," which we all supposedly know as soon as we become Christians. But this approach encourages us to think of the gospel as a pill that will cure all. We, as doctors, dispense it freely. We need not worry about the patient's symptoms. No matter what the symptom is, the pill will cure it. Thus, many of us abridge our diagnosis of the disease (sin), instead of taking time to explain the person's sinful nature which creates the sickness. Our object has become merely to convince people to take the cure. They do not need to know the problem—just the answer. Such treatment, however, makes the gospel vulnerable to being molded by the worldly desires of the sinner or the fads of the secular world (Jesus as the quintessential marketer, liberator of the abused, ultimate therapist, affirmer of my worth, movie star and so on).

If we carry through with the logic of simplistic evangelism, we need not carefully and persuasively explain and illustrate the doctrines of the gospel. Therefore, our evangelism training is directed toward *mobilizing everyone* (no matter what doctrines of the gospel he or she holds) *quickly* (enter population growth statistics and world-to-end-soon prophets). This large-scale unity of Christians for evangelism is on the basis of a common need to get the job done and a vague belief in the conversion experience, not by theological agreement on gospel truths.

Have you ever noticed that most conferences on evangelism concentrate on methods and not on the message content? This methodological emphasis is not the property of one denomination, mission or organization alone. It has become a hallmark of the evangelical subculture. Most Christians have read only post-1980 popular Christian literature. Is it any wonder they have unconsciously imbibed this "methodism" along with its truncated gospel posing as the whole gospel?

The person who has known only plain vanilla ice cream might look on cherry vanilla with suspicion at first. Have extraneous ingredients been added to it? My plea is that we taste and see the difference between modern evangelism with its methods/me-centered gospel and the historic God-centered gospel. Let us not be oblivious to the clear teaching of Scripture nor ignorant of the wise perspective of the people of God who stand in the stream of historic Christianity in ages before our own. Me-centered evangelism also shortens the message. It so focuses on relationships and its attractiveness that it reduces God. It so fears further doctrinal division among true

Chart 1. Some Contrasts in Gospel Content

Me-Centered	God-Centered
View of God Point of contact with non-Christians is love (God loves you). God's authority/ownership is blunted.	Point of contact with non-Christians is creation (God made you). God has ownership rights over your daily life and destiny.
Love is God's chief attribute.	Justice and love are equally important attributes of a holy God.
God is impotent before the sinner's will.	God is able to empower the sinner's will.
The persons of the Trinity have different goals when planning and accomplishing salvation than when applying it.	The persons of the Trinity work in harmony—salvation is designed, accomplished and applied to the same people.
Conclusion *God is a friend who will help you.*	*God is a king who will save you.*
View of Humanity Fallen yet has the ability (or potential) to choose the good and God.	Fallen and unable to come to God by own willpower.
Seeks truth but lacks correct facts.	Mind at enmity with God; none seek God.
Needs love, help, friendship and a new life.	Needs new nature (mind, heart, will), regeneration.
Makes mistakes, is imperfect, needs forgiveness for specific sins.	Rebels against God, has a sinful nature, needs reconciliation.
Needs salvation from the consequences of sin—unhappiness, hell.	Needs salvation from guilt and the enslaving power of sin, hell.
Conclusion *Humanity is sick and ignorant.*	*Humanity is spiritually dead and lost.*

Me-Centered	God-Centered
View of Christ Savior from failures, sins and hell.	Savior from sins, sinful nature and hell.
He exists for our benefit.	He exists to gather a kingdom and receive honor and glory.
His death was more important than his righteous, law-fulfilling life.	His death and his life of fulfilling our obligation to God are equally important.
Emphasizes his priestly role—Savior.	Emphasizes his priestly, kingly and prophetic roles.
Conclusion *An attitude of submission to Christ's lordship is optional for salvation.*	*An attitude of submission to Christ's lordship is necessary for salvation.*
View of Response to Christ Invitation waiting to be accepted now.	Loving command to be obeyed now.
Our choice is the basis for salvation. God responds to our decision.	God's choice is the basis for salvation. We respond to God's initiative.
We give mental assent to truths of gospel—decision.	We respond with our whole person (mind, heart, will)—conversion.
Appeal is made to the desires of the sinner.	Truths are driven home into the conscience of the sinner.
Saved by faith alone—repentance omitted for it is thought of as "works."	Saved by faith alone—saving faith always accompanied by repentance.
Assurance of salvation comes from a counselor using the promises of God and pronouncing the new believer saved.	Assurance of salvation comes from the Holy Spirit applying biblical promises to the conscience and effecting a changed life.
Conclusion *Sinners have the key in their hands.*	*God has the key in his hand.*

Christians that it allows the most imprecise gospel messages to become common currency.[4] A method-centered approach views the Bible as a mere source of "evangelistic texts" rather than as a book whose total focus is Christ. In reality the entire Scripture can be used in evangelism because it is entirely about Christ.

To obtain a clear view of the whole gospel we must first cut away the sprawling overgrown weeds of a me-centered emphasis. I use the term *me-centered* to refer both to the way Christians present the gospel in their witnessing and to the way non-Christians interpret life. Christians often rely on their own abilities and methods and on a deficient gospel. They also become me-centered when they focus on their fears, guilt, weaknesses and so on. Non-Christians' desires are me-centered, revolving around their worthiness, abilities and surface needs. They shrink God and identify faith with reforming their lives by self-effort. The Christian can end up presenting a what's-in-it-for-you gospel, to which the non-Christian will readily respond. Primarily, me-centeredness refers to a theology that assumes that the Trinity is not coordinated regarding who is to be saved and that people have the ability/potential to choose Christ. Sinners hold the key that admits them to salvation.

What then is method- or me-centered evangelism? How does it differ from God-centered evangelism? Let me continue my definition by contrasting in chart 1 some aspects of the content of the gospel that each view emphasizes. Much evangelism falls between the two.

Since salvation benefits us, *there is not a complete antithesis between the two views.* We are helped, loved and rewarded in God's gospel. God centers his designs on saving people. Yet he does it in a way that magnifies himself. When reading chart 1 many will find themselves somewhere in between the two views. It is important to be charitable in our dialogue within the Christian community. Yet we dare not neglect to deal with substantive issues involving pivotal truths. If the chart stimulates you to reexamine your evangelistic message, it has achieved its purpose. The point is that theology is foundational and will (consciously or unconsciously) mold our methods of witness.

I want now to elaborate on what seems to me a big difference between biblical evangelism and modern evangelism. It can be summarized in three ways:

a whole gospel versus a truncated gospel; a message-centered gospel versus a method-centered gospel; a God-centered gospel versus a me-centered gospel.

WHOLE GOSPEL/SHRUNKEN GOSPEL

How dangerous a half-truth can be when presented as the whole truth! For instance, the truth that God is love is a wonderful part of the gospel. However, if the whole presentation of the gospel is built primarily on this truth, distortion develops. Sinners can relax with the thought of God's love for them and find an excuse to delay repentance. This biblical truth is inverted by non-Christians to mean, "Love is God." Then a human definition of *love* (nice, tolerant, nonjudgmental) is substituted, and sinners find great comfort in this personification and deification of love. The love deity is programmed to only treat us kindly. We have a "mush" god. A biblical truth thus becomes twisted into an excuse for complacency. Such a view of God contributes to the pervasive idea (even among Christians) that God is *obligated* to save me. Created humanity is put on a par with the Creator and his autonomy, and salvation by grace is devilishly undercut.

But what if the truth that God is love was balanced with the truth that God is light? God is morally pure, holy. He is a just judge. He is angry with sin and will punish those who persist in it. The love of God is now given a backbone. It is seen as a tough love, not as sentimentalism. That he can still love sinners and freely offer himself to all who believe becomes astounding news. One good question to evaluate any gospel presentation of God is, "Was the nature of God defined clearly and its implications impressed on the mind and heart lovingly and firmly?"

Another example of a half-truth found in much gospel literature is this: "To become a Christian is to become happy, fulfilled, and to live an adventurous and exciting life." But what about the other side of the coin? In evangelism we should also mention the suffering and cost of discipleship.

Perhaps reading for yourself an example of some evangelistic literature will help you see my point. Three examples follow—they all purport to contain enough of the gospel so that by responding to what is written, you will be saved. They are not just for pre-evangelism. Here is a gospel pamphlet consisting mostly of Scripture. What do you think of the title, the ending and the overall thrust?

Meet My Friend

He is faithful.

"When my father and my mother forsake me, then the Lord will take me up" (Psalm 27:10).

He is the way to God the Father.

"Jesus saith . . . I am the Way, the Truth, and the Life: no man cometh unto the Father but by Me" (John 14:6).

He already loves you.

"But God commendeth His love toward us, in that, while we were yet sinners, Christ died for us" (Romans 5:8).

"For all have sinned and come short of the glory of God" (Romans 3:23).

He wants to give you eternal life.

"Believe on the Lord Jesus Christ, and thou shalt be saved" (Acts 16:31).

"For God so loved the world, that He gave His only begotten Son, that whosoever believeth in Him should not perish, but have everlasting life" (John 3:16).

He is the only one who can give you eternal life.

"Neither is there salvation in any other: for there is none other name under heaven given among men, whereby we must be saved" (Acts 4:12).

He won't refuse anyone.

"Him that cometh to Me I will in no wise cast out" (John 6:37).

Now that you have met my Friend, don't you feel that you want to commit your life for time and for eternity into His hands? Right now you can take the Lord Jesus Christ as your own personal Savior and Friend.[5]

A lack of understanding of the doctrines of the gospel can mislead the sinner and the saint in their duties. The sinner is misled regarding who God is and the danger that awaits. The saint presents a half-gospel—like the one-sided ads beckoning people to "join the Navy and see the world." Many of our gospel tracts and much of our evangelistic training, if not in actual error, are woefully lacking in helping us define precisely who God is, who we are and what sin is. Well-meaning Christians have adopted easy formulas leading many into easy believism and cheapening grace. A renowned preacher and author in the Alliance Church, A. W. Tozer, comments, "All unannounced and mostly undetected there has come in modern times a new cross into popular evangelical circles. It is like the old cross, but different: the likenesses are superficial; the differences are fundamental. . . . This new evangelism employs the same language as the old, but its content is not the same and its emphasis is not as before."[6] Without judging motives, let us call one another to renewed study of the whole counsel of God as it pertains to the planning, initiating, achieving and fulfilling of salvation.

MESSAGE-CENTERED/METHOD-CENTERED

What is method-centered witness? Peruse the content of most seminars on evangelism and compare the proportion of material given to clarifying the gospel message with that given to methodology. Consider the technique of singing many songs coupled with long and urgent appeals at the end of an evangelistic service. Such a method is validated with the argument that "a decision from the non-Christian must be evoked." Have you ever urged someone to "try God"? There is a whole method of evangelism based on this idea of experimenting for one week. You pray, and put God to the test—try him out for a while and see if he doesn't work better than anything else you've tried. Presumption is not faith.

In the new evangelism, doctrinal content is slighted, and the emphasis falls on methods of selling the gospel to people. Often this takes the form of recommending that a non-Christian's conversion experience should parallel that of the evangelizer. However, Scripture declares the priority of truth over experience. The thrust of the Bible is to conform our experience to revealed truth, not to start with our experience (no matter how beautiful or helpful it may have been to us) and then make a doctrine for others to emulate. The model for our witness is not to be a smooth-talking public relations agent but an ambassador with a proclamation from a King.

Doctrine and life, truth and the practice of that truth have been joined

together by God. Our message will mold our evangelistic methods and reg-
ulate our spiritual experiences. We must not use an incongruous medium to
present the God of truth. Modern electronic media (radio, TV, film, comput-
ers, multimedia and so on) have great potential for evangelism if they preserve theological content and avoid manipulation.

By knowing truth, we will be set free. People are to be led to seek Christ
by the force of gospel truths alone and not by our reliance on either the
latest persuasion techniques from the business world or the newest psychological tricks dished out through self-help proponents. We are not to
try to entice people by methods appealing mostly to their desires. It is
wrong to key into the non-Christian's interests by saying the gospel offers
the same thing as the world does: success, admiration, health, emotional
cures and so on. Tozer points out that whatever the sin-mad world happens to be clamoring after at the moment is cleverly shown to be the very
thing the new gospel offers, only religion's product is better. Felt needs
should be an entry point only.

I have found three questions helpful to guard against this aberration:
Were the truth points of the gospel elaborated on clearly so that a meaning-
ful response was possible? Did appropriate Scripture probe the conscience,
or only reinforce their sinful desires? Was the impression given that they can
decide for Christ by their own abilities whenever convenient?

Take a look at this tract that was written to lead a person to Christ, keeping these questions in mind.

What Is Your Favorite Game?

Playing games is a common pastime, whether you realize it or not. Not check-
ers or dominoes or chess, but social games which we devise to make us feel
closer to other people.

One girl turns on her radio every night just in time to hear the announcer
say, "And now we bid you a very pleasant good night." It is a human voice
speaking to her.

A grandmother goes shopping and buys another unneeded hat. She is disappointed because her husband has been called out of town again. So she is
off to grab a new thing to try to cure that empty feeling.

One woman calls another to have lunch. They sip their coffee and talk all around themselves; but they never really make contact.

A bachelor plays house with an eager co-ed he has met. He wants someone in his apartment to talk with.

What is it that we hunt for in life? What do we really want? What moves us through day after day, month after month, year after year?

Our needs are many. We cry "gimme" by our attitudes, our glances, our conversation, our actions. We find many stopgap answers, but always there is the big hole, begging to be filled. We pour into it an astonishing collection of things: work projects, television, athletics, clubs, travel, entertainment, volunteer service, parties, barbiturates. But if we are honest, we have to admit that the human satisfaction we gain creates a longing for even greater fulfillment than anything we have yet experienced. The deepest want of all is to find what some people call an "at-oneness." Some call it "peace of soul" or "peace with God."

The truth about our human involvements is that they both meet and do not meet our deepest needs. Life is spent in an effort to overcome the separation that is common to persons everywhere. The expectation of really belonging to someone drives us on in constant search. We know the superb moment of discovery as we find a kindred spirit. But we also know the dawning realization that even this special person is not enough!

There is no substitute for knowing God. He made us in His own image, and our reunion with Him is the foundation for everything else we seek. There is no relationship or game serious enough to satisfy our restless search for completeness. The only way to realize satisfaction and fulfillment is to say "yes" to God, who is love. When we say "no" to His will, we are not only out of place with Him but out of relationship with our fellowman.

People have been trying to bridge their separate existences since the world began. But God has already stepped over the gulf. Christ Jesus came to our world in a human form we can understand. He came as a servant, to say yes to everything God asked of Him. He became obedient to the death of the cross so that we might be saved from our isolation.

If all this is true, then you are wasting your time playing games to win satisfaction. Consider saying "yes" to Jesus Christ, because that's what you were made for. And you won't ever be satisfied until you are "at one" with Jesus Christ.[7]

GOD-CENTERED/ME-CENTERED

Me-centered evangelism contains some biblical truths. Yet these are distorted, for error comes when truth is given out of context. Allen Harris has described the effects of centering only on the person as threefold:

1. Deceiving non-Christians—unbelievers trust in their "response" for assurance.

2. Distorting Christians—believers look for another stage in their Christian life, often becoming disillusioned.

3. Disgracing God's honor—people profess salvation with unchanged lives.

Most of us probably fall somewhere between being God-centered and me-centered evangelists. May God help us not to contradict the character of God in our witnessing. May the God to whom we witness be consistent with the God we worship. Our evangelism needs to stress a God of holiness, not just a God who exists to give us good times and pleasant feelings. We gained redemption through a sovereign Savior rather than through a relationship to him as a mere friend. The life of a Christian is to be radically different from, not relatively similar to, the world.

Me-centered evangelism is not radical enough in its opposition to sinful human nature. Tozer again helps us see this, calling it "the new cross."

> The new cross does not slay the sinner; it redirects him. It gears him into a cleaner and jollier way of living and saves his self-respect. To the self assertive it says, "Come and assert yourself for Christ." To the egotist it says, "Come and do your boasting in the Lord." To the thrill-seeker it says, "Come and enjoy the thrill of the abundant Christian life." The idea behind this kind of thing may be sincere, but its sincerity does not save it from being false. It misses completely the whole meaning of the cross. The cross is a symbol of death. It stands for the abrupt, violent end of a person. God salvages the individual by liquidating him and then raising him to newness of life. The corn of wheat must fall into the ground and die. God then bestows life, but not an improved old life. Whoever would possess it must pass under the rod. He must repudiate himself and concur in God's just sentence against him. How can this theology be translated in life? Simply, the non-Christian must repent and believe. He must forsake his sins and then go on to forsake himself. Let him cover nothing, defend nothing,

excuse nothing. Let him not seek to make terms with God, but let him bow his head before the stroke of God's stern displeasure and acknowledge himself worthy to die.[8]

In light of Tozer's words, what do you think of this next tract?

You're a Beautiful Person

But—even beautiful people have problems. Problems like Life(?) Sin(?) Eternity(?) God(?) God(?)(!) What's He got to do with it? Everything, Like, try this—

Jesus Christ said:

> As it is written, There is none righteous, no, not one. I am the way, the truth, and the life; no man cometh unto the Father, but by me. I am the light of the world; he that followeth me shall not walk in darkness, but shall have the light of life. I am the door; by me if any man enter in, he shall be saved. He that believeth on him is not condemned; but he that believeth not is condemned already, because he hath not believed in the name of the only begotten Son of God.

Sound Strong? Hang on!

I gave you this because I believe it is the most important message in the world. God loves you, no matter who you are or what you are. He sent His Son, Jesus Christ, to die as payment for your sins. That's love! But Christ not only died for you, He arose from the dead and now lives! Jesus Christ is a living Saviour. He lives to give you real joy, real peace, and an eternal hope.

Now, how can you know this Christ as your personal Saviour?

Well, Christ said, "Behold, I stand at the door, and knock; if any man hear my voice, and open the door, I will come in to him."

Receiving Christ involves completely giving yourself to God, trusting Christ to forgive your sins, and allowing Him to have control of your life. The Bible says, "Whosoever shall call on the name of the Lord shall be saved."

Listen! Now is the time for you to accept Christ as your SAVIOUR! Don't put it off. God warns in His Word, "Now is the accepted time; behold, now is the day of salvation."[9]

Even if you dismiss tracts as a good medium, nevertheless most of our gospel conversations and outlines reflect similar defeciencies. Why are we so complacent about inadequate expressions of the saving truths of God's love and rule?

Questions: Is there anything misleading about becoming a Christian, about the Christian life? Is a person left defenseless, realizing that God would be just in delivering them to eternal hell? Is repentance explained? Is there an emphasis on self-denial and the cost of following Christ? (For more evaluation questions, see appendix A.IX.)

IS THE GOSPEL REALLY BEING COMPROMISED?

In a God-centered gospel, grace is central. God is exalted at every point in the outworking of it—from its design in all eternity through its outworking in Christ and its application to his people. Our King is assured of a kingdom and will neither be frustrated by human resistance nor be obligated to save his creatures because of their supposed rights to his favor. We rejoice in the benefits we accrue from a gracious God, but we glory in our God alone and the vindication of his honor above whatever good may (or may not) come to humanity.

Some may say the ogre of me-centered evangelism is not as prevalent as I have indicated. I say it is. We have only to look into the subculture of the evangelical church to find it. Peruse the shelves of a Christian bookstore and discover the bestsellers. Watch TV evangelists. Listen to contemporary Christian radio. Find out what, if anything, is taught in church youth groups after the fun and games are over. Survey what happens to all those "converts" after two years. Ask students from Christian schools who gave up the faith, saying, "I tried it, but it didn't work." What gospel was it that they tried?

We can also look at our own hearts and evangelistic practice and find how woefully inconsistent we all are. Our inclination to downplay the existence of hell reflects the tendency we have to compromise the gospel. I used to avoid even mentioning hell. I didn't want to frighten people. I was aware that people could be manipulated and seek salvation as merely a "fire escape."

But part of telling the truth is reinforcing the reality and danger of hell, of which the Bible speaks clearly. Jesus said, "Fear him who, after the killing of the body, has power to throw you into hell" (Lk 12:5). The writer of the letter to the Hebrews said, "If we deliberately keep on sinning after we have received the knowledge of the truth, no sacrifice for sin is left, but only a fearful expectation of judgment and of raging fire that will consume the enemies of God. . . . It is a dreadful thing to fall into the hands of the living God" (Heb 10:26-27, 31). Wise King Solomon said, "A man who remains stiff-necked after many rebukes will suddenly be destroyed—without remedy" (Prov 29:1). And John the apostle said, "If anyone's name was not found written in the book of life, he was thrown into the lake of fire" (Rev 20:15).

I once asked a young athlete to read a booklet *Ultimate Questions,*[10] which is a thorough, succinct, readable description of the gospel. At the end of our second discussion, we left our restaurant table and stood outside at a busy intersection. I had changed the topic to sports, thinking I should be affable and careful not to convey any pressure to respond to Christ. But he suddenly blurted out, "Will, if I were to be hit by one of these cars and die, I know I'd go straight to hell." Taken aback, yet not wanting to appear unconcerned, I quickly confirmed his conclusion. Two weeks later he asked for God's mercy to save him. He saw the implications of unbelief and was humbled and motivated to come to Christ. Too often people do not see they are in *real danger*. They often have an uncanny sense that evil is real and that some sort of hell or punishment exists, but they don't believe they will ever be affected by these realities.

Being complacent, they continue to ignore the issues of life and death. As Christians, we are too accepting of this. There is a time for warning against procrastination. Sitting on the fence (claiming to be neutral) is not an option when a King issues a command to believe and a Savior lovingly invites you to follow.

Tim Keller is pastor of a thriving church reaching the cosmopolitan population of New York City. An Ivy League MBA who was financially successful and had lived in three countries voiced to Tim the main objection secular people have to biblical Christianity. "I cannot believe people are going to hell just because they don't believe in Jesus. . . . God is loving." Here is an outline of Tim's response:

Sin is slavery. I do not define sin as just breaking the rules, but also as "making something besides God our ultimate value and worth." These good things, which become gods, will drive us relentlessly, enslaving us mentally and spiritually, even to hell forever if we let them. . . . When sin is seen as slavery, and hell as the freely chosen, eternal skid row of the universe, hell becomes much more comprehensible.

Tolerance is exclusive too. Nothing is more characteristic of the modern mindset than the statement "I think Christ is fine, but I believe a devout Muslim or Buddhist or even a good atheist will certainly find God." This approach is seen as more inclusive.

I point out that the universal religion of humankind is: We develop a good record and give it to God, and then he owes us. The gospel is: God develops a good record and gives it to us, then we owe him (Romans 1:17). In short, to say a good person, not just Christians, can find God is to say good works are enough to find God. But this apparently inclusive approach is really quite exclusive. It says, "The good people can find God, and the bad people do not." What does this mean for those of us with moral failures? We are excluded.

So both approaches are exclusive, but the gospel's is the more inclusive exclusivity. It says joyfully, "It doesn't matter who you are or what you've done. It doesn't matter if you've been at the gates of hell. You can be welcomed and embraced fully and instantly through Christ."

Salvation in Christianity is more personal. The postmodern "sensitive" approach to the subject of hell says, "It doesn't matter if you believe in the person of Christ, as long as you follow his example." But to say that is to say the essence of religion is intellectual and ethical, not personal. If any good person can find God, then the essential core of religion is understanding and following the rules.

There is no love without wrath. I answer people who say, "What kind of loving God is filled with such wrath as to send people to hell to suffer eternally?" by pointing out that a wrathless God cannot be a loving God. In *Hope Has Its Reasons*, Becky Pippert writes, "Think how we feel when we see someone we love ravaged by unwise actions or relationships. Do we respond with benign tolerance as we might toward strangers? Far from it. . . . Anger isn't the opposite of love. Hate is, and the final form of hate is indifference."

Pippert then quotes E. H. Gifford: "Human love here offers a true analogy: the more a father loves his son, the more he hates in him the drunkard, the liar, the traitor."

She concludes: "God's wrath is not a cranky explosion, but his settled opposition to the cancer of sin which is eating out the insides of the human race he loves with his whole being."

Ultimately, it is only *because* of the doctrine of judgment and hell that Jesus' proclamation of grace and love is so brilliant and astounding.[11]

Today's evangelism often tones down the awesome majesty of God. Mike Yaconelli, a writer aware of cultural trends, reminds us that an appropriate big fear can actually answer and assuage our many painful but small fears.

The tragedy of modern faith is that we no longer are capable of being terrified. We aren't afraid of God, we aren't afraid of Jesus, we aren't afraid of the Holy Spirit. As a result, we have ended up with a need-centered gospel that attracts thousands . . . but transforms no one.

Unfortunately, those of us who have been entrusted with the terrifying, frightening Good News have become obsessed with making Christianity safe. We have defanged the tiger of Truth. We have tamed the Lion and now Christianity is so sensible, so accepted, so palatable.

Our world is tired of people whose God is tame. It is longing to see people whose God is big and holy and frightening and gentle and tender . . . and ours; a God whose love frightens us into His strong and powerful arms where He longs to whisper those terrifying words, "I love you."[12]

TRUTH: THE MEASURING STICK OF EVANGELISM

We should be concerned because the gospel message is being blunted in our day, and one effect is scorched earth in many youthful hearts. I meet those who say, "I know I'm a Christian; here's the card I signed five years ago. Besides, the counselor told me never to doubt my salvation." We sadly notice the dust-laden Bible on the shelf. No one, not even the most consistently God-centered evangelist, can avoid dropouts and deformed babies. On the other hand, I do not say the gospel is wholly lost or that God may not often work through a defective evangelistic presentation. He is a sovereign God. No one can claim to have the perfect gospel outline or the right approach for each situation. We all are humbled by the sovereign and compassionate God who works as he wills to bring someone to himself. The *amount* of truth God will use to regenerate a person is something we cannot dictate. God, in the wind of the Spirit, blows where he wills. Yet, it is *truth* God always uses; it is never our *tool* (pamphlet, outline, program or famous speaker) in evangelism that works. All success is God's. To him alone be the glory.

However, the sovereignty of God never excuses us from responsibility. If we are not concerned to learn the complete gospel, then we are unconcerned to glorify God in all that we do. Are we content to follow the pattern of programmed witnessing dictated by me-centered evangelists (albeit well-meaning) who have abbreviated the message and unconsciously adopted techniques inappropriate to convey the gospel of God's grace? Are we willing to evaluate humbly our personal witness and all else that we use that professes to be "evangelistic" by this yardstick: what *truth* was taught?

In this attempt to evaluate the character of contemporary evangelism, it has been necessary to speak forcefully and by way of contrast so that I could communicate what disturbs me in the new gospel reduction. Differences among Christians must be understood and honestly faced. Under the cloak of Christian unity, a cease-fire has been declared on doctrinal discussion regarding evangelism. *Doctrine* becomes a word with a bad connotation, for it is labeled as the source of division among Christians. I am not interested in theological nit-picking over minor teachings in Scripture. What I am saying is that major gospel truths are being ignored. In the interest of unity, "some evangelicals are jettisoning any serious attempt to exhibit truth and antithesis. This often finishes up by denying, in practice if not in theory, the importance of doctrinal truth as such. Cooperation and unity that do not lead to purity of life and purity of doctrine are just as faulty and incomplete as an orthodoxy which does not lead to a concern for, and reaching out towards, those who are lost."[13] I believe it is ignorance of an overall systematic theological frame of reference that will bring about divisions among us as each person exalts his pet doctrine. A balanced theology would unite us (Eph 4:13-16). It is ignorance that often divides while doctrine can unite us. (See appendix D.)

None of us is so naive as to think all differences among Christians would be solved in our day if we returned to a theological basis for evangelism. Nevertheless, it is still imperative to challenge each other to look into the Scriptures again and again in order to make us more self-conscious of the doctrines that shape our methods. Even if we must agree to disagree on certain points, we will know clearly what they are; our fellowship will be more honest, and our children can take up studying where we have left off. We must never give up praying that new light will break upon the church as she seriously studies the Bible.[14]

One place to start could be an agreement to alter the unbiblical practice of separating doctrine from experience, thus making doctrine secondary in importance to practice. The movement in the New Testament is *from* doctrine *to* experience. To reverse this order or to say it doesn't matter leads to a contentless Christ trip. Doctrine and life have been married by God. It is not moral declension that leads to doctrinal declension, but the reverse. Romans 1 clearly shows that when men and women turn away from the truth, moral declension follows. So, let us not hush up any Priscilla or Aquila who will take us aside to expound the way of God more accurately to us (Acts 18:26). Let us be willing to test our spiritual experiences and evangelistic practices by Scripture.

At times we may reach an impasse over doctrine and go our separate ways in evangelism. Does this mean we cut ourselves off completely from other true Christians? In such a case we must also manifest love by looking to specific activities we can share, because in some areas we do possess a unity of truth. Christians must display their calling to manifest the character of God's chief attributes of holiness/purity and love/humility in all their personal relationships.

In seeking the recovery of the gospel for our day, God forbid that we should ever cover it with complexity for the unbelievers. "No sincere Christian intends to deceive sinners. In love for souls, true evangelicals invariably present some profound truths in their witnessing. Yet by the unconscious omission of essential ingredients of the Gospel, many fail to communicate even that portion of God's Word which they mean to convey. When a half-truth is presented as the whole truth, it becomes an untruth."[15] God help us to teach the maximum amount of truth about the glorious God who is Creator and Redeemer in a winsome, lucid, bold way to as many of this world's children as we can.

There is a "truth bomb" ticking away in evangelical Christianity that could explode misconceptions in evangelism. This bomb's ingredients are the sovereignty of grace, dependence on prayerful pleading, truth-centered witnessing, genuine love and friendliness. Could these, under God's Spirit, be the explosive device that will bring true revival to God's people, spreading to worldwide renewal (new birth) of sinners?

The Gospel Recovered

It is one thing to be painfully aware of weaknesses in evangelistic messages and attempt to evaluate them. It is another thing to try to put forward a positive example of the direction in which we must head. With all the abuses in simplistic gospel approaches, we must be careful not to rule out attempts to elucidate clearly the main elements of the gospel. It is a temptation to be only critical and not to try honestly, humbly and lovingly to build toward a remedy.

I have used the biblical theme of God's call to "come home" to a new relationship with him for connecting five pillars of gospel truth: Who is God? God-Centered Living, Self-Centered Living, Jesus—The Way Back, and Coming Home. (Please see the Amplified Version [appendix B.II], which is intended to help Christians learn the gospel's contents. The Simplified Version [on page 54] is for memorization to share with others.)

GOSPEL GRAMMAR: THE FIVE PRIMARY POINTS OF THE GOSPEL

1. God: our Owner, Father, Judge. It is instructive to compare Paul's evangelism among the Jews with his evangelism among the Gentiles.[1] When he was speaking in the synagogue (Acts 13:16-42), he knew his audience had a good foundation on which to build. He could assume a biblical worldview. He knew that terms such as *God* and *sin* would communicate accurately because his hearers, steeped in Old Testament revelation, packed the right content into the words.

Far too many Christians today are making this wrong assumption about their hearers—thinking that they understand some basic concepts in the

Come Home: Simplified Version (for sharing)

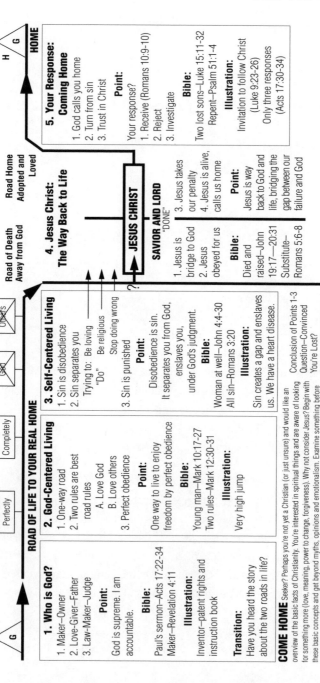

ROAD OF LIFE TO YOUR REAL HOME

Love God Perfectly — Love Others Completely

HOME

G H

1. Who is God?

1. Maker–Owner
2. Love-Giver–Father
3. Law-Maker–Judge

Point:
God is supreme. I am accountable.

Bible:
Paul's sermon–Acts 17:22-34
Maker–Revelation 4:11

Illustration:
Inventor–patent rights and instruction book

Transition:
Have you heard the story about the two roads in life?

2. God-Centered Living

1. One-way road
2. Two rules are best road rules
   A. Love God
   B. Love others
3. Perfect obedience

Point:
One way to live to enjoy freedom by perfect obedience

Bible:
Young man–Mark 10:17-27
Two rules–Mark 12:30-31

Illustration:
Very high jump

3. Self-Centered Living

1. Sin is disobedience
2. Sin separates you
   Trying to: Be loving
   "Do" Be religious
   Stop doing wrong
3. Sin is punished

Point:
Disobedience is sin. It separates you from God, enslaves you, under God's judgment.

Bible:
Woman at well–John 4:4-30
All sin–Romans 3:20

Illustration:
Sin creates a gap and enslaves us. We have a heart disease.

Road of Death Away from God

4. Jesus Christ: The Way Back to Life

JESUS CHRIST

SAVIOR AND LORD
"DONE"

1. Jesus is bridge to God
2. Jesus obeyed for us
3. Jesus takes our penalty
4. Jesus is alive, calls us home

Point:
Jesus is way back to God and life, bridging the gap between our failure and God

Bible:
Died and raised–John 19:17—20:31
Substitute–Romans 5:6-8

Road Home Adopted and Loved

5. Your Response: Coming Home

1. God calls you home
2. Turn from sin
3. Trust in Christ

Point:
Your response?
1. Receive (Romans 10:9-10)
2. Reject
3. Investigate

Bible:
Two lost sons–Luke 15:11-32
Repent–Psalm 51:1-4

Illustration:
Invitation to follow Christ (Luke 9:23-26)
Only three responses (Acts 17:30-34)

Hell

Conclusion of Points 1-3
Question–Convinced You're Lost?
Dilemma–How to Get Right with God?

COME HOME Seeker? Perhaps you're not yet a Christian (or just unsure) and would like an overview of the basic facts of Christianity. You're interested in spiritual things and are aware of looking for something more (love, meaning, power to change, forgiveness). Why not consider Jesus? Begin with these basic concepts and get beyond myths, opinions and emotionalism. Examine something before you judge it. Don't be biblically illiterate or one who takes ideas out of their context. This booklet could be the means to introduce you to the biblical Jesus who is still fascinating and transforming people of all cultures into a new international family. By beginning with understanding these basic truths you will come to realize that Christianity is both something to be believed and someone to be received.

Bible. Although most Western countries have a Christian historical background, the dominant worldviews of people are not Christian at all. This is true for non-Western countries as well. Even if the audience is Jewish, most of them have imbibed a relativistic worldview and are ignorant of the real meaning of many biblical words.

What purports to be the most modern and up-to-date evangelism is, in fact, outdated at this point. Evangelists rattle off "God words" like *justified, holy, salvation* and *sin,* fling truth at people, and then ask their hearers to "decide" for a contentless Christ. Any such decision amounts to a leap in the dark. This form of evangelism opts for solutions to surface problems by means of an emotional encounter with minimal engagement (therefore little humbling) of their minds. We must always be careful not to assume too much on the part of our hearers, even though they may use the same words that we do. For the few outspoken atheists we meet, we will encounter droves of people who use biblical words to which they attach their own definitions.

I remember being in Florida one year at the time of spring break for many college students. As I ambled from person to person on a sunny beach I would inquire about their schools and interests, then pose two questions. "Do you believe in God?" Most replied, "Yes." Then I asked, "Does sin separate you from God?" Their replies were brief but astounding. "No, why should it?" or "I don't believe in that kind of a God," or "My concept of God is one who loves." How many times have each of us talked to someone who does not balk at the word *God,* and may profess to believe in him, yet defines God out of personal and cultural values?

The concept we want to drive home, highlighted under "Main Point" in the "Coming Home" outline, is God's ownership of each of us. An individual must be brought to see that he is not the master of his fate nor the captain of his soul. In the words of a James Ward song, "I must be brought down, all the way down—till I come to you with my face on the ground." What does this ownership mean?

In the ancient Middle East there existed suzerains—sovereign monarchs of a land. These rulers held absolute sway over their subjects. It was a suzerain's prerogative to initiate a treaty with his subjects. This was no bilateral agreement negotiated between two equal parties; rather, it was a sovereignly imposed law. He bound his subjects to himself, in effect owning them. In return, not because he was in any way obligated to but purely out of his self-determined will, he pledged himself to protect, defend and show mercy to his subjects. If they kept covenant with their suzerain king, all was well—they would experience blessing from his mercy. If they broke covenant, they would be liable to his righteous indignation, his terrible curse. God is our suzerain king.

Now let's look at how Paul emphasizes God's ownership as he moves among the Gentiles. When he enters the pagan marketplace (Acts 17:22-34; see also Acts 14:11-18), he begins to amplify his proclamation into a work of teaching because he was concerned to *communicate*. He was not trying to intellectualize the gospel for certain audiences. Anyone who makes the gospel sophisticated and abstract is not making a New Testament proclamation but is trusting in human understanding and his own wisdom (1 Cor 2:4-5). It is precisely because Paul knew the crude polytheism of his audience (note how observant he was even as he entered the city) that he is careful to delineate the true God from his hearers' false religious notions. As mysticism and pantheism become an increasing part of the syncretism in religions around us, we must carefully distinguish the biblical God by patiently instructing others in his nature.

In Acts 17 Paul teaches the basics about the nature of God. The Lord is transcendent and immanent. He controls history and our destiny. He has a purpose for humanity. He is the Creator; we are his creatures. Paul first fixes his definition of God by positives and then negatives, teaching antithetically. He emphasizes to the conscience of his audience the difference between their concepts of God and the world and the biblical view.[2] God is personal (pronoun *he*). He is holy ("will judge by righteousness"). He requires repentance and obedience to his authority ("commands"). History has a goal ("he has set a day"). Christ is the resurrected mediator of all judgment (v. 31). It is amazing how much instruction is given about who God is in this summary of a powerful evangelistic sermon. Here's a content-filled gospel message that can be the basis for the conversation with a philosopher or a child. I know; I've used it effectively with both. Luke tells us we are to witness to the necessity of Christ's sufferings (Lk 24:46-48). How can we do this without going into the nature of God's character as *just* and *loving*? These two attributes sum up God's moral character and form the motive and shape the means of God's plan of salvation. We cannot explain the work of Christ unless we present a true picture of God.

We must give people a thorough grounding in the character of God as the self-sufficient *Creator* as part of our basic gospel. The theory of macroevolution (evolution between species, versus microevolution, which is evolution within species) is uncritically assumed by the college student and the ghetto grandmother. We preach the gospel in a space age in which all people sense their finitude to a new degree and see technology as the creator and sustainer of life. We are insignificant, and only animals at that—this is the common attitude. The erosion in the Western world of the Creator-creature distinction, which is foundational to all biblical thought, constitutes a serious challenge to our evangelism. The absence of this crucial distinction forms a barrier to unbelievers seeing their responsibility before their Maker. We labor to communicate that people are responsible for their actions and attitudes. Beginning with God as our Maker is the foundation for this concept. "Be perfect as your heavenly Father is perfect" (Mt 5:48).

When we speak to people who have no foundational concepts about the true Creator God, let us be thankful God has spoken and defined himself. Much of my time in witnessing is taken up with defining the nature of the biblical God and implications of his love and justice. You can find joy in witnessing; and with God's definitions on our lips, we reinforce the "law written in the heart" (Rom 2:15), that God-implanted sensor. As we witness we touch that light-sensitive nerve deep in the heart of nonbelievers with the hot iron of revelatory truth.

I like using a story about a super-computer failure to illustrate this first point of the gospel. The giant computer responsible for the overseas operations of one of the largest corporations in Japan would not function. An urgent message was sent to the American manufacturer to send their best technician immediately. Later that day a young man, unshaven and dressed casually in Levi's, arrived. The corporation's CEO was furious. "I told your boss to send me their best, most experienced technician. We're losing millions because this computer is down. It must be fixed immediately. Who are you, anyway?"

The young man replied in an offhand way, "Sir, I invented this technology. Please show me to the computer." Within an hour the computer was functioning. On the way out, the inventor handed the CEO the instruction manual, which he had found filed away unused. "Sir, I deeply care about this machine and how it is used. It will operate just fine if you take time to read and obey the instructions in this book. It was made to function by these guidelines." So also God made us and loves his creation deeply. He has given us a book (the Bible) describing procedures for our "optimum operation." Call on your Maker when your life isn't working.

2. God-centered living: the two rules of the road. What if a surgeon was in the midst of a life-saving operation and discovered his scalpel was missing? In anguish he would complain, "I don't have the right instrument for this incision!"

We too have been called on to be doctors—physicians of the soul. We've been given a scalpel, and yet at times we've failed to use it. However, it is of absolute necessity for our operation on the hearts of nonbelievers. This scalpel has never failed, no matter whose hand held it. It has always accomplished its purpose. Its edge is so sharp it can cut between thoughts and intentions of the heart. Of course, I'm speaking of the scalpel of the Scriptures. It compels conviction of sin and reveals a compassionate Savior, guilt (law) and forgiveness (love).

Although all of Scripture carries this double message, there are some passages that make especially keen scalpels. Repentance before God and faith in the Lord Jesus Christ (Acts 20:21) are the goals of the gospel, so let us examine in turn the use of law and love to achieve this goal in our witness.

Understanding the place of the law in evangelism is of tremendous importance. With the aid of the Holy Spirit (who is in the business of convicting of sin, righteousness and judgment, Jn 16:8-11) we can use the sharp-edged scalpel of the law to expose the abscess of sin in the nature of unbelievers.[3] As noted previously, most people aren't hostile to Christianity; they're just indifferent. Psychology and sociology have told people their guilt is not real; they just haven't adjusted to their environment or social situation yet. They are not responsible for many of their actions. Such "modern" people do not measure themselves by God's absolutes but by comparison with others—what is normal in society. So their conscience is quieted, and they become unconcerned.

What will show people like this their spiritual poverty? They need to be lovingly shocked. They will never submit to radical heart surgery if they do not see their true guilt before a holy God. Their security is false. They think there is peace when there isn't. No wonder indifferent sinners look askance when told, "You need Christ as your Savior!" You can read their minds even if they do not say it: *Me? Need a Savior? That's for people who are lost!* They think their house is in order—not perfect, but not badly out of line either. They have never used the level of God's law to check the angles of their soul. Our job is to bring that true level alongside their emotions, thoughts, actions, words, desires. Some passages of Scripture are ideal for telling this aspect of the story to a non-Christian. Here are four that are scalpel sharp.

The Ten Commandments (Ex 20). Ask non-Christians to take a test. Go quickly through the commandments; ask how many they have broken. Many people think they have done fairly well on half or more—and the ones they have failed to keep were those that all of us slip up on now and then. Then go back over the commandments one by one and show the extent of them. Most people then see they have broken every one. If they remain unconvinced, mention James 2:10—breaking even one law brings condemnation from a wholly righteous God. (See appendix B.V.)

The Sermon on the Mount (Mt 5—7). This address describes the Christian's inner life (Beatitudes) and actions. You may use this to explain the full implications of the Ten Commandments. For the climax you can show that unless a person's righteousness exceeds the righteousness of the scribes and Pharisees that person shall never enter the kingdom of heaven (Mt 5:20). You can detail the scrupulous life of these Jewish religious people and ask, "Have you done better?" You can then explain the difference between external righteousness and heart righteousness.[4]

The moral young man (Lk 18:18-30). Here is a moral person. Jesus explains that in breaking one commandment (coveting, the tenth commandment), the young man is not right with God. His heart is far from loving God; he is

guilty. We can see why the disciples ask, "Who then can be saved?" (If any-
body would have made it, this fellow should have.) Christ points out that it
is impossible for humans to save themselves; however, with God all things
are possible. (See appendix B.VI.)

Paul's life (Phil 3:4-11; Rom 7:7-13). Paul was another person who seemed
to have everything in a religious sense. He was a very moral and zealous individual. What made him give up all of his credentials? What led him to
make the statement that those things that formed the basis of his security
were no longer of any importance? Why did he desire to be identified with
Christ? He had had a formal adherence to God's law. Now he saw this was
not sufficient. He needed the righteousness of another—a perfect representative—with whom he could identify by faith.

What brought this proud man low? It was God's law; again, it was the last
commandment. Coveting is something we do with our hearts, not our hands
or feet. Suddenly Paul saw the deep spirituality of the law, and it "killed" him.
It revealed his sinfulness to him and put a sentence of death over any of his
self-righteous efforts, leaving mercy as the only remedy that could save him.

The second point of the gospel shows that God has designed a way for us
to live. Thinking of life as a long road that leads to our real home with God
is a helpful analogy. To follow his road in life is to live with God as the center
of all we do. It is the only way to truly be alive and enjoy a relationship with
him now and in his eternal home. Living with God as the axis puts all else
(other people, the physical universe) in a proper relationship with us. The
authority of the Maker over our lives is focused in two commands. These
rules of the road fit with how we were made to operate. You may think
you're really free when you drive at one hundred miles per hour, but if the
road was designed for thirty-five miles per hour, you will soon destroy yourself and harm others.

God's rules for life do not destroy our freedom but tell us *how* to live, and
result in our safety and happiness. But they must be obeyed perfectly. God
is not like the police, who may overlook a violation for going five or ten
miles per hour over the speed limit. He knows we could hurt ourselves, and
he is displeased with the slightest moral disobedience. To break just one
point of his law is to bring his fatherly displeasure on us (Jas 2:8-13).

The law of life is actually the entire revelation of God, yet it is summarized in Mark 12:30-31 as loving God perfectly and loving others completely. I always ask people to respond "yes" or "no" to whether they have kept these two rules of the road of life. I then reinforce this with a paraphrase of the Ten Commandments or sections of the Sermon on the Mount. With the story of the moral young man who couldn't break the hold that money had on him (Mk 10:17-27), I try to expose the desires and secret idols of a person's heart. It is *essential* that they measure themselves by God's requirements. Otherwise they will only pick and choose aspects of Christianity that they agree with, or reject the need for a Savior altogether.

I like to elaborate on the idea of a pole vault set at one hundred feet—illustrating God's high standard. They should conclude that the biblical God requires an impossibility from us! Although mental acknowledgment is not the same as personal conviction of this truth, it can be a step in the right direction. Truth concepts lodged in a person's mind have a way of filtering into the conscience and heart as they are watered by our love and the Holy Spirit. Very few gospel outlines sufficiently emphasize God's law, and this means God's grace loses its sweet flavor.

In *Pilgrim's Progress* John Bunyan has illustrated that it is the function of the law to reveal our sin. Initially, Pilgrim (Graceless) finds out the strength of the law when he wanders out of the narrow way to the Celestial City. He is duped by Mr. Worldly Wiseman, who points him to a broad and easy way which "will get you to the same destination." So he heads toward the town of Morality, where he is to get help from Mr. Legality. Soon the road becomes exceedingly steep, and he finds himself climbing a mountain. The rocks hang over the road and threaten to crush him. Smoke and fire come out of the hill. With each step the pack on his back (a symbol of sin) gets heavier. Evangelist brings Pilgrim back in the way and rebukes him for trying to climb Mount Sinai (the place where the law was given in the Old Testament).

Later, Pilgrim, now called Christian, is shown the meaning of certain principles in Scripture by a guide called Interpreter. Let John Bunyan tell this in his own words:

> Then he led him into a very large parlor that was full of dust. When they had
> observed it for a moment, the Interpreter called for a man to sweep it. When

he began to sweep, the dust rose and filled the whole room so that Christian almost suffocated. Then the Interpreter said to a maid who stood by, "Bring water and sprinkle the room," which she did. Then the dust settled and the maid swept the room clean.

CHRISTIAN: What does this signify?

INTERPRETER: This parlor is the heart of man that has never been sanctified and cleansed by the grace of God through the gospel. The dust is his original sin and corruption that have defiled the whole man. The man who began to sweep at first is the law. The maid who brought the water and finished the job is the gospel. The man, though working with all his might, could not clean the room; he only stirred up the dust and made it worse to live in. This shows you that the law, by its working, instead of cleansing the heart from sin, only revives sin, causes sin to show its strength, and increase its activity in the soul. Though it discovers and forbids sin, it does not give the life and power to subdue it. So man cannot of himself give up his sin, without first receiving divine life and help from above. This is why the maid came, sprinkled the room with water, and cleaned it with all ease, to show you that when the gospel of Christ comes to the heart, with all its sweet and gracious influence, new life comes in, sin is subdued and vanquished and the soul is made clean by simple faith in Christ. Consequently, man is made fit for the habitation of the King of Glory.[5]

Calvin explains that the law is a preparation for the gospel. Its function is to call the conscience into judgment and alarm it with fear. Scripture describes the law as a schoolmaster (an old-fashioned pedagogue with stern words and a whip) who leads us to Christ (Gal 3:24). The teaching of God's standard is needed today. To use this schoolmaster would do much to humble nonbelievers and remove superficiality from me-centered evangelism.

The law sends us to the gospel so that we may be justified. The gospel sends us to the law to find out what our duty is now that we are justified. The place of God's moral law in the life of a Christian has also been neglected.[6]

3. Self-centered living: separated and enslaved. *Sin* and *God* are correlative terms. If you redefine the biblical God, you can deny the seriousness of sins. But with a biblical God, it follows that he must disapprove and take action against much that is acceptable in today's world. By reminding people who God is, we show them who they are, both in terms of their significance and in terms of the horror of their sinfulness. The human individual is noble, a special creation of God, built to reflect God's moral characteristics. Yet the same individual is also horribly ignoble, spoiled by the Fall and the spoiler of all creation. The corruption of what is best will lead to the worst results. This incongruity between our nobility and our ignobility is revealed in every newspaper. A human interest story tells how the people of the neighborhood have pooled their resources to help a child cruelly crippled in an accident. Two pages later a story reveals that some of the same people are shunning a South Vietnamese family "because they're different." How can human beings be so inconsistent? At one time they display self-sacrifice, and the next moment they are all selfishness and pride. This point of tension is explained by the Christian view of human nature. When people are able to see a reason for the human paradox, they may begin to admit sin is in their nature and a radical solution is therefore needed. Man plays God and man fights God.

When we fail God's two-question test, to love God perfectly and love others completely we become separated (cut off) from a relationship with our Maker. Like cut flowers, the beauty may last for a while, but with no nutrients and root system to sustain them, they die. When we don't center our life on God, it's not as if we don't have anything at the center. Other things rush into the vacuum. They can all be summarized in one word: *selfishness.* This "meism" is our idol. The Bible calls it foolish (stupid), a recentering of our worship (what I most highly regard) on ourselves and other created things. "They exchanged the truth of God for a lie, and worshiped and served created things rather than the Creator" (Rom 1:25). In this great exchange one thing is sure—people were shortchanged. They find themselves in a downward spiral, away from real living and God, and toward eternal homelessness and hell.

People sometimes sense the loneliness and meaninglessness of life without God and try to recapture a relationship with him based on their own efforts. Although sincere (but not necessarily true), their efforts at meeting God's favor fall short. We have only to refer back to God's rules requiring *perfect* obedience to see how powerless we are. We can never *do* enough. Our disobedience is called sin, and it arises from our sinful *nature*, so we can't just change our outward actions and be okay. That's reformation and resolution, which never bring deep change. For religious people and "do gooders," the story of Paul (Phil 3) or the elder son (Lk 15) may connect them with their need. The woman Jesus met at a well (Jn 4) is superb for storytelling about sin. She, like all of us, had a "heart disease" that could not be cured by an aspirin or any other superficial remedy. She needed a new heart and a return to worshiping her Maker-Redeemer in spirit and truth; she needed to be re-created. "Therefore no one will be declared righteous in his sight by observing the law; rather, through the law we become conscious of sin" (Rom 3:20). Misdiagnosis of our real disease is spiritual malpractice. Superficial diagnosis is a crime in the medical world because it's life threatening. Shouldn't we be even more concerned about evangelism that misinforms us about our heart disease?

The gospel challenges each of us with the question, What is man? The naked ape or the genetic freak? The chemical machine or the quirk of chance? We must help people to personalize the theories they hold in order to see if they are practicable. We need to get them to answer the question Who am I? in terms of the logic of their own position. If they finally admit, for example, that being a naturalist means they believe people are quirks of chance or complex machines, then we can point them back into God's world and cry with them as they long for relationships, love, communication, personality. These gifts from God show human beings they are significant. But the worldview of most non-Christians gives no basis for these gifts.

In all our emphasis on teaching the truth of the whole gospel, we would be denying part of this gospel if we were not listening and being sensitive to the person we face. If we don't treat people as persons when we witness to them, we deny a basic tenet of the very gospel in which we believe. If we turn this outline into a formula, we have depersonalized those we encounter. We can be blunt about the hard subject of sin with a person, if at the same time we treat that person as a unique individual.

In explaining what it means to be human, we must vividly contrast Genesis 2 and 3 (creation and Fall) and personally punctuate Romans 1:18-23 (creature tries to be the Creator). That is, from these Scriptures people should be shown what they were made to be, and then discover what they have instead become. As soon as we talk about man, therefore, we of necessity talk about sin.

Sin is a term like the word *God* that is part of common conversation. To most, it's become limited to dramatic wrongs done to others—rape, embezzlement, killing, child battering. Well and good, but people who think of sin only in these categories (horror and horizontal relationships) will have a difficult time seeing why *they* need Christ. Other people might—because they are the "real sinners." But to admit I am sinful in my *nature* (not just that I make mistakes or am imperfect), and by simply not loving God (vertical relationship) I have offended his holiness, making me liable to punishment—this is a concept of sin totally foreign and distasteful to our minds.

Since everybody's life includes acts and attitudes that cause dissatisfaction and shame, everyone has a bad conscience about something.

> The danger is that in our evangelism we should content ourselves with evoking thoughts of these things and making people feel uncomfortable about them, and then depicting Christ as the One who saves us from these elements of ourselves, without even raising the question of our relationship with God. Unless we see our shortcomings in the light of the law and holiness of God, we do not see them as sin at all. For sin is not a social concept; it is a theological concept. To preach sin is not to make capital out of peoples' felt frailties (the brainwasher's trick), but to measure their lives by the holy law of God. To be convicted of sin means not just to feel one is an all-around flop but to realize that one has offended God.[7]

If you now think that we're stumped in our evangelism unless we can obtain a confession of hideous misdeeds and thoughts from non-Christians, let me explain. We do not only try to expose peoples' failures, but in addition, we admire their strengths. We acknowledge the fine qualities that they may have. These are areas of their lives in which they consider themselves to be self-sufficient and secure. We point out that such a thought is in fact evidence of the depth of their depravity and of the Father's alluring love. People need to discover their strengths are gifts from God. They have experienced God's goodness that is designed to bring them to humility, thankfulness and repentance (Rom 2:4).

Many people have a naturally bad conscience from mistakes, imperfection and inability to live up to their own standards. We must guard against equating this conscience with a spiritual conviction of sin. Packer points out that true conviction of sin includes

1. Awareness of a wrong relationship with *God*—not just with self or others, or a general sense of need, but a specific need of reconciliation with God

2. Conviction of *sins*—a sense of guilt for particular wrongs

3. Conviction of sinfulness—a sense of helplessness to do right and consequent need of a new heart or rebirth. Any goodness I claim is not inherent but derived from God. Our righteousness is not good enough, either quantitatively or qualitatively[8]

So let us not fail to impress upon sinners the basic truth about their condition before a holy God. Yet we are not in the business of judging too closely the amount of conviction needed before a person is ready to receive Christ. Good evangelists are doctors who use the surgical knife of the law summarized in the Ten Commandments and elaborated in the Sermon on the Mount to expose the sinful character of sin. By our comprehensive teaching of such passages from Scripture, we free the religious Sauls of our day by exposing them to the high standard of God's law, even though the commandment may slay them at first. Repetition and perseverance are important here. It was not until the tenth commandment that the moral young man (Lk 18:18-30) and Saul recognized their sin. "Indeed I would not have known what sin was except through the law. For I would not have known what coveting really was if the law had not said, "Do not covet" (Rom 7:7).

Here are two illustrations that I've seen God use:

Describe a diseased tree as a modern parable of human nature. What do you do when you find deformed and diseased fruit on a tree? Can the problem be solved by simply picking off the bad fruit? Of course not. You have to get to the root of the problem; you must change the very life of the tree, found in the sap. So also with our sinful natures. We cannot be changed by altering a few of our bad habits. Reformation will not do, for the disease of sin has captured our very life system. We need regeneration, a new heart.

Recite a story of someone recording every action and thought for the last twenty-four hours in a diary and then losing it. How would they feel? Sin not only separates us from God, it enslaves us. We're addicted to a self-centered lifestyle, and no one can break this addiction without God's intervention. What seems to be an innocent "doing it my way," like the younger son in Luke 15, becomes an enslavement to self. God knows our inmost thoughts, and one day we will stand before him and nothing will be hid (Mt 10:26; 1 Cor 4:5). After the dark clouds of the bad news, the good news shines in a rainbow of bright colors. Paul announces his theme as the gospel in Romans 1:16-17, yet immediately portrays nothing but bad news all the way until Romans 3:21! Unbelievers must see themselves as guilty rebels under judgment and unable to save themselves. Are you afraid to sound the alarm?

Conclusions of the first three points of the gospel should be reviewed when witnessing to a person before continuing. Guilt is what Christ came to deal with. It is real, not psychological or merely sociological; it is theological and very painful. We dare not minimize sin, with its resulting mental and emotional impact of guilt. It is God's way of convincing people of their utter dereliction. We also dare not manipulate people whose conscience registers guilt. This is cultic, destructive and cruel. Holy Spirit-induced conviction of our sins is awesome and humbling. Leaving people alone with Psalm 51, a description of King David's realization of need for forgiveness and his genuine repentance, is one way to help them discern whether their sadness is merely self-centered or is a godly sorrow (2 Cor 7:10).

In the gospel diagram "Come Home" (appendix B), I've built in a "pause for reflection" at this point, to give time to ask a listener what they are thinking and feeling. I've listed serious questions to help them personally face the implications of the truths of points one to three. Give them time to absorb, letting the Holy Spirit impact them. Find out if they have any understanding and alarm about the dilemma the Bible (not just your opinion) says they are facing. How can a holy perfect God forgive a sinful person?

4. Jesus Christ: The way back to life. The law *convicts*, but it is powerless to *convert* a person. Such a turning occurs as unbelievers are wooed by God's love, for instance, as they hear the story of Christ's life and death. The Holy Spirit in regeneration instills in the hearts of unbelievers a change of mind about their former life (repentance) and an irresistible drawing toward the One who shows mercy (faith). Conversion is then both a turning from *and* a turning toward. Paul knew that the Thessalonians were elect because of the effect the gospel had in heir lives. They had turned to God from idols (1 Thess 1:4-10).

As we've looked at the place of law, now let's look at the place of love in evangelism. It is necessary for an unbeliever not only to be convicted of sin but to apprehend the grace of God, thus laying hold of Christ crucified and risen. If we only show sin as exposing people to God's justice, then God will be a monster from whom a person will run. God, outside of Christ, will be terrifying to unbelievers who have enlightened consciences. Therefore, the doctrine of repentance is always to be presented in conjunction with grace. "Repentance and forgiveness of sins will be preached in his name" (Lk 24:47). This last phrase does not just mean "in his authority," but in the Old Testament sense of "name" it denotes the full mercy and character of God. In Acts 26:20 we see Paul summarizing his ministry as a preaching of repentance and turning to God. But what encourages a person to turn to him? Three verses later we see Paul holding up a crucified Savior and promising life. Yes, we need to face unbelievers with the law as seen in judgment passages in Scripture, but it is the dying Savior on a cross who causes us to hate sin and surrender to love.

First, the cross shows us how heinous sin is. Why was Christ hung there? To give his life as a ransom for lost sheep. What was happening to him while there? He was taking on himself all the punishment that should have been meted out to sinners. He was being made sin. So the meaning of the cross is to be found not in the example of self-sacrifice, the physical suffering, the scorning, the forsaking by the disciples. God did not spare his own Son but freely delivered him up so that we might go free. Every other manifestation of divine judgment against sin has always been deserved. At Calvary, the innocent Son was punished. Here we see the exceeding sinfulness of sin.

Second, the cross reveals a way of forgiveness consistent with the justice of God. How can God be just and do anything other than condemn the sinner? He provided a way out by having the judge stand in the place of the condemned.

Third, the cross demonstrates the love of God. God so loved that he *gave*. God's attributes of mercy and his disposition to pardon are made clear. How can one look on his sins in the face of Calvary and not be moved?[9]

C. John Miller, founder of World Harvest Mission, often reminded would-be evangelists that we should be careful of separating repentance from the love of God. If we do, we will only lead people to penance. Rather, we need to present the law of God within the context of the love of God. Yes, we have sinned against law, but we have also sinned against grace! Even so, God still loves. He has free grace for sinners. No one should think of grace as locked in a box. Like John Newton, the converted slave trader turned hymn writer, we proclaim grace as costly but free. If you are thirsty, you can come and buy it. But you will not need money because the price has already been paid by another. Without money, come to Jesus Christ and buy (Is 55:1-8)!

In our witnessing let us do all we can to picture Christ as standing, arms outstretched, offering grace to sinners. They have sinned against God's goodness (which was designed to lead them to repentance). They have sinned against Christ himself, not just an abstract ethical standard. As Miller says, grace is available to repentant sinners. It will cover even the sin of despising the cross.

Let us open up the love of God to sinners in a striking and winsome way. How? By holding up Christ before the eyes of unbelievers. Then they can look to Jesus just as Israel in the wilderness looked on the bronze serpent (Jn 3:14-15). As the Jews forsook all other remedies, faith poured itself in through their open eyes! Can we say with Paul that before the eyes of unbelievers we have clearly portrayed Christ as crucified (Gal 3:1)? There is a need for more preaching from the Gospels in our day. We should be using episodes from the Gospels in our personal witnessing as well. The loving encounters Christ had with the poor, sick, blind, leprous, tax collector, religious hypocrite and prostitute need to be vividly recreated in the minds of sinners. They need to identify themselves with these people. The sheer power of these simple stories can reveal the inmost thoughts of many unbelievers, showing Jesus as the intriguing, attractive and overwhelming Savior that he is. Again and again we must focus on the stunning and extensive love of Jesus. There is too much moralizing in evangelical preaching and not enough magnifying of grace in Jesus. Many sections of Scripture shock us with God's love. Here are some passages that melt hard hearts:

The woman at the well (Jn 4). See how tenderly Christ puts his finger on her sin. He speaks the truth in love. How apt is his use of water as a thirst quencher for a dissatisfied lover. She was looking for the right thing, but in the wrong place. He knows her sordid life, yet he offers her himself. Compare the story of Hosea choosing a promiscuous woman for his wife.

The blind man (Jn 9). Jesus heals this man and lets him see again. But he doesn't see too clearly for a while. He has limited understanding of the person who healed him. He is doubted by friends, forsaken by parents and ridiculed by the ministers. Jesus goes and finds him, completing his understanding and fortifying his faith. Yet all this display of God's love is consistent with this man's God-ordained blindness. For the really unfortunate people are those who claim they can see but are spiritually blind, and therefore their guilt remains. His blindness was to display God's glory, and it worked out for his good. Since he was blind he could see his need of Jesus more clearly!

The lost and the found (Lk 15). The three stories in this one chapter all have the same point. Jesus had been criticized by the religious people for spending time with the needy. He shows in the incidents of the lost sheep, the lost coin and the lost sons that it is his nature to seek that which is lost. Don't miss the story of the elder son, whose lostness is demonstrated by his dutiful legalistic (graceless) relationship with the father. When you are found there is joy in heaven. God loves sinners. They are precious to him. He rejoices in them. His banner over them is love.

The woman with much to be forgiven (Lk 7:36-50). A woman who lived a very sinful life came to Jesus while he was eating dinner at the home of a religious leader. She washed Jesus' dusty feet with expensive perfume and tears. Then she dried them with her hair. The religious people objected to Jesus having such a woman touch him. He replies that God loves to be generous, canceling even the largest of debts. She was displaying the magnanimous love that she experienced in forgiveness of her numerous sins.

One of the oldest and wisest of the Protestant creedal statements is the Westminster Confession (1640). In it we read this definition of *repentance* (italics are mine):

By it [repentance] a sinner, out of the sight and sense, not only of the danger, but also of the filthiness and odiousness of his sins, as contrary to the holy nature and righteous law of God, *and upon the apprehension of His mercy in Christ* to such as are penitent, so grieves for, and hates his sins, as to turn from them all unto God, purposing and endeavoring to walk with Him in all the ways of His commandments.

Today's surgeons of the heart are not using their best knife! No wonder the conviction of sin and repentance, signifying the soon recovery of the patient, are often lacking. The Holy Spirit uses the law to convict. For an example of the heart language of a convicted sinner, study Psalm 51. Both law and love are basic ingredients in telling the gospel story.

Once we have helped people see the true nature of their disease, there is only one cure. Other religions do not have this radical view of sinfulness; therefore, the salvation they offer is also not as radical. Those who have difficulty understanding why Christ is the only way to God and who want to argue the unjustness of this (the all-roads-lead-to-heaven theory) have probably not seen the real character of man (a creature with a sinful nature) nor the true character of God (the Creator who is holy and loving). Much of witnessing is bringing people to understand and feel the extent of their helplessness and corruption. Since most come to us with sparse God-consciousness and little sense of their sinfulness, often the content of the first two points of the outline (character of God, the two qualifying laws) must be reinforced creatively again and again.

Francis Schaeffer was once asked the question, "What would you do if you met a really modern man on a train and you had just an hour to talk to him about the gospel?" He replied, "I've said over and over, I would spend 45-50 minutes on the negative, to really show him his dilemma—that he is morally dead—then I'd take 10-15 minutes to preach the Gospel. I believe that much of our evangelistic and personal work today is not clear simply because we are too anxious to get to the answer without having a man realize the real cause of his sickness, which is true moral guilt (and not just psychological guilt feelings) in the presence of God."[10] You will find that as people begin to grasp the significance of God as Creator and man as the sinful creature, they begin to sense that Christ has done exactly what is needed for their dilemma.

Yet, here again me-centered evangelism is often deficient. It tends to focus on one of Christ's roles to the exclusion of others. It may be well versed in presenting Christ as sin-bearer who, via a substitutionary sacrifice of himself for sin, effected a reconciliation between the sinner and God. Yet unhappily, it often misses the importance of his life of perfectly fulfilling all obligations of the law (active obedience) and thereby gaining a perfect righteousness for those whom he represents. In the death of Christ (passive obedience), the broken law's penalty is borne for us. Yet Christ has not just put us back in the garden (a state of innocence or of moral probation) but has put a robe of righteousness on us. A simple pencil can be used to illustrate this. The eraser is the blood of Christ cleansing us from all sin (1 Jn 1:7). The lead is the righteous life of Christ by which he fulfilled all the commands of God required of us. Not only are all our sins erased, but a mark of righteousness is written next to our names (Rom 8:3-4). He is sin-bearer and purity-bestower.

There are two other terms to summarize Christ's functions. He is a *master* (king) and a *teacher* (prophet). Let us look at his kingly role first. Can you have only the Savior (sin-bearer) Christ in your heart? No, it is impossible to divide Christ. If he truly comes into your life, *all* of him enters. The overwhelming usage of the word Lord in the book of Acts shows us clearly how Christ was presented to nonbelievers. The phrase "accept Christ as your personal Savior" is not found. Rather, "God has made . . . Jesus . . . both Lord and Christ" (Acts 2:36); "Who are you, Lord?" (Acts 9:5); "Believe in the Lord Jesus" (Acts 16:31).

These apostles were not preaching salvation by "making Christ Lord of your life" in a good-works fashion. He is already Lord; therefore, our evangelistic call must be to come to him as to the feet of a monarch, in submission to his person and authority. We cannot come to a king with one hand behind our backs, standing upright, signifying secret reservations and unwillingness to give over control of our lives. We are not in a position to bargain. We must bow with both hands outstretched and open. Part two will discuss the ramifications of this.

This is the picture of the true penitent's *attitude* of heart (not that we are able to render perfect obedience). Because we are not whole people we cannot give a holistic response. Yet God receives the part for the whole, the seed as evidence the flower will bloom. In the mercy of God, it is later in our Christian lives that we are shown the implications of our initial submission to him as king.

I cannot point to the specific day on which I crossed over the line to be on the Lord's side. I can remember well that I was sixteen when I first began to have an attitude of love to Christ and surrender to his will. I used to live for the fun of the weekends, but by Sunday night I would return to the loneliness of my bedroom and express my deep dissatisfaction, telling him to take over. I knew very little of the theology of Christ's lordship, but I still embraced it. I wanted someone to rule my unruly heart.

I realize now how gracious Christ was to not overwhelm me at that point with the specific forms his mastery over me would take. I did not comprehend that his lordship would include my custom-built car, dating life, money, vocation. Nevertheless, I handed him the notebook of my life and sincerely asked him to write in it what he wanted. All new Christians are born spiritual babes; we don't expect them to be full-fledged disciples immediately. Yet there is an instinctive attitude of wanting to embrace Christ's lordship in every truly converted person. Christ will exercise his sovereignty by daily bringing us to a willing bondage under an easy yoke and light burden in which his commands are not grievous. What a tremendous liberation!

There's *good* news! God the Father has provided a bridge back to himself so you can return to the road of life. As loving Father and just Judge he sends his Son, the God-Man Jesus, to save you. He does this not because of anything deserving in us but because he desires to glorify himself by showing mercy. This is called *grace*—love for those undeserving of love and empowerment for those unable to save themselves. He provides for us the two things his Father required of us. First he keeps the rules of life. He never sinned. Our obligation to live a morally perfect life is fulfilled by Jesus for us. He is our substitute law-keeper. Second, he takes the punishment we deserve for disobeying God's holy law. He dies by a cruel, painful crucifixion in our place. He is our substitute sin-bearer. Then he rises from the dead, showing that he has defeated the power of sin that enslaved us. Christ has *done* all that's necessary for our salvation. There is no more trying to do good; we rest in what he has done. The way is opened for us to cross over to a relationship with God, to be adopted into his family and come home. In "Come Home" I have departed from the normal verses given in gospel outlines to commend the simple reading of the crucifixion and resurrection story. Perhaps this is because it was pivotal in my conversion. Many do not know the story and find it very powerful.

The "Do Versus Done" illustration is also helpful. You pique the person's curiosity by saying that there's a big difference between religion and Christianity.

> Religion is spelled D-O—people *do* good deeds, like praying, being nice to others, or giving money to the poor, in order to try to earn their way to heaven. The problem is, they never know how many good deeds they need to do. Even worse, the Bible says they can never do enough to merit eternal life.
>
> But Christianity is spelled D-O-N-E. Jesus has *done* for us what we could never do for ourselves. He lived the perfect life and died as our substitute to pay for all of our wrongdoing. But merely knowing is not enough. We must receive Jesus as our forgiver and leader. Are you ready to take that step?[11]

As our teacher-prophet, he is the one who supremely reveals God himself and his will. When we make this clear in evangelism we set the stage for a person to know where he must go from now on for guidance and who is the only one who has the words of eternal life. In his special commission to his disciples, Jesus appointed them to give the written, inspired interpretation of his revelation in history. Christ as our prophet did this through the Holy Spirit by bringing "all things to their remembrance," so that the believers since then will have a "more sure word of prophecy"—the Bible (Jn 14:26; 2 Pet 1:19-21). We are *not* to look to seers, mystics, mediums or even our own hunches, supposed prophecies or personal revelations and feelings for determining God's will.

Jesus is alive today.—a truth that gripped and fired the early evangelists in Acts. He really rose from the dead; if he did not, then we are wasting our time. Picture a ship in a raging storm being broken up on cruel rocks just offshore. The people of the town man a small boat and struggle against seemingly insurmountable odds to rescue the ship's crew. In anguish the people on the shore wait and watch for the first sign of the return of the rescue boat. At last it appears through the wind-whipped sea. Too anxious to wait any longer someone yells out from shore at the top of his lungs, "Any survivors?" Each second seems an age, and then the brief and crushing reply comes, "No, all are lost." The group on shore, bewildered, does not know what to do or say. Finally, one man cries out with the little that is in him, "Three cheers for the attempt," and the crowd does its best to raise its voice in compliance.

And what of the resurrection of Jesus? If he did not really conquer death, then the best that can be said is "Three cheers for the attempt."

We wish people to see Jesus as the God-man who is the only way to life. A prairie fire was whipped along by the wind so fast that it overtook all creatures in its path. One family, seeing the impossibility of outrunning the blaze, began a backfire and then covered themselves with earth as they lay in the midst of the already burned-out circle. The roaring fire met the backfire and it burned only up to the edge of that burned-over area, then went right around it, continuing its hungry race. That family was saved. They knew the only safe place was where the fire had already burned.

The fire of God's wrath has touched down at one particular point in history. And when it did, it utterly consumed a man as he hung on a cross. It did not burn a large area, but it finalized God's work of judgment. The fire of God's wrath will come again in history. This time it will consume the whole earth. Will there be any place to hide? Only on the hill where that cross stood, where the fire has already burned. A person is forgiven if he identifies with Christ who on the cross bore God's judgement for sin. Jesus Christ is our burned-over area, the only safe hiding place.

In presenting the whole gospel, we must vividly present the whole Christ in all his roles.

5. Our necessary response: coming home to Jesus. An inherent part of the biblical gospel is the call to respond. No evangelist is worthy of our support, no matter how superb his presentation of truth about God, man and Christ, if he then walks away without lovingly urging people to respond.

On the other hand, method-centered evangelism is too active. Considering how important it is not to "let the fish get away," whole manuals have been written for "successful" fishing. Often sinners are confused rather than helped at this point. A physical action (signing a card, repeating a prayer, walking forward, raising a hand, standing up and so on) are made the sign of an inner spiritual reality. The me-centered evangelist turns into a salesperson, creating undue psychological pressure. It is here we most graphically betray our weak theology. If God is sovereign, and if the person's conviction is of the Holy Spirit, then God can finish what he has begun. Our mistrust of the Spirit's power is serious at this point.

Instead of these tactics, offer passages like Isaiah 53:1-11, Psalm 51:1-17 and Galatians 2:20, and then in many (but not all) cases leave them alone. God will finish what he has begun. We can urge them to pray and seek mercy and to keep on doing so until God answers. We need to direct seeking sinners to come and rejoice with us when they know God has answered (inner witness, Rom 8:14-16), and they see their motives and actions begin to change (outer evidence, 1 Jn). Then we can complement the work of the Holy Spirit by helping them to become grounded in Scripture and involved in fellowship.

We must not usurp the work of the Spirit whose task is to bring people to repentance and faith, and then to seal new believers. Too often we have tried to give assurance of salvation by listening to their prayers, seeing their tears and thus judging them sincere. We then instruct them to put their name in John 3:16 and never doubt God again ("For God so loved _____"). But the Spirit witnesses to our eternal life assurance policy not some counselor. No wonder the church is full of professors but few possessors!

Repentance and faith. The command to "turn to God in repentance and have faith in our Lord Jesus" summarizes the gospel invitation (Acts 20:21). It is important to have both these elements urged upon non-Christians who are under conviction. The lack of emphasis on repentance in "easy believism" teaching is regrettable. Although turning and trusting may be presented separately at times in the Bible, as we compare Scripture with Scripture, we see that they are two sides of one coin. We must avoid pressing one on unbelievers without the other. Repentance without faith will lead to sorrow and mere legalistic resolutions (2 Cor 7: 10; cf. Cain, Saul and Judas). Faith without repentance is unfounded optimism, leading to self-deception. As J. I. Packer so aptly puts it, "Mere creedence without trusting and mere remorse without turning do not save."[12] Again, we see the importance of defining our words and not speaking in general terminology without specific application to the life of non-Christians. (See chapter thirteen, "Our Goal: Disciples.")

Wrapping up this brief commentary on a few distinctives of a God-centered gospel, I conclude with the importance of defining faith. Saving faith has as its object the person of Christ, the Atoner, not just certain facts about the atonement. The latter view makes faith equivalent to mental assent. And the church is filled with people who add one more fact to their minds. The whole person is to respond to the whole Christ. The essence of real faith is trust—pictured as drinking, eating, submitting, identifying with a person. Such faith does not receive half of Christ but a whole Christ. There is not one exhortation in Scripture to Christians to "accept Christ as Lord." Rather, they are to live out the implications of their *initial* relationship to him. Christians are urged to daily surrender after their initial and basic surrender that took place at their regeneration (Rom 6:17-18, 22; 12:1-2; Col 2:6). Saving faith is not a look backward to the cross in the past but a look forward to Christ today and in the future. It is the implementation of an attitude.

The story in Luke 15 of the two lost sons is perfect for showing people how they should respond to God. Although the application of the younger son's response is obvious, the older son's story may not seem as applicable, because it doesn't include a response! Yet it *is* appropriate, for it shows how religious people can "live with" God the Father (be acquainted and work dutifully for him) yet not have a saving relationship with him. "His Father went out and pleaded with him" (Lk 15:28). So he is pleading now with self-righteous and bitter people who have never experienced grace to come home, find salvation and celebrate. The illustration I suggest to people is of a *person* standing before them, because becoming a Christian is entering into a relationship, not just following a code of ethics. This sets up the proper focus for a *personal* response, of which there are only three possibilities. People may balk at this, but I believe we see this in the three reactions to Paul's sermon in Athens (Acts 17:32-34) and Jesus' own invitation (Lk 9:23-26). The option of being neutral or having no response is not available; it is the same as rejection.

As we discuss the call for both repentance and faith in our gospel proclamation, I want to make a special plea for teaching the magnificent doctrine of justification by faith. Picture a courtroom scene. God has on his robes of justice, and we are standing before him. We would expect to hear the word *guilty* as the gavel of God's judgment comes down with a thud. But what do we hear? *Acquitted.* Yes! Justification is God saying, "Go free," to undeserving sinners. We are not condemned because his anger against our sin has been fully satisfied by the free donation of an alien righteousness on our behalf.

It is astounding how little evangelicals really understand this; consequently, they have a wrong emphasis in both evangelism and the Christian life. The truths of justification give the foundation for Christian witness. Robert Horn says, "Justification holds all the aspects of the Gospel in focus. Indeed it is the Gospel: without it we have no good news to tell; leave out justification and we leave out a great deal more than just a word. . . . Without justification, everything becomes superficial. . . . The point is that justification represents a whole perspective."[13] As we respond with the gratitude inevitably kindled by free grace, our turning and trusting pleases God.

Assurance. The Bible teaches that when people respond to the gospel, they both *can* and *should* have assurance of their salvation. This was John's purpose in writing his first letter: "I write these things to you who believe in the name of the Son of God so that you may know that you have eternal life" (1 Jn 5:13). There are those who consider themselves saved who need to discover they are lost. There are also those who still consider themselves lost who are truly saved. How can this be? Let me describe two types of people.

The first type has assurance that is based on self-deception. They believe God has saved them, but they continue to live a deliberately sinful life. This is presumption, not assurance. They presume on God's grace rather than being assured of it. They are still lost, and they need to examine their basis for assurance.

A second type vacillates in the certainty of their own salvation. They do not doubt that God can save, but doubt rather that God has saved *them.* They can have many reasons for this vacillation, and they may or may not still be unbelievers. Since assurance of salvation may not be immediate on becoming a Christian, people can be true believers yet lack assurance that they are. True believers can be confused about their salvation because of unresolved doubt, failure to deal with known sin in their lives, temptation, physical and emotional fatigue, an overly sensitive conscience, wrong teaching or God himself sending a trial and withdrawing from them.[14] So the confused, along with the presumptuous and the uncertain, need a clear understanding of the theology of assurance.[15]

The question is, How do I know that I am a Christian? This is a different question from How do I become a Christian? and therefore has a completely different answer. Yet too often people respond to these questions in the same way, and those who seek help in their quest for assurance do not find it. The answer to the second question is "You become a Christian through repentance toward God and faith in Christ alone as Savior and Lord." The answer to the first question is "You know that you have become a Christian (that God has answered prayer and regenerated you) by a threefold result in your life."

The first pillar of assurance is a trust in the promises of God as being promises to you. You count them true and take them personally. The second is the beginning of a change in your attitudes and actions corresponding to the fruit of the Spirit (Gal 5) and the marks of salvation (1 Jn). The third is the inner witness of God's Spirit to your spirit that you are his child (Rom 8). These three pillars are like giant candles whose light reveals our regenerated nature. Scripture tells us to "examine yourselves to see whether you are in the faith; test yourselves" (2 Cor 13:5). This is not morbid introspection. In biblical self-examination we look to what God says should be true of a believer and see if it is true of our lives during the past week or month. We must not only consider the last hour or day but also a longer time period, for we find winters when no fruit is evident, even in the souls of true Christians.

We must not, however, condone persistent and prolonged disobedience to the known will of God on the part of professing Christians. God's purpose is to smash such "assurance," for it is mere presumption. This is the point of all the warnings and "ifs" in the letter to the Hebrews. Professing Christians will not escape if they neglect God's great salvation. If such people are merely labeled "carnal Christians," they are led into a dangerous false security. Using the term *carnal* as an adjective to modify the word *Christian* leads to the misconception that a person can be both of the world (continuing in a life characterized by fleshly attitudes and actions) and of Christ. The Bible nowhere allows this. It speaks of Christians who have *areas* of carnality in their lives (jealousy, quarreling, personal loyalties; 1 Cor 3:1-4), but never of Christians whose whole lives over a prolonged period are saturated with disobedience. How can Christ be in a life but not on the throne of that life? Where else in our hearts could Christ the king reside if not ruling from the throne of our lives?

What do the first type of people lacking assurance need to be told, those professing believers whose lives are characterized by sin? It would be confusing to urge "more of the Spirit" on them when they may still be unconverted! The kindest thing we can do is to turn them to the Scriptures so they can evaluate their *present* lives, not past deeds or experiences. Here they will find objective descriptions of the attitudes and actions of true believers. They are not to measure themselves by their own (or others') traditions and subjective standards of true spirituality, for this would lead them into a quagmire of uncertainty. Educating their consciences with God's teaching about the three marks of saving faith will free them from enslavement to their darkened consciences, the expectations of others, and the use of feelings as the criterion for and content of faith.

Is it kind to shatter a person's hope of salvation? Yes, because without scriptural grounds, it is nothing more than a false hope. A hope of acceptance by God based on such things as going forward in a meeting, praying a suggested prayer, imitating the experience of others, joining a church, attending many Christian meetings, being baptized, studying the Bible regularly, helping others, feeling good in a religious service or having a strong conviction that they are right with God is a hope not founded on biblical truths. Perhaps people may trust in the doctrine of election or in theological precision or in baptism. They may have a sentimental belief in the general providence of God: "God has been good to me; God will take care of me." Yet people can be involved in any or all of these activities without ever looking to Jesus Christ as the only Savior and Lord. Without this there is no salvation. Without this there is no assurance. Let us in kindness alert these people to what Christ will say to them on the day of judgment. "Not everyone who says to me, 'Lord, Lord,' will enter the kingdom of heaven, but only he who does the will of my Father who is in heaven. Many will say to me on that day, 'Lord, Lord, did we not prophesy in your name, and in your name drive out demons and perform many miracles?' Then I will tell them plainly, 'I never knew you. Away from me, you evildoers!' " (Mt 7:21-23).

Suppose we are dealing with the second type of people lacking assurance, true believers who are really tormented and need to know of their security in Christ. Again, the kind thing is to bring the sure Word of God, with its infallible promises, alongside the grace they find exists in their changed hearts. The Spirit will then enable believers to say with assurance, "I am a child of God and will be forever." This great comfort and encouragement does not come through a private revelation of the Spirit (a witness of the Spirit apart from or in addition to the Bible). Assurance is effected not by imparting new revelation to a person's heart, but by applying what is already revealed in Scripture, namely, the truth that believers shall be saved.[16]

When we sin it is to be expected that our assurance of salvation will be weakened. God is keeping us from complacency and warning us not to play with sin. God, in mercy, will not allow children of his to be comfortable in sin. He makes us restless, even to the point of questioning our salvation, so that we may not presume on his favor but, instead, relish his grace. Often we recognize our salvation not by victory over sin but by the warfare that is still going on within us. Comfort and encouragement do not come from outward circumstances of "success" but rather from drawing near to God with a true heart in full assurance of faith, from knowing that nothing can separate us from the love of God in Christ Jesus our Lord. Boldness coupled with humility is the result. Our assurance must be founded, built up and established on the mercy of God alone. It can be further established when we review ourselves before God and find evidence of his dwelling and reigning within us in the deeds he has enabled us to do.[17] Our eternal security should be focused not on remote past actions but on our present attitude toward Christ. Just as earthly parents can expect physical growth in their children, so we can expect to see a gradual change in the lives of God's children.

Let me conclude by specifically mentioning some guidelines. Since we cannot read other people's hearts and discern their true standing (saved or lost) before God, we should not try to take over the work of the Holy Spirit.

Rather, we should help them to measure themselves by God's standard. We refrain from minimizing sin, we portray grace as truly free, and we remind them of the three tenses of salvation: I have been saved (Eph 2:8), I am being saved (1 Cor 1:18), I will be saved (Rom 5:9). The basis for assurance of salvation is threefold: the promises of God made real to the heart, the inner testimony of God's Spirit to our spirit, and the production of attitudes and actions congruent with the fruit of the Spirit and God's commandments. This last objective pillar is delineated in John's first letter. It is helpful to suggest that a person who has made a profession of faith read this epistle keeping the following points in mind:

1. Test of consciousness of sin (1 Jn 1:8, 10)

2. Test of obedience (1 Jn 2:3-5, 29)

3. Test of freedom from habitual sin (1 Jn 3:9; 5:18)

4. Test of love for other Christians (1 Jn 3:14; 4:7-8)

5. Test of belief (1 Jn 5:1)

6. Test of overcoming the world and Satan (1 Jn 2:13-14; 5:4)

The vocabulary of the five pillars of God's gospel is molded by the empowering love of the Trinity. Meditate on these words of the poet John Donne:

> Batter my heart, three-personed God; for You
> As yet but knock, breathe, shine, and seek to mend;
> That I may rise and stand, o'erthrow me, and bend
> Your force, to break, blow, burn, and make me new.
> I, like an usurped town, to another due,
> Labor to admit You, but Oh, to no end!
> Reason, Your viceroy in me, me should defend,
> But is captived, and proves weak or untrue.
> Yet dearly I love You, and would be loved fain.
> But am betrothed unto Your enemy;
> Divorce me, untie or break that knot again,
> Take me to You, imprison me, for I,
> Except You enthrall me, never shall be free,
> Nor ever chaste, except You ravish me.[18]

GOSPEL TELLING: "COME HOME" DIAGRAM

Importance of a gospel summary. I have a vivid recollection of reading through the entire book of Acts in one sitting with some friends. Ernie Reisinger, a friend from church during my college days, took a half-dozen students one Saturday out into the woods and hills of central Pennsylvania. We did a survey of Acts, looking for the content of the gospel proclaimed by the early church. I never forgot what I read of the evangelistic message of those early believers. Their approach, like that of Jesus, was never stereotyped. It was theological and personal.

In studying Acts we discover that the evangelists brought out certain gospel truths again and again. Their witness was also versatile. They were aware of unbelievers as individuals in unique situations. Yet, there was a basic grid or "pattern of sound words" that proved a useful springboard for the memories of evangelists. It kept them on the track. They turned again and again to the pivotal points of the gospel. It was not, however, a straitjacket, inhibiting any creativity on their part.[19]

The "Come Home" outline is not perfect, but it is an attempt to fix in our mind certain poles around which truths cluster so that we will have a clear understanding when we talk with nonbelievers. Any attitude of "now I have it" betrays ignorance and pride. Likewise, an attitude of "holding back" in my witnessing until I comprehend the gospel is sinful.

Often, along with the idea of learning such an outline comes the concept that there are many people just waiting to hear these several hundred words and anxious to believe. This assumption is not generally true. There are exceptions, as we find people quickly converted in the New Testament (such as the thief on the cross or the Philippian jailer), but these people were under conviction of sin and prepared by God's Spirit.

We must not make the mistake of thinking that people are converted because they follow our line of reasoning as we explain the gospel. It is very helpful for nonbelievers to see the overall picture, but they may be far from any sense of awe of God as Creator, conviction of personal sin and hunger for redemption.

On the other hand, it is certainly helpful for believers to have a framework on which to begin building a more systematic comprehension of our great salvation. Any such outline should be filled in by thorough meditation in the Scriptures, personal communion with Jehovah, and active listening to solid preaching that exposits and applies the Word. It will help to thoroughly learn the central points of the outline by first studying the Amplified Version, then role playing the Simplified Version. (Both versions and a procedure for learning are located in appendix B in a format for copying.)

Gospel diagram: coming home to God and a family. Inherent in each person is a God-imparted longing for significance and loving relationships. At the foundation of the cosmos is the one personal God existing in three beings. This means that *both* unity and individuality are the essence of existence. We do not have to choose either the *One* or the *Many* as the ultimate origin/center of the cosmos. The uniqueness of the biblical Trinity (one in three and three in one) has incredible ramifications for intellectual thought and practical living. I will leave the unraveling of this to others and focus on the application to the gospel.

The biblical God is a person. Therefore, he has various names, and he is referred to by a personal pronoun, not *it*. References to a triune God—Father, Son and Holy Spirit—abound in Scripture, with divine attributes given to each. This means there is interaction, *relationship*, at the center of life. Making humanity in his image means he created us to be in relationship with each other. Men and women are commanded to combine and produce children so there will be more relationships. The achieving of one flesh (unity, although their individuality doesn't cease) glorifies God, even if no children are forthcoming.

Nevertheless, *family* relationships are at the heart of his plan for humanity. People are to live in loving relationship with their creator God, their nuclear family (mother, father, siblings), their extended family of blood relations, and with all other people as their brothers and sisters. We share in a common humanity from a common origin. As the apostle Paul expressed to some intellectual polytheists in ancient Greece: "The God who made the world and everything in it . . . gives all men life and breath and everything else. From one man he made every nation of men . . . so that men would seek him and perhaps reach out for him and find him. . . . 'For in him we

live and move and have our being.' As some of your own poets have said,
'We are his offspring' " (Acts 17:24-28).

Believers in Christ are adopted into God's family. He becomes their spiritual Father, Christ is their elder brother, and other believers are spiritual brothers and sisters—a new family transcending and incorporating all racial, ethnic, gender and cultural differences; a unity in diversity displaying the nature of a triune God; having spiritual equality yet diverse roles and talents. Redemption reestablishes the relationships that were meant to be, both on earth now and in the new heaven and earth to come. Home and family were meant to be places of security, interaction, safety, love, joy, friendship, creative endeavor and joint worship of God. This now becomes a reality, although imperfect, in the Christian family and the church. When we enter the eternal kingdom, adopted both legally and experientially, the perfect fulfillment of a real home and family will be beyond our wildest dreams and will meet our deepest longings. We will say, "Somehow, I just knew it was meant to be like this!"

The universal desire for relationships is obvious today. This thirst can be a doorway into the satisfaction of finding true friendship (deep fellowship) with God and others. It may involve a divorce from current friends and your natural family. Jesus warned that our love for him must supersede our love for anyone else, and that even our own family may become alienated if you follow Christ. Nevertheless, the promise made to his disciples who left all to follow him has not been rescinded:

> "I tell you the truth," Jesus replied, "no one who has left home or brothers or sisters or mother or father or children or fields for me and the gospel will fail to receive a hundred times as much in this present age (homes, brothers, sisters, mothers, children and fields—and with them, persecutions) and in the age to come, eternal life."
> (Mk 10:29-30)

I have used the theme "come home" to link the five pivotal truths of the gospel: God, his law, our sin, Christ's salvation and our response. Key concepts are organized under these five headings. The five "truth clusters" are linked by the Road of Life, which leads either to hell or, if Christ the bridge is crossed, to heaven and home. Beginning with God as Creator establishes his authority and our responsibility. Outlining the two "Rules of the Road," God's law, establishes standards for living—a missing element in many gospel outlines. Concise yet thorough teaching on sin (self-centeredness) shows what our real need is. The fourth point expands on the grace of God in providing Christ as our Savior and Restorer, who guides us back onto the God-centered Road of Life. Lastly, the response of repentance and faith is required of us to enter into a *relationship* with God and therefore to be at *home* in the universe.

Then we will live out the great design of our God who wishes to be in covenant with his creation: "I will be their God and they will be my people" (Jer 31:33). Although this covenant relationship has its background in the sovereign provision by a king for his servants, the Bible makes it clear that the fruition of this is a loving family of the Lord and his children. "They will follow the Lord; he will roar like a lion. When he roars, his children will come . . . [and] I will settle them in their homes, declares the Lord" (Hos 11:10-11).

PART TWO

To the Whole Person
Conversion of the Total Person

4

Professors but Not Possessors

While I was revising this book, my phone rang. What follows is a paraphrase of what a frustrated woman said to me. She identified her affiliation for thirty-five years with a local church and denomination that are considered to be theologically sound and evangelistically zealous. In its creed the "doctrines of grace" are explicit. Its evangelism training has been widely used. Its school has educated thousands. In addition to teaching at the church school for twenty years, this woman has engaged in an evangelistic ministry to children for twenty years. Why was she upset and asking my advice? "There is so little evidence of deep change in the lives of many of those who have professed faith in Christ, especially the young people I teach."

This is a woman who has been trained in what many consider to be the best evangelism program. She has observed for two decades or more the "results." What she describes is widespread throughout the evangelical subcul-ture. It is a global problem: "saved" Christian young people who are merely adapting externally to the patterns of their church culture. Churches who are operating on the principle of "presumptive regeneration," a term used among the Puritans in early America who faced the same dilemma, presum-ing children of Christian parents are born again as long as they conform out-wardly and have a head knowledge of Scripture. Young people who show no outward evidence of moral deviance at the age of twelve (or there about) are enrolled in the church membership class for about six weeks. At completion, a church leader listens passively to their testimony. If they use the right phrases they are formally received into the local church the next Sunday. In Baptist churches, the procedure is immersion in water based on a credible profession of faith. But are any searching questions asked? How can we guard against cheap grace and mere intellectual assent with little evidence of a changed life? How can we discern any idols still lurking in the heart?

We begin to notice the prevalence of the "two-stages" testimony, typically summarized in words like these: "I received Jesus as my Savior when I was six and prayed with my Sunday School teacher, *but* I made him Lord when I really started living like a Christian at twenty-two in my first year of grad-uate school." Complacency in doctrinally orthodox churches regarding both the content of evangelism training and confusion on how to evaluate profes-sions of faith lead to "Christians" who are self-deceived and to a God who is dishonored. There are helpful resources discussing whether Christ can be your savior but not your Lord.[1]

What can we do to avoid misleading people, resulting in a profession of faith in Christ without actually possessing Christ? It is sad to realize that false professions of faith are frequent in the church. Most of us know people who seemed to be drawn toward the gospel and yet didn't step over the line of faith. Can this be the explanation for the conflict between statistics that show a large number of professing born-again Christians and the continuing moral tailspin in the world? What I wish to do in this section is set forth the biblical view of conversion, a conversion of the whole personality in all its faculties, and contrast it with types of synthetic conversions.

Our desire must be nothing less than to see the whole individual converted. We are looking to God for changed persons, not just a response from one segment of a personality. God's regenerative work is a thorough renewing that involves all the faculties of mind, emotions and will. Scriptural language calls this a "new creation," a "new birth." People are either saved or lost. To weaken this radical but scriptural cleavage of mankind by suggesting a third category for people is an attack on the biblical doctrine of regeneration. There is no such thing as being a half Christian—for instance, being a "Christian" but not a Spirit-baptized Christian; being a "Christian" but not accepting Christ as Lord; being a "Christian" but living a life continually characterized by being carnal (spiritual adultery).

A Christian has the Holy Spirit, being baptized, indwelt, sealed and sanctified by him (Acts 2:38-39; Rom 8:9, 11, 13-15; 1 Cor 3:16; 12:12-13; Eph 1:13). A Christian has acknowledged the lordship of Christ (Acts 22:10; Rom 10:9-10; 1 Jn 5:1-5). All Christians turn away from sin (Rom 6:1-14; 1 Jn 3:3-10). The low level of spirituality among us has caused the term *Christian* to become so insipid that we propose various adjectives to restore its flavor. I have no argument with any movement to raise the norm of our spiritual life. I suggest, though, that the best away to raise it is to deepen our understanding of regeneration, not tack on new dimensions. If God has already given us the greatest present in the world, will he withhold the ribbon? Nevertheless, we find our joy in the gift not decorations (Rom 8:32).

Mere Conversion

Regeneration and *conversion* are words to describe two different ways of viewing salvation. *Regeneration* is viewing salvation from God's side; it is an instantaneous impartation of new life to the soul. We may or may not be conscious of the exact moment this happened to us. *Conversion,* on the other hand, is viewing salvation from our perspective. It is a *process* of the entire work of God's grace from the first dawning of understanding and seeking to the final closing with Christ in new birth. For some, this is a period of years; for others merely an hour. We respond in time to God's action in eternity.[2]

Lack of understanding of the normal stages of conversion has led to confused counseling on the part of well-meaning evangelists. To dispel this confusion, a closer look at the phases is helpful. But be advised, the Spirit does not always work according to our timetable. God does not limit himself to a specific design. There is a pattern, however, even amidst the unique circumstances surrounding a conversion like Paul's.[3] It helps to realize people are not always regenerated the first time they begin to call on the name of the Lord. To confuse the *first* workings of response in the conversion process with the *final* is extremely dangerous, for non-Christians can be deluded into thinking they are saved before they really are. Our forefathers made some helpful distinctions in these areas. They called an unbeliever, apparently untouched by any saving operations of God's Spirit, a "sleeping sinner." An "awakened" or "seeking sinner" was one who had begun to respond to God's prior working of his Spirit. The positive response would manifest itself in a conviction of sin and an active call on Christ for salvation, which would result in the sinner willingly exercising faith and repentance. Each of these stages emphasizes a different relationship with God. Today, however, the tendency is to rush a person into the kingdom at the slightest indication of an interest in spiritual things. Jesus was cautious at times (e.g., Nicodemus, the moral young man) and tested the spiritual conviction of his would-be disciples.

What a joy it is to meet people prepared by God's Spirit to receive the gospel! We pray that the convicting power of the Holy Spirit will come on these seeking and awakened sinners. We don't require them to stand outside the kingdom for months, but say, in the words of a hymn,

> Come, ye needy, come, and welcome;
>   God's free bounty glorify;
> True belief and true repentance,
>   Every grace that brings us nigh;
> Without money . . .
>   Come to Jesus Christ and buy.
> . . . Jesus ready stands to save you,
>   Full of pity joined with power:
> He is able . . .
>   He is willing; doubt no more.[4]

We are anxious, in a good sense, to see such people move beyond a general sensitivity to the gospel, so we point them and urge them toward Christ, the door. What can we do when we find someone who seems to be coming under conviction? Sometimes these people get stuck at the brink of decision. Here are some principles in guiding them.[5]

First, counsel them in a way that focuses on action, not talk. In other words, resist counseling at length without giving them imperatives on which to act.

Second, urge them to cast themselves on the mercy of the Lord. We are not to hear their confessions and become their priest, for this may be a way they relieve their guilt.

Third, use the Bible in an effort to impress them with God's counsel, not your wisdom.

Finally, we must be genuine. Our entire emotional concern is to represent the Lord and to help the seeker. Specifically we should:

1. Encourage them. God is bringing them to a crisis.

2. Warn the hesitant and stubborn—not that they can't be saved but that they are not choosing to be saved. Tell them to ask God for faith.

3. Emphasize the sin there is in relapse—greater judgment accrues from greater knowledge (Heb 6:4-6; 2 Pet 2:21).

4. Encourage them not to neglect Christian meetings—"faith comes from hearing" (Rom 10:17).

5. Point them to a personal Savior—not just to meaning in life, peace of heart or the like—because the root of our rebellion is personal sin against God (Jer 29:13).

6. Stress urgent, earnest seeking (Deut 4:29).

7. Challenge them to admit what sin they are clinging to.

8. Show them how to pray; suggest Psalm 51.

A PARTIAL RESPONSE TO THE GOSPEL

Is it possible for a person sincerely to *profess* faith in Christ but not possess the real thing? Yes, certainly. A friend told me how he awakened to the fact that something was amiss in the body of Christ. He had been striving to incite love and obedience among some church young people and had been invited to speak to these "Christians." The weekend retreat was fast approaching, but he had no peace about the message he should bring. He began to wonder why it was that the faith of these young people always needed "jacking up." He began to wonder if they had any real faith in the first place. He was afraid of being thought of as fanatical or supercritical, but he decided to begin by asking the group some basic questions.

The first night of the retreat arrived, and he opened up with two questions: "How many of you, if you died tonight, would know you'd go to heaven?" All raised their hands. "How many of you really want to do the will of God—allowing that you can't obey *perfectly*—but you truly *purpose* in your heart to do it?" Only one-fifth raised their hands. How could he square the responses to these questions with clear biblical teaching that says that true salvation not only secures the forgiveness of rebels but their obedience as well (Heb 5:9)? He decided to preach evangelistically that entire conference and saw many come to faith in Christ.

At a women's college I was having lunch in the dining hall with a student who had regularly attended the InterVarsity Christian Fellowship Bible studies. She seemed to have high morals and was kind to others. She had very little to say when it came to how the Scriptures were part of her life; she also failed to express any specific biblical content in her witness to non-Christians. She was friendly and outgoing. Many assumed that she was a Christian. I asked her to what she attributed her confidence that she was converted.

"When I was thirteen," she replied, "I remained in my church sanctuary after the morning service. It was a lovely day, and the sun was shining through the stained glass windows, creating vivid patterns. I felt all warm, good and peaceful."

I sat there waiting for her to say more, but that was it! Many people have a good hope but with absolutely no foundation for it.

Another girl at a state university came to me full of frustration. For a year she had been quite active in various Christian activities. She prayed, read the Bible and sang heartily. Her peers assumed she was a Christian, but these were her words: "I need the friendship and acceptance of others. This school is so big. It's a lonely place. I didn't fit in with the wilder girls. The Christian group is so friendly. I fit in easily, but I can't face it any longer. I'm not really one of you. I've come to admit I'm not a Christian."

Without a thorough understanding of the holistic approach to evangelism, such people who have never been converted may continue being deceived about their true state and thus become a hindrance to the church, or they will drop out, joining the ranks of the disillusioned and become either numb or hostile to religion. Hardened by years of no response to the Word of God, relatively few of these people seem to convert. We must help them and not mislead them.

God's Word is not silent on this issue either.

Parable of the four soils (Mt 13:1-23). Two of the seeds sown by the sower begin to grow but do not mature because the soil is bad. There is an initial response of joy, hearing, growth, but that response does not continue because of a lack of roots and shade. The thorns showed that the soil of the heart was not good.

Simon the sorcerer (Acts 8:9-24). This man is described as believing and desiring more spiritual power in his life. He was also baptized. Yet he is not truly converted for he offers money for spiritual power (simony). Peter says he should perish and that Simon has "no part or share in this ministry, because your heart is not right before God. . . . You are full of bitterness and captive to sin."

Herod (Mt 2:1-18). Because we are so familiar with the outcome of Herod's inquiry for Christ, we forget that he impressed many with his "Christian" zeal at first. He took an interest in the Bible; he sought out wise men to help him with prophecy; he went to the trouble of finding Christ. He did not ask Christ to be brought to him but, in apparent humility, wanted to go to him. Not only that, he professed a correct view of Christ, for he said he wanted to worship him.

The Passover crowd (Jn 2:23-25). Here are personal witnesses of Jesus' miracles who even "trusted in his name." Yet their lack of saving trust is clear, for it says that Jesus did not entrust himself to them. He knew all men; he knew what was in a man. In John 8:31-59 we see again a group of people described as believers yet who do not hold to Christ's teaching; they end up trying to stone him!

The enlightened Jews (Heb 6:4-9). These people experienced the influence of

God's Spirit but not his saving influence. What is said of them (that "they are crucifying the Son of God all over again and subjecting him to public disgrace," and that it is impossible for them "to be brought back to repentance") cannot be said of a true Christian. In verse 9 the writer shifts his address to those who are Christians: "Even though we speak like this, dear friends, we are confident of better things in your case—things that accompany salvation."

The lordship people (Mt 7:21-23). These professors seem to have it all. Not only do they confess the lordship of Christ, but they do so fervently. Their theology and piety seem sound. They manifest spiritual power by prophecy, driving out demons and performing miracles. But their wills have not been converted. Their lack of true regeneration is evident because Christ consigns them to hell as evildoers.

Clearly, we have sufficient warning from both our experiences with others and in Scripture that a partial response to the gospel is not only dangerous but prevalent. We should be cautious in identifying outwardly favorable reactions with regeneration. *Inquirer* or *seeker* is a more lucid and helpful way to denote people who indicate an interest in the gospel. Initially, its better to say a person professed faith, rather than became a Christian last week.

What an awful thought that many will come before Christ thinking they are included and yet find they are excluded. We cannot shirk our responsibility to encourage people to "examine yourselves to see whether you are in the faith; test yourselves" (2 Cor 13:5). They need a confrontation in love, not a spiritual quick fix designed to make them feel at ease with disobedience. They need salvation. We can turn them to the Beatitudes, the first letter of John and Psalm 51, urging them to read these and ask God to show them where they stand with him. This is biblical self-examination—using that aspect of God's law that gives the evidences for new life. It differs from morbid introspection in that it uses an objective criterion and avoids wallowing in subjective analysis.

What then are we trusting God to do? What do we mean when we say the whole gospel is for the whole personality? To respond adequately to these questions we need to examine the faculties comprising our personality. We also need to see how a false conversion can result when any one of these faculties is not touched by the Spirit of God.

The Whole Gospel to the Mind
Not Intellectualism but
Using Truth to Inform and Humble the Mind

I made a courtesy call to the chaplain's office while visiting a small private college. I was greeted by a big smile and warm handshake. We talked amiably about our concern for ministering to students and the needs of the campus. The *Bible, Christ* and *witness* were all words falling naturally from his lips. I was excited to meet a Christian with this calling. All the right bells seemed to be ringing as he said the words I wanted to hear.

ALL HEAD KNOWLEDGE

Later that day, I investigated the programs he was offering. I talked with students who knew him. Some questions were raised in my mind, so I returned to ask the chaplain about his own beliefs. Although somewhat taken aback by my boldness, he agreed in a condescending way to respond. Having grown up in an evangelical Christian home, he had always wanted to help people. He felt the role of a campus minister would give him the most freedom from supervision and stereotypes to influence others in developing their potential.

At one of the leading liberal seminaries he had "come of age" and repudiated the naiveté of his evangelical roots. The Bible was a source book of the "faith of the early church," and the Judeo-Christian tradition was one of many valid expressions of the human search for the ultimate. Jesus? Well, he was an enlightened man, but you had to peel away the myths and legends that had grown up around him to find the "real" Jesus.

I walked away from that chaplain's office saddened to know the truth about a man with religious knowledge but no personalizing or proclaiming of the truths of the gospel. I had poured my interpretation into the words he used as mere symbols.

Unfortunately, this is not an isolated example. Often Christians think they have led someone to Christ but, in fact, the person was only giving the answers the Christian wanted to hear.

The opposite extreme, however, is equally dangerous.

LITTLE HEAD KNOWLEDGE

In my ministry to college students, I have the opportunity to welcome new students into the world of the college campus. I remember one fellow who seemed happy to meet other "Jesus people," as he called us. His enthusiasm was contagious. Later I found that his previous encounters with Christ and Christian fellowship were in a milieu that distrusted and despised the mind. Spontaneity, authenticity, joy and openness in relationships were the hallmarks of the group in which he was nurtured. But there was not much Bible teaching.

In hardly a month he was missing from our fellowship and was not in any other Christian group. He didn't have time to study the Scriptures, and when he did, he had the habit of opening the Bible anywhere, looking for a "blessing."

He had enthroned vivid, firsthand, emotional experiences as the criteria and content of faith. Now at college he met others with a variety of experiences and opinions that were not even close to Christianity.[1] But their experiences were just as intense. Why was his "religious trip" any more valid? they asked. Before long he was openly denying the faith and continues to do so to this day. He had never really been converted, for he did not make truth the criterion of experience. There was no submission of his rebellious mind to the authority of Scripture or his thoughts to the review of higher thoughts.[2] If the *content* of the gospel is Jesus Christ, the *intention* of the gospel is to bind the mind of the unbeliever to the authority of the New Testament and to the lordship of Jesus Christ. These are not two separate entities. The New Testament is the Word of our Lord, and therefore, one of the signs of saving faith is a willingness to keep his teachings (1 Jn 2:3-5).[3]

THE BALANCE: THINKING GOD'S THOUGHTS, NOT JUDGING GOD'S WAYS

Briefly, the biblical teaching on the mind is that our mind is not to be bypassed in our Christian faith, nor is it to be ultimately trusted. Our mind is God-given. John Stott puts it this way:

> Our rationality is part of the divine image. . . . To deny our rationality is therefore to deny our humanity, to become less than human beings. Scripture forbids us to behave like horses or mules which are "without understanding" and commands us instead in our understanding to be "mature.". . . Many imagine that faith is entirely irrational. But Scripture never sets faith and reason over against each other as incompatible. On the contrary, faith can only arise and grow within us by the use of our minds. "Those who know thy name put their trust in thee"; their trust springs from their knowledge of the trustworthiness of God's character. Again, "Thou dost keep him in perfect peace, whose mind is stayed on thee, because he trusts in thee." Here trusting in God and staying the mind on God are synonyms, and perfect peace is the result.[4]

The Fall has infected our minds so that apart from the Spirit they cannot come to the right conclusions morally. They do not interpret "facts" (evidence) as God does. The proper function of the mind is to think God's thoughts after him. The improper use is to sit in judgment on God and his ways. Our minds are not "neutral"; they will not naturally respond and follow the truth of the gospel though they may still operate on certain principles of rationality such as the law of contradiction. They suppress moral implications of the truth (Rom 1:18). They are at enmity with God (Rom 8:7). As fallen men and women, we must repent of the desire to be mentally autonomous. We must cast down our vain imaginings and proud thoughts of ourselves. None of us will be called who *continues* in his own wisdom.

A rather humorous story illustrates this truth. A man walked into a psychiatrist's office one day, insisting he was dead. After several sessions with this "dead" man, the psychiatrist at last thought he had hit on a solution to his patient's problem. He assigned him to go to the library and write an extensive paper on the characteristics of dead people. The doctor did not hear from him for several months. Then one day he received in the mail a large manuscript, the fruit of his patient's labors on this topic. One of his main conclusions was the interesting fact that dead people do not bleed. Over-joyed, the psychiatrist called the man in for an appointment. As soon as the man arrived, he began once again to proclaim that he was dead. At that moment the doctor whipped out a large hatpin and pricked the man's finger. Blood rushed out profusely. "There now, what conclusion do you draw from that?" asked the doctor. After a moment's hesitation, yet without blinking, the patient looked the doctor straight in the eye and exclaimed, "Well, what do you know; dead people do bleed after all!"

Likewise, in spite of all the evidence, the minds of sinful men and women cling to twisted views like a child clutching a favorite toy. We change all evidence to fit our presuppositions.

We are not in any way, however, to encourage non-Christians to put their minds on the shelf in considering the claims of Christ. We invite them to use their minds. " 'Come now, and let us reason together,' says the Lord" (Is 1:18).[5] Paul disputed or argued. He used logic. He did everything possible to clarify and to help unbelievers understand. The apostles used educational evangelism. Indeed, the very vehicle by which God gave his revelation—words—assumes engagement with our minds.

In witnessing to the whole person we should use methods that communicate to the mind. Admittedly, our culture (and worse yet, some parts of the church) rely on another approach to influence people—distracting the mind so that it can be bypassed. (Francis Schaeffer uses the illustration of the burglar who uses meat to distract the dog while he goes about his real business of robbery.) Thus elections are won, products sold and converts produced by creating a pleasing image and obtaining an uncritical response—rather than by reasonably discussing issues or merits.

We must forsake any kind of evangelism that either overly exalts the mind or unduly neglects it.

The Whole Gospel
to the Emotions
Not Emotionalism but Showing Love
and Touching the Heart

Jill sat next to me crying—and I never carry a handkerchief in church! I overheard someone say it had been a "powerful" service. It was over now, and I sat with my friend in the pew trying to recall the meeting. One of those testifying had choked up and was unable to finish. Then the preacher started in on the love of God. Why, you'd be a fool not to respond.

ONLY EMOTIONAL REACTION

My friend Jill then broke into my recollections. "How did he know how much I want to be loved? It seems he was speaking right to me. Everything I ever wanted he says Jesus will give me. . . . Then that long song at the end. The music just did something to me, and he kept pleading with us. After a while it got to me—how I'd messed my life up. I wanted to do something. I didn't want to disappoint the speaker so I raised my hand. Something, I'm not sure what, was making me feel sorry, hopeful and confused all at once. I was so shaken I couldn't think straight about anything. I don't know what's happening to me."

Was Jill converted? What do you think? Let's look at the opposite end of the emotional spectrum.

NO EMOTIONAL REACTION

"Well, that's the truth and you can take it or leave it." I'm not sure the preacher said exactly that, but that certainly was the impression he conveyed. His complacency and bored matter-of-factness permeated the entire sermon, and he ended it the same way—so abrupt, so cold. He spoke on Christ's love for sinners, but he gave no indication that he wanted people to respond. He showed no interest in his audience. There was no pleading with them to come to Christ. It reminded me of the student who approached me on campus and wanted to show me a gospel booklet. He was half-way through his presentation before he looked up at my face and saw that I wanted to speak. It was all so mechanical. So impersonal. So unreal. He also talked of a God of love, but I felt he didn't care at all about me.

THE BALANCE: EMOTIONS LED BY TRUTH

The particular evangelical subculture in which we have been converted will often set the pattern for much of our subsequent growth, attitudes and view of spirituality. One subculture will bring forth emotionally stunted converts who often wear masks. They sometimes seem stiff, unnatural, embarrassed when the talk goes beyond clichés and into "what does this mean to you?" Another subculture has many who effect an exuberance that is all the more hollow. Perhaps they are trying to cover over what is lacking in their faith; maybe it's an unconscious mimic of what their group leaders convey as "spiritual." What can we do to safeguard our evangelism so that it does not run to either extreme of stoicism or emotionalism?

On the subject of emotions, evangelicals are schizophrenic. Some have been so threatened by the accusation of emotionalism that they backpedal as hard as they can. They fall into an unloving smugness. A religious publisher lauds the academic credentials of his writers, or the Christian school president points to her large percentage of faculty with Ph.D.s. Others have been so bored with the sterility of the lives of supposed believers that they rush forward, seeking experience after experience and follow anyone who exudes a warm glow. All evangelistic endeavors must be positive, peppy and have a leader who can "attract young people" (good looking, athletic and humorous). If you believe my analysis is extreme, I simply invite you to peruse some evangelical magazines and popular books, and visit churches and fellowship groups outside your normal circles.

Once again, we hold on to part of the truth while missing the beautiful balance of Scripture. Emotions are part of the image of God in us. If our feelings have been legitimately roused, they should be expressed, not suppressed. Emotions have a valid place in our lives, but they are not to *lead* our lives. Truth is to lead, with emotions and will conforming. We must allow truth to grip us.

> Nothing sets the heart on fire like truth. Truth is not cold and dry. On the contrary, it is warm and passionate. And whenever new vistas of God's truth open up to us, we cannot just contemplate. We are stirred to respond, whether to penitence or to anger or to love or to worship. Think of the two disciples walking to Emmaus on the first Easter afternoon while the risen Lord spoke to them. When He vanished, they said to each other, "Did not our hearts burn within us while He talked to us on the road, while He opened to us the Scriptures?" . . . What was the cause of their spiritual heartburn? It was Christ's opening the Scriptures to them! . . . As F. W. Faber once said, "Deep theology is the best fuel of devotion; it readily catches fire, and once kindled it burns long."[1]

Paul burst into an exhilarating doxology over doctrine (Eph 1:6-10)! It is gratifying to see some new thinking by evangelicals on our emotions.[2] God made us in his image. He has emotions. Let's quit denying ours!

In witnessing we must be emotional. How can we not? We're talking of the deepest *love* in the world. We're pressing on the conscience the awful *anger* of God against personal sin and social injustice. We're communicating the reconciling *peace* of God. Our theme is the liberating *joy* of no condemnation for those in Christ Jesus, the Jesus who *wept* over Jerusalem's unbelief. Have you? It is said that some of the Puritans stained the floor with their tears as they prayed. Is there pain and unceasing sorrow in our hearts for anyone who is yet unconverted? What if we do experience these emotions for sinners in private? Is it wholesome to expose them in public? *Very.*

One fall night my wife, Suzanne, and I were at home together. The phone had rung several times with calls of one sort or another. I was beginning to become a little protective about my privacy. Just then the phone rang again. I reluctantly answered and heard the rough voice of an older man say, "Is this the Willie Metzger that used to live in Baltimore?"

"Yes," I replied with hesitation. When he called me "Willie," I knew this must be a voice out of the distant past. I was hoping that he wasn't going to keep me guessing. He didn't.

"Do you remember being on a busload of students headed for the IVCF Urbana Missionary Convention in Illinois?"

My reply was, "Of course." But I was not completely honest, for by now I had been to many of these triennial conventions, and they were becoming one blurred recollection. It was now seventeen years since that particular bus ride.

The gruff voice continued, "Well, I was the driver for that bus, and you stayed up during the overnight drive and talked with me about my family problems and about Jesus Christ. I was housed near the convention, and you even came by my room one night to ask me to come with you to a meeting. I refused and kept drinking my beer and watching TV. Then, on the long ride home you urged me to consider becoming a Christian. I was skeptical and cynical. How could a young kid like you know the solution to the hard problems of marriage and job and money that I was facing?"

At that point I broke in, "Al! Yes, yes, I do remember you now. Go on." I listened intently as the bus driver told me how he had put the Bible and a note I had given him on his closet shelf together with a letter his dad had written him urging him to get right with God. Then, five months ago he reached up to get his jacket from that closet shelf. There he found the Bible and the two letters. He took them down and began to read. His heart was softened. Later that summer he went to hear a gospel preacher at the invitation of his son.

"I really got converted," he said. "Since we last met I've become a truck driver. You know, those big eighteen-wheelers on interstate hauls. I've miraculously survived two bad crashes. God kept after me all those years. I've been baptized and joined a little church here. My wife and others in my family are Christians too. I found your phone number in Baltimore written in that Bible. So I called up, and your dad gave me your new number. I often thought of you, and I just wanted to let you know what's happened. I don't remember much of what you said to me years ago, but I remember your concern and sincerity, and I still have your note and the Bible. Keep loving people to the Lord, Willie, no matter how long it takes."

We need to let our non-Christian friends know how we feel. Many of us are unemotional, numbed by our culture. We need verbally to affirm others as we see God's gifts to them. We should struggle to express to others that we love them. How well I remember the time when I knew I couldn't say anything more in a conversation with a younger relative. It seemed right to hug her, and the words came out, "Oh, how I wish you'd become a Christian!" On another occasion I was unconscious of the deep tone of concern that was coming through during an intense talk with an uncle of mine. He remarked that he hoped I would not suffer frustration and depression as a result of his unwillingness to be converted. He could see that I cared.

Would it surprise you that not only students are coming to Christ but people of all ages? The woman who cuts my hair found that Jesus' words cut open her heart. The man who came to my office to sell me insurance became "sold" on Jesus and is now in the ministry. Who has God brought into your life?

In witnessing we endeavor to touch the heart of unbelievers. We want them to fall in love with Jesus. Isn't it the love of Christ that draws sinners? Let's allow for differences in the emotional makeup of people. But let's never forget to involve their emotions.

One word of caution. If you have an especially forceful personality and can talk people into most anything, beware of manipulating others. This is a grave danger in evangelism among children or with an emotionally unstable person. To treat children or anyone else as saved on the basis of emotional reactions without further evidence may actually hinder them from seeking God truly and may result in their becoming bored with the gospel. Enthusiasm is easier to generate than continued obedience.

I realized the difficulty in refraining from pronouncing my sons "saved" when they were young because they said a spontaneous prayer, showed interest in Bible stories or sang loudly "Jesus Loves Me." As their father, I was so excited to see them react emotionally to Christ. But were they converted? It is such a temptation to say yes, but were they acting out of conformity or from the heart? Only time and the tests of life would tell. It is only when we face a choice in which our will must be overridden in order to do the will of Christ that we have insight into the reality of our salvation. I rejoice in the fruit of grace that is now seen in their lives as men of God, radiating Christ in their family, church and workplace.

The Whole Gospel
to the Will

Not Appealing to Natural Desires but Inviting, Persuading and Commanding Allegiance to a New Leader

The desire for success and status is strong. Sometimes the church feeds it instead of calling it by its true name—pride. Here's part of a letter written by a pastor to a young person going through a period of depression.

> I'm writing to help you shake this feeling of uselessness that has overtaken you. Several times you have said that you don't see how Christ can possibly use you—that you're nobody special.
>
> The church must bear part of the responsibility for making you feel as you do. I have in mind the success-story mentality of the church. Our church periodicals tell the story of John J. Moneybags who uses his influential position to witness for Christ. At the church youth banquet we have a testimony from all-American football star Ox Kickoffski, who commands the respect of his teammates when he witnesses for Christ. We've led you to think that if you don't have the leverage of stardom or a big position in the business world, you might as well keep your mouth shut. . . . Nobody cares what Christ has done for you.[1]

In addition, we make appeals stressing the "adventure of the Christian life," or we say, "Try Jesus because things go better with him." These are direct appeals to the will couched in terms of an exciting challenge. People get the impression that they can take up Jesus the same way they would take up jogging! These are attempts to trigger the will of a person by appeal to his or her human desires. It becomes a what's-in-it-for-me gospel.

On the other end of the spectrum, I've met people whose story goes like this:

> I had been putting off getting serious with God for quite a while. I enjoyed my Christian friends, and I knew I didn't have what they had; but I just didn't want to face up to becoming a Christian. It was kind of easy just to slide along with the meetings. Nobody ever really put me on the spot about my salvation. Now that I am a Christian, I wish someone had confronted me earlier. I needed to hear that it was something I shouldn't put off.

Or like this:

> I'm not ready yet to come to God. My motives are so selfish. Besides, I don't understand enough yet. I want all my questions answered first. I want to prepare myself more and come to God in just the right way. The pastor encouraged me to wait for God to move me. He didn't try to persuade me at all.

THE BALANCE: GOD MOVING SINNERS THROUGH PERSUASION

It is a mistake to appeal to the unbeliever's will directly if we do not accompany such an appeal with biblical content. Why? Because such content is needed to instruct the mind in its choice and humble its sinful desires.[2] It is possible to encourage unbelievers to arrive at decisions from false motives. They "become Christians" for what they can get out of it, such as coveting the speaker's experience or happiness or success in life. The true reason for becoming a Christian is not that we may have a wonderful life but that we may be in a right relationship to God. Too many of our evangelistic methods are benefit-oriented. Phrases like "the adventure of the Christian life," "the thrill and excitement," and "Christ made me happy every day" are not balanced with the cost of discipleship. "The most serious of all dangers is that of seeking to produce decisions as a result of pressure brought to bear upon the listener's will."[3] There is the danger of using our personality or stories to force listeners to respond to our appeal. Truth has neither convinced nor convicted them. Music can produce the same effect. People can sing a chorus repeatedly until they eventually become intoxicated. There is value in such things as music, fun, drama and videos to accompany evangelism, but they should not take the supreme and first position. They are aids and helps—not what actually produces the results. Connecting with people through their felt needs/desires is a start. Yet to mold the content of the gospel to satisfy such misleads people and produces me-centered "Christians." Instead, confront the extreme narcissism of our culture (self-idolatry), redirecting even legitimate human needs and humbling the sovereign self. Is your evangelism only relational? Take heed.

On the other hand, Scripture does appeal to the will. It is no laissez-faire approach. "Choose for yourselves this day whom you will serve" (Josh 24:15). "Come, all you who are thirsty, come to the waters" (Is 55: 1). "Come to me, all you who are weary and burdened" (Mt 11:28). "Believe in the Lord Jesus, and you will be saved" (Acts 16:31). True evangelists *do* pop the question. In fact, we are to plead, command, invite and beg! It is uncomfortable for us when we put people on the spot, yet we must not neglect to call for a response. I can recall times when I have struggled to do this.

I have found myself saying to someone, "This is really important; you ought to make up your mind. Perhaps you feel like I'm pressing you, but I only want to reflect the pressure of God's Spirit who is calling you to respond. If you feel in your conscience the force of truth as contained in Christ (not just because you don't want to disappoint me), then surrender your whole life to him." Our sobering words may bring spiritual conviction to people. We want them to face God now, for it is a matter of life or death. There is to be a tone of urgency and persuasion in our voice.

The sermons of great evangelists like Bunyan, Whitefield, Edwards and Spurgeon were all marked by direct questions and pleas put to unbelievers. So was their personal witnessing. We are told in the autobiography of Spurgeon of a woman who had come to him several times for counsel. She had seen her need of Christ after listening to his sermons and wanted further instruction on how to become a Christian. Spurgeon tediously went over the gospel with her on each occasion. She would always end the session with "Mr. Spurgeon, please pray for me." Spurgeon became exasperated and finally said, "Lady, pray for yourself, for I will not." This shocked her so much that she sought God directly and was soon converted.

There are astounding benefits that of course do come to believers (the assurance of heaven, forgiveness, joy, love and peace). Nonbelievers may only desire these things in a selfish way, so we should not convey to them the idea of waiting until they have only right motives for coming to Christ. They never will, simply because they cannot. Sinners are commanded to come *now*.

THE LABELING FALLACY

This matter of the will and our need to call for a response is an especially sensitive area among evangelicals because of certain theological assumptions. There are those who are theologically self-conscious and concerned to define carefully every aspect of their evangelism. They remind me of the saying, "After all is said and done, there is more said than done!" They so fear doing anything unscriptural that they resist anything new and different. A desire to be scriptural is commendable; but if taken to an extreme, it is bondage to the letter and not the spirit of the law. It is one thing to hold strongly to your principles; it is another thing to fall into an overly scrupulous application of a principle in mechanical fashion. As Thomas Jefferson wisely said, "Every difference of opinion is not a difference of principle." To be so unwavering is bondage to tradition or to a pastor or to a principle—but not to the Lord. We must not be merely orthodox critics but Spirit-motivated doers.

Other evangelicals are theologically ignorant of why they do certain things in calling for a response to the gospel. These evangelicals should be willing to examine their theology. Instead of blindly imbibing a certain approach to the will evolved from unbiblical assumptions, they should critically look for the biblical basis of their methods. Evangelists should be more self-conscious of their theology for the sake of their own ministry and for their followers. Too many organizations and churches "do evangelism" a certain way only because "that's the way we've always done it." As the years go by, there is less and less examination of the theological basis for a particular method. As a result, people are loyal to a certain approach and not to the Scriptures. This breeds snobbish Christians. I'll never forget the reply given to me by a student when I asked about his style of evangelism. "I picked it up from my leader who told me this is the way our group has always done it on campus." When pressed further he could give no scriptural reasons for his method of evangelism. This did not make him any less certain, though, that "the people in the other Christian groups were doing it all wrong."

Labels are deadly in Christian circles. For example, when it comes to the topic of the will, immediately certain views are categorized as Reformed or Arminian. The discussion then ends because it is thought (wrongly) that as soon as you have given a name to something, you understand it. Instead, there should be continued dialogue in the Scriptures by all of us. Let's fight this labeling fallacy. What exactly underlies these views on the will?

One view is that the Fall has only weakened the will of sinners and that we have the potential (or ability) to believe. This seems to provide a basis for appealing to unbelievers to respond, thus safeguarding the scriptural doctrine of human responsibility. In practice this view may lead to approving any method that evokes the latent potential to believe. This is the me-centered approach. Beginning with a well-meaning desire (sinners are responsible and should be urged to believe), an unwarranted conclusion is reached: since in Scripture people are commanded to believe, they must have the ability.

The other view sees clearly that the will is dead in trespasses and sins. There is none that does good (Rom 3). This honors God's initiative in salvation and establishes grace; but if the will is in bondage, some may hesitate to make an appeal for all people to believe. Beginning with a desire to exalt God, what also seems to be a logical (but not scriptural) conclusion is drawn.

Both views have at least this in common: as a result of trying to be faithful to Scripture, you might begin with either view and go beyond Scripture, not keeping the doctrines of divine sovereignty and human responsibility in balance.

The writers of the Bible are not embarrassed to put side by side teachings that do not fit our logic.[4] For example, Peter charges his hearers on the day of Pentecost with wickedness in killing Christ yet admits it was all in God's plan (Acts 2:23). Jesus says, "No one can come to me unless the Father who sent me draws him." Yet "Whoever comes to me I will never drive away," also is true (Jn 6:37, 44). How can this be? To our finite minds such teachings seem to be at odds with each other. We try and try to reconcile them. Perhaps we should not consider these two doctrines of sovereignty and responsibility as enemies but rather see them the way the Bible does—as friends!

Me-centered theology is people pleasing (centering on the ability, potential, capacity of fallen man) and takes human responsibility to an extreme. Its historical basis is found in the work of Pelagius in the fifth century and later the writings of Jacobus Arminius (1560-1609), who reacted against a wrong emphasis he felt existed in the churches of the Netherlands. Arminius thought the creeds accepted in these churches denied that humans are responsible for their moral actions, and indeed the preaching in the churches may have neglected this aspect of Scripture. So his followers taught that divine sovereignty is not compatible with human responsibility and that human ability limits our obligation.[5]

Horrified by the implications of this teaching, the church synod reemphasized God's sovereignty in salvation (sinners do not save themselves or contribute to their salvation in any way), insisting it was a work of grace from beginning to end. Five statements were formulated in reaction to five articles proposed by the Arminians. We make a mistake, therefore, if we consider the five points of this synod to be a balanced creedal statement. The "five points of Calvinism," as these later became known, are orthodox theology but are in need of further filling out with the whole counsel of God because they are merely a reaction to a theological distortion. A scriptural emphasis on divine sovereignty and human responsibility should be at the heart of a right view of the human will and a recovery of fervent evangelism today. In witnessing we trust in the inherent power of "the word and the Spirit." We speak truth to and pray for sinners, and by this God-ordained means, the God-ordained end is accomplished. God has ordained both the means and the end. I deal with this extensively in part three.

REACHING THE WHOLE PERSON

To analyze human nature I have divided it into the three segments of mind, heart and will. But these are only aspects of a unified human personality; I do not mean to leave the impression that these are independent of each other.[6]

People cannot give a holistic response. Because sin has brought fragmentation we are not whole people. The way in which people come to Christ will vary depending on how sin has incapacitated them (it may have a stronger hold on one aspect than on another) and on their unique temperaments. Some will lead with their emotions, letting their minds catch up later. A cerebral person, on the other hand, may have difficulty responding emotionally. And people today seldom use their will in making decisions because our sensuous culture influences them to react according to their desires.

At the same time, I do not intend to say that people can make a proper response to Christ on one level but not on the others. The mind, heart and will are all involved to some extent in every action. Our evangelism must therefore be to the whole person, allowing that the response will be in accord with each unique personality.

May God grant that as we direct unbelievers to Christ we shall see more and more wholly converted people, people of whom we can say, "But thanks be to God that, though you used to be slaves to sin, you wholeheartedly [from the center of your being] obeyed [will] the form of teaching [mind] to which you were entrusted" (Rom 6:17). Directing people to trust in Christ alone can be hard work. It requires boldness and keeping our eye on pleasing God, not others.

Hundreds of years ago John Bunyan commended this ministry of "faithful dealing" with people who are merely talkers, having no true faith.

> You [Faithful] did right to talk plainly to him. There is not enough of this faithful dealing with souls these days, and lack of that causes people to undervalue the Christian faith. Then when these talkative frauds, whose religion is only in word and who are debauched in their living and vain in their conversation, are admitted into the fellowship of Christians with the hope that they may be converted or contribute money, the people of the world are puzzled, the sincere are grieved, and Christianity is blemished. I wish that all Christians would deal with such as you have done. Then they would either be truly converted, or they would show their colors and leave the congregation of the saved.[7]

Theologically examining regeneration and saving faith has resulted in a change in the personal testimony of some, including me. I now understand my initial interest in Jesus Christ as the beginning of my awakening and not my conversion. I find myself dating my conversion much later, though I still don't know the day. I now think of my conversion as closer to a time when

I began to follow Jesus as my leader. As my life slowly took on a new direction, I had assurance of salvation. This new insight into what God was doing in my life seems to coincide with scriptural teaching. I would suggest we ask two questions to people who have made a profession of faith and have come to us for counsel:[8]

"What has Christ done *for* you?" (Is there an objective understanding of the main content of the gospel?)

"What has Christ done *in* you?" (Is there any objective evidence of new life, a changed heart?)

Often grace and the message of the cross mean little to people because they have no understanding of their peril. God is seen as a genial Santa Claus who has no wrath toward sin. They see themselves as basically good people who pretty much deserve heaven. To tell them "Jesus died for you" sounds nice and comforting, but they may wonder, why did he go to all that trouble? To get the idea straight, complete this story based on one in James Denney's *The Death of Christ*.

> A man is sitting on a pier fishing on a calm summer day. Suddenly another man comes running down the pier, dives into the water, and drowns. Having witnessed this, I explain to the fisherman, "This man died for you!" The fisherman, however, has great trouble understanding why the man needed to die for him. After all, he was in no danger that he could see.

Now, rewrite the story so that the fisherman can see that he is in peril and has a desperate need.

Denney says that the parable of the fisherman unaware of his peril reflects the way modern evangelists and pastors often present the gospel. They minimize human depravity, and so the preaching of the cross loses its power. Why is the human will considered an impregnable fortress that God can't storm? The human predicament is seen as more psychological than judicial before a holy God. With that in mind, why is such a mild evangelism so popular today?[9]

PART THREE

Wholly by Grace

The Foundation for Evangelism

8

Grace Is Only
for the Powerless

] was late. Lunch with Rob[1] was something I was looking forward to with a mixture of excitement and apprehension. I removed my coat and looked around the room. In the bustle, I didn't see him. My heart began to sink. Then, on the far side of the lunchroom, I saw an arm waving in welcome.

Rob and I were merely acquaintances due to a mutual interest in football. One time coming back from a game I asked him about his religious background. He shrugged and said he used to attend church during high school but didn't have the time or interest now. I said, "Really, what made you lose interest?" (I had learned to not let a complacent response end the conversation on this topic.) I smiled and waited.

He responded, "Well, it was a number of things, but mostly I didn't see the relevance, and I got sick of seeing all those hypocrites pretending they were holy at the Sunday church service. I knew what they were like the night before."

I listened and chose my words carefully. "Rob, you might be surprised to know that Jesus would have had a similar reaction. I'd like to hear more about your experiences. Want to have lunch next week?"

So, here we were. I shot up a quick prayer and sat down. For the next hour, I did a lot of listening as I entered into Rob's world. I told him I wanted to hear his criticisms, doubts and whatever else he wanted to tell me. I let him know that I was a Christian and could learn from him how others view Christianity. That seemed to help him open up. At an appropriate point I re-iterated, "Jesus would identify with some of your thoughts. Have you heard the story Jesus told about a religious leader who said, 'I thank God I am not like other people. Especially that sinner over there.'" As the conversation went on, I wove in misconceptions that I used to have. I summarized, saying, "I thought religion was simply trying hard to be nice. I used to find security in all my religious activities. Then I found out I could never *do* enough. I needed to just trust in what Jesus had *done* for me." Rob's face lit up. "Really? Jesus met and exposed hypocrites? Good for him." Right then the bill arrived and after quickly dividing up the cost, Rob said, "Thanks. You've given me something to think about. It's good to know Jesus is on my side against religious hypocrites. I'm going to try harder to keep my New Year's resolutions, and be a better person. See you."

For the second time my heart sank. How many times, after the clearest explanation that self-effort doesn't reconnect us with God, had I heard the reply, "Well, I'm not a very good person, but I'm trying." Even true Christians regularly fall into the mentality that good works get them extra points with God. A compulsion to earn salvation is deeply rooted in the nature of fallen mankind. What will root it out? We'll begin by seeing why self-effort is doomed to fail.

SALVATION IS IMPOSSIBLE FOR NICE PEOPLE
We have an Owner. We belong to the One who made us. We are responsible to serve him with loving obedience. The goal is to be God-centered, not self-centered. We exist to benefit God, not vice versa.

As God's creatures, we are worthy, unworthy and owned. Nothing could indicate more clearly the worth that God gives us than the story of Adam and Eve in Genesis. The special attributes we have that come from being made in God's image set us apart from all other creatures. The entrusting to us of the careful management of the rest of creation is a high privilege. The pronouncement that we were "good" in God's eyes and the companionship of our personal Creator speak of the worth he bestows on us, as well as the opportunity Adam and Eve had to freely choose to take him at his word by living in obedience each day.

As humans, we are also unworthy. We were to glory in our role as created beings, vice regents under our Creator King. No inherent rights. No claim to obligations from our Maker. All rights granted were gifts; derived, not intrinsic. We were made to be dependent. However, our first parents, acting as our representatives, made a choice to disobey their Maker, and their sin has affected every human since then except one. When Adam and Eve sinned, the image of God was defaced but not erased. Our wills became captive to our desires, which, unless God influences, are always me-centered. Therefore, we no longer have a will that is free to choose what is good and right, leaving us with a big dilemma. We are unable to save ourselves, and we are undeserving of God saving us.

The following fictional stories describe two "nice" individuals trapped by their sinful nature. One was committed to his dutiful performance of good works, and thus forgiveness and grace were incomprehensible. The other was married to her desire for wealth and reputation and thus not free to choose "marriage" to Jesus. Could they change themselves?

Story 1. Hi Chon Son had just received a letter regarding his brother, who was in Amsterdam without food or money. Years ago his brother had disregarded his father, taken his part of the money from a lucrative family business and disappeared.

Over dinner one evening, Hi Chon Son shared his reaction to the letter he had received.

"My younger brother deserves every problem he has. Do you realize what effect his actions have had on me, Dad and the business these last four years? Nobody knows, and my brother certainly wouldn't even care to know. Yes, there was my part of the property left, but the impact of quickly getting that much cash together for him was

horrendous for the business. A lot of employees lost their jobs, and I had to pick up the slack. I thought after the first two years of working almost 24/7 I could have some relief. Well, it's still that bad.

"He's not having fun! Well I'm not either! I never have. I have had to take on even more responsibility in the past two years. Dad's aged a lot in these four years. Now don't you dare let him know about this letter. I'm the one who is caring for him as well as the office stuff. He always knew he could depend on me, not on his younger son. That son of his was always whining about being independent. He shirked working for the company even when he was still at home. He never helped. Freedom was his cry—like a baby. I gave up my freedom to work hard. He should think about that. Even Dad doesn't comprehend what I've done for him. He doesn't show his appreciation much either. My conscience is clear. I've done my duty—and Dad can always count on me. You Americans have no idea of how my Dad was dishonored. All our relatives knew. Even business associates changed their opinion of Dad and me. It's an Asian thing. You wouldn't understand. Sometimes I don't think even God does."

At this point I made what I thought was a rather innocuous observation. "Look, you're really emotional about all this. It sounds like you're mad with everyone, not only your brother but also your dad."

His face became flushed and his hands clenched. He spat angry words at me in a decibel level that made quite a few other diners uncomfortable too. "Let me tell you something. I have a right to be angry. At the very time that son of his split, I was in love with a girl—and she was in love with me! But with all of the added responsibility, I lost her. There was no time for anything but work. You think that doesn't still hurt? Here I am, thirty-three and still single. I've never had any fun. Since my duty to Dad comes first, I probably never will. Friends? They're all married and gone. Do you know the only kind of men and women who are still single at my age? Forget it. Even if I had time, I wouldn't be interested anymore. I lost the only one who did love me.

"Why am I telling you all this? Look, the bill is here. I'll pay—like I always have to. If he wants to take his life, let him. It would be better for Dad too. He constantly thinks about him for some crazy reason. I think it's a weight on his mind. His suicide would be better for me and for the business too. I've always suspected he'd show up on his knees one day, waiting to be accepted. Why? For more money, of course. Remember that song 'It's My Party and I'll Cry If I Want To'? Well, there won't be a party for him to whine at if he does try to come back. Nobody's going to give one. Don't bother me again about him. I've honored my father. I've done my duty.

Let's identify who this angry man is. I've updated, with many liberties, part of a story told by Jesus in Luke 15:11-32. Both brothers in Jesus' story were lost. They were estranged from their father, who represents God. Neither was seeking God. God, the true seeker, sought them. The story reminds us that we are undeserving of the Father's love.

The older son's unworthiness for salvation may seem less obvious. What does his life of hard work reveal? An attempt to earn the father's favor without loving the father. Good works cannot save us. His anger is revealing. He blames the father and despises "his father's son." He has not experienced saving grace even though he has been with the father all these years. This is the sad portrait of many nominal church members and leaders—as lost as the younger son (who will be discussed later), but not realizing it.

We are left with the older son standing on the outside of the family celebration. What will happen to him? He is unwilling and undeserving of saving grace. Will he continue to be like so many religious leaders (nice people) that mutter criticism when Jesus celebrates with sinners (Lk 15:2)? The father goes out to seek this son too. We are not told of his final response, making us ponder what he, and we, might do. Henri Nouwen, a contemporary writer, has seen himself as the older brother and has written a moving exposition of Rembrandt's painting *The Return of the Prodigal Son* in his book by the same title.

> When I listen carefully to the words with which the elder son attacks his father—self-righteous, self-pitying, jealous words—I hear a deeper complaint. It is the complaint that comes from a heart that feels it never received what it was due. It is the complaint expressed in countless subtle and not-so-subtle ways, forming a bedrock of human resentment. It is the complaint that cries out: "I tried so hard, worked so long, did so much, and still I have not received what others get so easily. Why do people not thank me, not invite me, not play with me, not honor me, while they pay so much attention to those who take life so easily and so casually?"
>
> . . . This experience of not being able to enter into joy is the experience of a resentful heart. The elder son couldn't enter into the house and share in his father's joy. His inner complaint paralyzed him and let the darkness engulf him.
>
> . . . Can the elder son in me come home? Can I be found as the younger son

was found? How can I return when I am lost in resentment, when I am caught in jealousy, when I am imprisoned in obedience and duty lived out as slavery? It is clear that alone, by myself, I cannot find myself. More daunting than healing myself as the younger son is healing myself as the elder son. Confronted here with the impossibility of self-redemption, I now understand Jesus' words to Nicodemus: "Do not be surprised when I say: 'You must be born from above.'" Indeed, something has to happen that I myself cannot cause to happen. I cannot be reborn from below; that is, with my own strength, with my own mind, with my own psychological insights. There is no doubt in my mind about this because I have tried so hard in the past to heal myself from my complaints and failed . . . and failed . . . and failed, until I came to the edge of complete emotional collapse and even physical exhaustion. I can only be healed from above, from where God reaches down. What is impossible for me is possible for God. "With God, everything is possible."[2]

The story of the elder brother is on target for respectable sinners. He was fixated on *doing* the right things. He had a duty-based religion but lacked a personal relationship with God as Father. He complained that his father never gave him anything. Think of what he missed all those years of living legalistically. Because of his spiritual blindness, he became bitter and unable to love either his brother (his heart was void of forgiveness) or his father (he knew nothing of a love relationship). His bitterness judges that a celebration is unfair, but the father said it was not only fair to celebrate, it was *right* to do so. They *must* celebrate.

Two brothers: one an out-in-the-open sinner, the other an inward, respectable sinner. Their wills are hardened by selfishness and arrogance. Both are totally hopeless and helpless—unless saving grace intervenes.

Story 2. Late one night the following e-mail mysteriously surfaced on my screen.

I've realized that I'm stuck in my situation. I'm not talking about my career or single lifestyle, but spiritually. How I got to this point is a mystery. All I can do is rehearse the facts that led up to my realization. Since I can't be sure I'm putting the correct interpretation on them, I'll try to give an objective description. You tried to help me a long time ago. I didn't listen.

As you know, I came from a hard-working, religious and very ethical family. We were not wealthy. There was a pervasive insecurity about not having enough money, which gave way to many anxieties in our home. The goal of our family was clear. My sister and I were to get into college, graduate and get good (defined as high-paying) jobs. My sister became ruthless in these objectives and soon jettisoned the family, ethics and religion. I did not.

Honesty and spirituality were incorporated into my climb up the ladder of success. Even at an early age I realized commitment to a man would sidetrack me. Not that I didn't date, but I knew how to control my emotions. I graduated, but my first job did not come easily. Women have to prove themselves more than men. It was not what I wanted, but my foot was in the door. Quickly I learned to make connections with the right people and other companies. I developed my resumé. It took five years, but then a timely opening in another company occurred. I heard of it through my network of associates. My qualifications were shining: experienced, professional attitude, poised, articulate, a hard worker with a no-nonsense approach. What stood out was my reputation for being trustworthy and honest. Integrity was important for the public image of this new company. I was hired and put onto the fast track for promotions.

I'm going to skip a lot of years. At thirty-seven, I am financially successful with investments, stock options, a large salary and benefits. I have all that I want: the wardrobe and the ability to always update it, a beautiful home, two vacation homes, cars, a boat, and a private plane on order (really!). What gives me most satisfaction, however, is not the wealth but the status and recognition I have. I love the titles CEO and Dr. (remember, I continued and got my Ph.D.). I really stand out, whether entertaining at home, out in the social scene or heading a corporation meeting. I'm known for my accomplishments. Topping all this off, and what many recognize as unusual, is that I've maintained my religious activities and become prominent in the world of charity. Of course, I haven't forgotten to provide security for my parents too. I'm still single and focused. I don't need a trophy husband. I have many trophies.

I'm 90 percent happy with my life. Yet it's in the very area that impresses people most—good deeds and spirituality—that I know something is incomplete. This may sound trivial, but it's similar to the feeling I get when I just can't find the right dress for a special occasion. I know what I want. I'll recognize it as soon as I see it. It's like that with the incompleteness in my spiritual life. Everything's fine for life in this world, but I'm convinced that there's an afterlife. I'm not confident I've done all the right things to give me admittance to that future world called heaven. It's this 10 percent missing factor that has been nagging me for quite a while. I have a library of books from the self-help and spirituality sections of the bookstore. Films have also provided insight. Yet, what I call my "Big Question" is still unanswered.

Then one day it happened. I had been observing a particular person from a distance for a while: read two of his books; saw an interview on television; ordered his video series. On his website was an announcement for a seminar the weekend of April 6-8 at the Hilton in New York City. I registered online that day.

By the end of the seminar, I was captivated. But he hadn't answered my Big Question! I calculated the right moment to approach him. He always exited from the same door with his entourage of associates. Reviewing my assertiveness training, I decided on a hand outstretched, puzzled facial expression combined with twinkling eyes and a winsome smile. He would have to stop. It worked—and then my B.Q. came out. "You seem to be such a good person. Can you tell me how I can be certain I will live forever?"

His initial response unnerved me. He seemed to deflect my real question and instead queried my assumption that he was someone who was super virtuous. "If you really believed that I'm good, there are implications," he said. I had only used the "good" adjective glibly. Perhaps I needed his mild reprimand. Fortunately he went on to give me a list of dos. They were what I expected. I had heard these rules before and incorporated them into my lifestyle. I was disappointed. I didn't have the certainty I longed for—that I would be OK forever. Blurting out, "I've already done all those steps," I immediately realized this sounded self-justifying (which it was). And he saw right through me. Then came what I would later call "The Crushing Insight From Someone Who Is Much Smarter Than I Realized." The exact wording I disremember, but his haunting yet love-filled stare gripped me. The gist of his response was

> Wait a minute—you've spoken without thinking again! There is an assumption underlying all my seminar steps. There can be only one absolute love in your life—and it can't be money and prestige. Your motivation is key. There must be only one supreme love. You must change the focus of your desires. This can't be done by implementing external regulations. You want something to do? Okay, here it is: Quit your job. Get rid of all you own. Empty your accounts and cancel that plane order (how did he know about that?). Come, be one of my associates.

At that point my composure was shaken. His words cut like a knife into my heart. I turned on my spiked heel and left him standing there. This was not what I wanted to hear. This was impossible for me and egotistical of him. Impossible! Without money and the status it brought, I would be nothing. This was asking too much. Egotistical! Join his company at entry level? Who did he think he was anyway—God? After *a sleepless night, I came to the realization that I couldn't let go of the image that hard work and money had gotten me. I was married to my lifestyle and the recognition it brought me. Enchanted by my achievements and the awe of others, I now saw I was enchained. I admitted it was impossible to free my heart from love of the fame that money brought me. My so-called spirituality shriveled up. I was too proud.*

This update of the story of the rich young ruler, which Jesus tells in Mark 10:17-27, reveals the grip that legitimate things can have on our hearts. Like the woman in the story I just told, the man in Jesus' story was well off financially, rigorous in personal ethics, a leader in business and community service, involved in spiritual activities—a self-made man but with one elusive goal unreached: a lack of confidence that he was doing enough to assure him of achieving a happy eternity. A nagging realization that there was more to life than just being successful in this world. How will he achieve this goal? The only way he knows: by trying harder and doing more. This is an extension of the only method he knows, one which has served him well so far: good works that merit an eternal reward. The problem with this method is that you never are certain you've done enough. Therefore he has no peace or continuing assurance of salvation. He pursues an authority who will give him the right self-actualization formula.

Jesus doesn't do this. Instead, he takes him a step deeper into his soul to examine his heart motives and desires. He does this by reminding him of a commandment that hadn't been mentioned yet, the tenth commandment: "You shall not covet." This exposes the interior of our lives and reveals the idols of our heart. What is implicit in all the commandments is now made explicit. True goodness begins with the highest love for God and neighbor. This man's heart was enslaved to his idol. He worshiped money and what it brought him. Therefore, his facial expression registers sadness as he realizes the reversal of priorities Jesus requires. Unwilling to pay the price, he leaves.

The disciples are astonished for two reasons. First, from all outward appearances, this person seemed to be a seeker for salvation and, because of his religious knowledge, a prime candidate for the new kingdom. They probably envisioned him soon joining with them. They may even have begun to count on a major donation to their cause. If this fellow couldn't qualify as a follower of Christ, who could? He seemed to have much to merit his inclusion. Second, Jesus seemed to set the entrance requirements too high. Nobody could pass his test. They recalled a hillside seminar in which he had said, "For I tell you that unless your righteousness surpasses that of the Pharisees and teachers of the law, you will certainly not enter the kingdom of heaven. . . . Be perfect, therefore, as your heavenly Father is perfect" (Mt 5:20, 48). Jesus didn't pursue this seeker but let him walk away. The disciples then ask an insightful question: "Who then can be saved?" It is impossible for anyone to ever do enough or always have the right motive. In Tolkien's *Lord of the Rings*, we read of a ring that gives absolute power by binding all. Evil is real, and when it rules it enslaves.

THREE MYTHS THAT OBSCURE GRACE

The myth of my inalienable rights. The Constitution of the United States has made famous the phrase "inalienable rights." The existence of certain rights that all humans possess is a noble idea. It safeguards the value of human life and liberty from people who would take these away. Is it true that no one can revoke these and other human rights? What about the One who made us? Is it not inherent in the fact that we are not self made that therefore any rights are derived?

We are creatures. Does it not also follow that God has all rights over his creation? As our Creator, he has creation rights (ownership prerogatives) over everyone. We were made for his purposes. God does not exist for our benefit, remember? Our wills are not sovereign, an independent, high-walled enclosure that God cannot enter. He alone is autonomous—a law unto himself. Whatever he does by definition is right and good; therefore, he can do anything to people that is his "good pleasure." He is supreme. God is God. Various people in the Bible express this truth.[3]

In this day of multiple human "rights," most people wrongly assume that God owes us something—salvation, or at least a chance at salvation. He shows astonishing favor to many, but he does not have to (that is the essence of grace). If he were obliged to be gracious, grace would no longer be grace and salvation would be based on human merit rather than being *sola gratia*. This is why the doctrine of election is opposed by so many. It doesn't seem fair to them. But as soon as we introduce the doctrine of fairness, we introduce a standard of right by which God has to save all or at least give everyone an equal chance of being saved. And that is not grace! If God were motivated only by what is right, without any consideration of grace made possible by the work of Christ, all would be condemned, and all would spend eternity in hell.[4] Humbled, we celebrate a "Declaration of Dependence," agreeing that we are endowed with *alienable* (transferred to us from our Creator) rights.

   The myth of human goodness. As a young Christian, I was not aware of the Bible's teaching about our total lack of moral goodness, rendering us unacceptable to God. However, I came to believe in this negative analysis of our moral ability, driven by two factors: the plethora of texts in the Bible on the pervasive effects of sin in behavior and my awareness of the depth of sin in my own life. Yet even then I couldn't bring myself to be consistent. I had a hard time believing that the "kind old ladies" I knew were under God's condemnation. I wanted these seemingly virtuous people who had no connection with biblical Christianity to be an exception. Four things helped me reevaluate my anemic view of sin. The first was God's providential kindness to everyone. "He causes his sun to rise on the evil and the good, and sends rain on the righteous and unrighteous" (Mt 5:45). Therefore, everyone experiences God's grace in a general way and this is the source of human kindness. We all experience his awesome creation, human love, family, physical and mental abilities, creativity and so on. God doesn't stop the rain at the edge of a nonbeliever's field. Some people show an appreciation for the good things in life and are softened in their behavior. But this is not connected with saving grace.

   Second, restraining grace is implicit throughout Scripture and explicitly stated in the story about the pagan king Abimelech (Gen 20:1-7). He refrained from sexual relations with Sarah, the wife of the great patriarch, Abraham. Why did he not pursue his sinful desires? Speaking to him in a dream, God discounted the king's pretensions of goodness: "I have kept you from sinning against me."

   Third, I realized my tendency to rank some sins as not as bad as others. I would overlook these sins, not realizing the implications of God's holiness. "For whoever keeps the whole law and yet stumbles at just one point is guilty of breaking all of it" (Jas 2:10).

Fourth, in my humanness, I was emotionally repulsed by God's judgment of "kind old ladies." As a human, my emotions would not easily align themselves with this idea or, for that matter, anyone going to an eternal hell. In my mind and will the Holy Spirit helped me to bow before God's ownership rights. But the pain is still there, as it was for Paul when his Jewish friends rejected Christ as Messiah (Rom 9:2).

What helped me most to accept that human goodness was a myth was realizing that what made something good in human terms was different from how God defined *good*. A right motive (love for God), according to a right standard (the revealed will of God in Scripture) and for the right goal (the glory of God)—this is what constitutes a good action in God's eyes.

The artist Michelangelo wrote a sonnet in his later years expressing his need even as a "good" person to have a Savior.

Whence the loving fancy that made of art
my idol and my king,
I know now well that it was full of wrong. . . .
Painting and sculpture shall no longer calm
The soul turned to that love divine
That spread its arms on the cross to take us in. . . .

O flesh, O blood, O wood, O extreme sorrow,
Only by you my sin is done. . . .
Thou alone art good.[5]

As it is written:
  "there is no one righteous, not even one;
    there is no one who understands,
    no one who seeks God.
  All have turned away,
    they have together become worthless;
  there is no one who does good,
    not even one." (Rom 3:10-12)

Why do you think salvation by good works is so ingrained in the non-Christian's approach to spirituality, and even carries over to the Christian's?

Let's nail shut the lid of the coffin of good works by teaching not only the debilitating effect of sin but also how *good works undercut grace.*

The myth of my free will. There are only three people who possessed a will capable of choosing good and rejecting evil. Adam and Eve, representatives of the entire human race, were tested in a perfect environment and failed. They freely chose to disobey God and to obey Satan instead. Because of Adam and Eve's decision, all who have come after them have wills that are bent away from obedience to God and toward self. Some people pridefully object to the negative consequences of a representative acting on our behalf. They wish to make their own choice because "It's not fair," or "I would have done differently." Yet these same persons are silent when the representative principle is operative through a second Adam (Christ) who freely makes right choices leading to innumerable positive benefits for many (Rom 5:12-21). God achieved his purposes by testing one couple. Would you really have chosen not to sin?

The effects of sin on human nature are pervasive. As a drop of ink disperses in a glass of water, so also has Adam and Eve's sin dispersed throughout the human race. All aspects of our nature are tainted: mind (thinking), heart (emotions), will (behavior). Our mind no longer thinks God's thoughts or recognizes God's handiwork in all facets of the physical world. We "naturally" suppress the truth (Rom 1:18-20). Our heart hates what it should love and loves what it should hate. Our wills are enslaved and self-serving. We freely choose what we desire, yet we never desire the will of God. Instead, we give preference to our self-centered desires. Even if we outwardly conform to moral standards, inwardly there is neither a motive of love for God nor a correct goal of giving glory to God. Martin Luther calls this "the bondage of the will."

"Free will" is a philosophical term, and its use confuses the discussion about our moral responsibility. Some Christians mistakenly rally to safeguard the freedom of the will and regard with suspicion those who question our freedom to choose or reject God. We still have natural/physical freedom, but not spiritual. The civil righteousness for which we strive stems from what Jonathan Edwards termed "enlightened self-interest." This righteousness is not spiritually meritorious because it is not motivated by love for

God nor by a desire to glorify God. God's general (nonsaving) grace and his restraining (from evil) grace are the real source of any human goodness. Edwards gives valuable insight into the will as "the mind choosing" according to our "motives" (desires).[6]

Acknowledging our inability to save ourselves requires humility because it gives God the lead role in everything. I can understand the reticence of many Christians to allow God sovereignty over their wills. Perhaps by citing reasons people cling to the idea of free will, those who are struggling may be able to pinpoint their own reluctance to surrender their wills to God's control.

The Top Ten Reasons Christians Believe in Free Will

10. A desire to hold humans responsible for actions

9. Confusion of the philosophical (nonscriptural) concept of free will with "human responsibility"

8. A lack of emphasis on the holiness, righteousness and justice of God

7. Encounters with Christians who play intellectual games about the sovereignty of God without lovingly living this truth

6. The display of outward morality by many non-Christians

5. Dislike for the alternative, which seems to make God responsible for our sin, or even the author of it

4. The concept that the ability to choose Jesus is necessary for doing evangelism

3. A human concept of God's love leading to sentimentalism and me-centeredness

2. Neglect by pastors and authors to emphasize the importance of theology and the avoidance of teaching on so-called controversial issues

1. A reluctance to allow God to be totally sovereign

I hope that what I have written below begins to refute those reasons.

UNABLE YET RESPONSIBLE

Once we've seen our inability to do anything good in God's eyes, we sometimes wonder how we can still be held responsible. Here are two thoughts to keep in mind.[7]

God has determined the end results. He has also determined (ordained) the *means* by which those end results will be accomplished. There is a very interesting description of this by Luke, the author of the book of Acts. A storm is raging in the Mediterranean, and the boat, which is taking the prisoner Paul to Rome, is about to wreck near an island. The crew has given up all hope for their lives. Paul speaks to them after God revealed to him that no one would die.

> *"But now I urge you to keep up your courage, because* not one of you will be lost; *only the ship will be destroyed."* . . . *In an attempt to escape from the ship, the sailors let the life boat down into the sea, pretending they were going to lower some anchors from the bow. Then Paul said to the centurion and the soldiers,* "Unless these men stay with the ship, you cannot be saved." *(Acts 27:22, 30-31, emphasis mine, cf. Phil 2:12-13)*

Whatever God has planned will necessarily come to pass. However, God's sovereignty is different from fatalism, in which an impersonal force compels events without the use of secondary causes. We are not subject to external compulsion, and therefore we are responsible. At the same time, we are not free to act except as God has planned. We are not independent of God, yet we are still responsible.[8]

When witnessing, we always point people to the door into his church, which is Christ. Nowhere in the Bible are we encouraged to dig up the foundation of his church to see if our name is on any of the foundation stones. Standing outside we respond to the invitation to "come." Once inside we read written on the wall, "chosen," and rejoice in the love that draws us in (see diagram 1).

·   Earlier we looked at the passage in John where Jesus, speaking to his disciples, says of salvation, "With man it is impossible, but with God all things are possible." We have discovered an astounding theme in Scripture from Genesis to the book of Revelation: God requires people to do things they are unable to do. The giving of the Ten Commandments is an example of God commanding obedience that was impossible for sinful people. No one could live up to those commandments. So also is the New Testament command to

Marvelous in their revelation of reality, the Scriptures teach twin truths—divine sovereignty and human responsibility. Sometimes we find them side by side in the same verse. More often we see only one at a time—like only seeing the one side of a coin. As we become familiar with Scripture we realize the other side of the coin is always there. So also God has welded together these two profound truths, which seem contradictory, in a mysterious way. God sovereignly grants specific individuals salvation; we are responsible to believe for salvation.

Divine Sovereignty
All that the Father gives me will come to me. (Jn 6:37)
No one can come to me unless the Father has enabled him. (Jn 6:65)

Human Responsibility
Repent and believe the good news. (Mk 1:15)
Whoever comes to me I will never drive away. (Jn 6:37)

Responsibility & Sovereignty in One Sentence
Work out your salvation with fear and trembling,
for it is God who works in you to will and to act according to his
good purpose. (Phil 2:12-13)

Faith and Repentance = Gifts of God for Which We Plead
Ephesians 2:8-10 and 2 Timothy 2:25

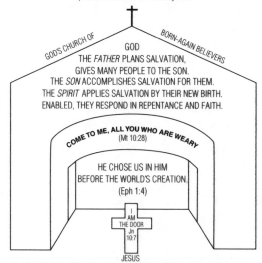

Mankind's Only Plea: God, Have Mercy on Me, a Sinner. (Lk 18:13)

The Revealed Will of God
Christ points all people to himself as the door to salvation.
We are not to try to discover if we are chosen, but to come to Christ.

The Hidden Will of God
Once inside the church of sinners saved by enabling grace,
we understand that we were chosen in eternity, and we respond in love and worship.

Diagram 1. God's Method of Salvation

believe on the Lord Jesus impossible to obey. We can no more keep this command, and do this good act, than we can keep any of God's commandments! So what does all this mean for evangelism? It gives us an *accurate* picture of the task before us. It's like preaching to dead people and telling them to live again, much the same way God, through Ezekiel, spoke life into dead bones.

> The hand of the LORD was upon me, and he brought me out by the Spirit of the LORD and set me in the middle of a valley; it was full of bones. . . .
>
> Then he said to me, "Prophesy to these bones and say to them, 'Dry bones, hear the word of the LORD! This is what the Sovereign LORD says to these bones: I will make breath enter you, and you will come to life. . . .'"
>
> So I prophesied as I was commanded. And as I was prophesying, . . . the bones came together. . . . Then he said to me, "Prophesy to the breath; . . . say to it, 'This is what the Sovereign LORD says: Come from the four winds, O breath, and breathe into these slain, that they may live.'" So I prophesied as he commanded me, and breath entered them; they came to life." (Ezek 37:1, 4-5, 7, 9-10)

When I was in high school, I recall traveling on a bus back from a Christian conference. My friends were telling me that I needed to become a Christian. I knew that. And I wanted to. But something was blocking my response. I couldn't believe it could be so simple. It sounded too easy. There must be something more I needed to do. Yet my friends kept saying, "Just believe." I found out that was my problem. I could not conjure up "faith" from anywhere inside me. It seemed like what they were saying was, "Keep trying to believe." I saw faith as a "work" for me to do . . . and I couldn't do it!

The idea that I can become a Christian just by trying harder or by pushing an imaginary faith button inside of me is unscriptural but prevalent. When I worked with my father in his tree service business, we would go to people's property and cut down trees that were old or dangerous. Quite often they would tell us to leave the stump; it was too expensive to take out. The problem was that the following spring that stump would begin to send up shoots. I remember one home that ended up having a large oak bush in its yard because there were so many shoots coming out of the stump. Unless we remove the stump of our belief in our ability to do good works, this idea will continue to sprout up. Teaching empowering grace does this.

God Is Grace-Full

Educating non-Christians about the character of God may help to correct the imbalance that has led many to assume God's main attribute is love. This fantasy is perpetuated by the belief that God is a sentimental servant of mankind, debasing the toughness of his love. Love becomes God, and complacency sets in as even the most despicable presume that God is only loving and will overlook gross evils. This belief is misguided though; biblical love has a backbone. It is a *tough* love. The trivialization of the word *love* is one of the reasons I have chosen the word *grace* to convey God's "love with a punch." Yet I am hindered in this attempt to revive a word which has rich significance. To most people, grace has deteriorated into an innocuous graciousness or vague kindness. One of our tasks in evangelism is to find new words, illustrations and stories to communicate eroded biblical concepts, such as grace. Let's draw vivid word pictures of the sheer beauty of truth before the glazed eyes of others.

GRACE MAKES SALVATION POSSIBLE

Let's think together about grace. Are you saying, "Well, *finally!* You've spent a lot of time getting me to think about sin, and I was beginning to wonder where the hope was." Good. You're getting the point. As much as I'd like to write only about grace, I can't.

> For the Christian church (even in its recently popular seeker services) to ignore, euphemize, or otherwise mute the lethal reality of sin is to cut the nerve of the gospel. For the sober truth is that without full disclosure on sin, the gospel of grace becomes impertinent, unnecessary, and finally uninteresting.[1]

It is only in the context of disobedience that mercy has relevance and meaning. Mercy is of such a character that disobedience is its complement or presupposition, and only as exercised to the disobedient does it exist and operate.[2]

What could have caused such indifference, even among churchgoers? It is a failure to understand and 'feel in one's heart' four great truths that the doctrine of grace presupposes: 1) the sinfulness of sin; 2) God's judgment; 3) man's spiritual inability; and 4) God's sovereign freedom.[3]

Below are two more stories that I have retold. Both have a happier conclusion than the two earlier stories where I emphasized the impossibility of salvation. Now we see that, as Jesus said, "with God, all things [salvation] are possible."

Story 1. At the age of twenty-four, Young Jun Son had burned out. He ended up in Amsterdam, sleeping sometimes in an urban men's shelter, other times in a rotting warehouse. He says:

> How could I have gone so far down so fast? Occasionally I worked washing dishes at a dingy restaurant. I took uneaten food right off the plates. I thought I might as well have it since it was just going to a farmer who would feed it to his hogs. I felt like an animal, and I lived like one. I had been acting like an animal for a long time. When I was fired I began working for the farmer—disgusting. Let me tell you how my problems all started.

> I grew up in Seoul, Korea, where I lived with my father and brother. I'm not sure where my mother was; "single-parent family" was what my high school teacher wrote next to my name in her grade book. What she didn't know was that my father had money—lots of it—from various properties that he owned. He never flaunted it, but I realized how rich he was when I sneaked a look at his accounts on the computer. Looking back, I see that's when my animal passions came to the forefront. I wanted to have it all; get the biggest part of the money for myself. Back then I called it "my passport to freedom." My desire wasn't really for the money; it was only to be independent, to live life at my speed and have fun. I was seventeen at the time, and the wealth wouldn't come to my brother and me until my father died. I had to be patient.

> I was patient for three years. During that time, I went to a community college and worked at an auto parts store because I liked cars. Actually, I loved them. But during those three years my desire for freedom grew stronger. I couldn't stop thinking about all that money. Why couldn't I get it now, when I needed it. I began to hate my father.

Not that he had done anything against me, but I couldn't keep waiting. The awful thought came to my mind, Why doesn't he die so I can get on with my life? I could get a really good car; that would attract the girls. I could have my own place and a boat too. I kept turning these things over in my head. I didn't realize how mentally deranged I had become. I began to pray for my father's death, and this led to plotting for it. I justified all this by telling myself, I deserve it. No one can be sure of the future, so let me live life my way now.

It's too painful to recount the details of what happened next, so I'll summarize. The gun jammed, and my father lived. He never told anyone except my brother. Boy, was my brother mad. He is older and a real goody-goody. I told my dad why I wanted him dead. I could see the astonishment in his eyes, but he never said anything harsh. Four weeks later he picked me up at work. At lunch he gave me a checkbook. He had opened an account in my name and put in my part of the money—$3,500,000. There were tears in his eyes. He was afraid that I would be gone soon and that he might never see me again. He was right.

I was gone for four years—many cities, many women, several cars and many friends. No job though. I didn't need one. Then my money evaporated. My friends left. I was full of bitterness (frozen anger is what I called it), and it was eating me up on the inside. I was becoming inhuman in so many ways. My human passions, which I had thought were just an innocent desire for freedom, actually controlled me. I was enslaved to them. But I didn't care. I didn't deserve to live; I contemplated taking my own life. I wasn't afraid of anything. I still hated my father and brother and God, if there was one.

Then it hit me like a shaft of light from heaven entering my mind. I'd been so stupid. I'd sinned terribly against both my heavenly father and my earthly father. I realized that my only hope at that point was mercy. I wasn't worthy to be part of the family— only a servant.

That day I left for the long journey home. Little did I know that every day my father had been looking toward the horizon with hope and love. When I neared home I saw him running toward me. I was stunned and unable to get out all my words of deep repentance before he smothered me with his embrace and kiss. I'll never forget the celebration. I was forgiven and free. He would hear nothing of my being a servant. I was family. I belonged. It felt so good to be home at last.

The story of Young Jun Son parallels the story of the prodigal son that Jesus tells in Luke 15:11-24. In contrast to the older son, whom we looked at earlier, we see in the Bible that the younger son experiences the power of saving grace. Grace brings him to his senses. In the culture of that day, his request was tantamount to wanting his father to die. The realization that his sin had not only a horizontal dimension (against his father) but also a vertical dimension (against heaven) is evidence of the work of the Holy Spirit calling to him. What was the son's mental state before this? By implication, senseless, insane, not in his right mind, crazy. This is the non-Christian's mental state. They have no true wisdom. Their thinking about how to live is eccentric, off-centered. But once the Holy Spirit breaks through, his mind changes. Conviction of sin and hope for mercy from the father moves him to come home. He is willing to be taken back as an employee, and he forfeits all claims as a son. He wants only to be allowed to work for his father. What brought about this change? God's enabling grace enlightened him to his sin and then provided the riches of sonship. Grace is being treated better than you deserve. He wishes to repay his father for his mistakes; but if the heavenly Father allowed this, grace would cease to be grace!

Story 2. Pedro arrived in the United States quietly. His small boat was the beginning of a flotilla of boats coming to Florida from Cuba. Many of the people were not the most respected of citizens. But Pedro was different. He was a leader, outspoken and bold. He was well educated, a professor. He was from a well-known family that had produced many religious leaders, and he would soon follow as the greatest and most zealous of them all. Here is his story:

> *My primary motivation in life has always been to serve God. I cannot remember ever not believing in God. He was the center of my life and the subject of my academic studies. I am proud of my family. I can trace them back to Spain, to a Spanish cardinal of the church. And I can go even further back in my family line, to Italy. I have a genealogy that links me to the family of the first pope, which means I may even be related to St. Peter himself! I come from a long line of priests and bishops. My great-great-grandfather arrived in Cuba and eventually was the bishop for the entire island. I was baptized in the largest cathedral on the island by the pope himself during his visit to Cuba. If you wish proof of my orthodoxy, I am a Jesuit and committed to that noble conservative group, Opus Dei. You can find no fault with my*

church heritage nor my theology. But more important, I do not just theorize about my religion: "The zeal of the Lord has consumed me" is my motto.

Erroneous teachers are the enemy of God and his Word. I have taken inspiration from my study of the Spanish Inquisition and have applied it to a situation that arose in Florida shortly after I arrived. Some fanatics from my parish were questioning the teachings of the Holy Bible and claiming they had a new interpretation as to who should lead the church. They began to follow a man who reinterpreted everything. I immediately took leadership in stamping out this new cult. Their heresy was obvious and very dangerous. I was even able to work up charges that led to the imprisonment of some. To sum up, I can say that when it comes to keeping God's law, I am blameless and righteous.

Well, I can tell you it took a voice from heaven to knock me off my high horse! For some time my conscience had been nagging me because I had begun to see that the motives and thought behind all my behavior had to be right in God's sight. There was also something eerie about the peace of the followers of the "reinterpreter," even when I put them in prison. The culmination came when the Spirit of God (I can attribute it to nothing else) forcefully got my attention with this thought: when I persecuted the followers of this new leader, I was actually fighting God Almighty—for he was God! Smitten with the seriousness of my sinfulness, I realized all my self-generated goodness was sheer junk to God. I was the heretic—totally blind to the fact that my zeal for God was uninformed and erroneous. Seeking forgiveness, I transferred the basis of my acceptance with God from myself to what another (Jesus) had done for me.

What has reminded you of yourself in my loose retelling of the preconversion life of Saul, recorded in Philippians 3:4-6, Romans 7:7-10 and Acts 9:1-19, who became the apostle Paul?

Paul was humbled by the tenth commandment, which says, "You shall not covet." This commandment was like a bright searchlight shining into his heart. The realization of his need for an alien righteousness led him to gladly give up all the good deeds he had in his spiritual bank account. Once his hands were empty, they could be filled with a gift righteousness: "not having a righteousness of my own [making] that comes from the law [keeping], but that which is through faith in Christ—the righteousness that comes from God and is by faith" (Phil 3:9). When did all this happen?

When Paul was extremely hostile to Christ, persecuting him by persecuting his followers. He was "arrested" on a road. Holy Spirit conviction of sin against his Maker came upon him. Saving grace melted his heart, and another unwilling, unable and undeserving sinner was regenerated. Immediately his re-created will responds. He obeys his Lord's command to wait, and we find him praying.

Paul had an abnormal spiritual birth in one sense. He was not part of the first new births among the early disciples. Yet he was born according to God's perfect timing. "But when God, who set me apart from birth and called me by his grace, was pleased to reveal his Son in me" (Gal 1:15). He sure wasn't expecting it or seeking it! In fact, his will was dead set against it. He was anti-Christ and was actively hostile to the risen Lord. He called himself the head honcho of sinners. Grace makes "salvation-change" possible.

OUR RE-CREATING GOD

We've looked at four lives: a dutiful older son, a wealthy young woman, a runaway son and a religious leader. Two of them surrendered to the pursuing love of Jesus. These two seems so different—a wild son and a zealous churchman. One traveled the road of sinful pleasure and self-centered living. The other traveled a road of legalism and hatred for those whom he considered irreligious. So different on the exterior; so similar on the interior.

"*But* because of his great love for us, *God, who is rich in mercy, made us alive* with Christ even when we were dead in transgressions—*it is by grace you have been saved* . . . through faith—and this [faith for salvation] not from yourselves, it is the gift of God—not by works, so that no one can boast" (Eph 2:4-5, 8-9). Thank God for the *but*—that attaining forgiveness and righteousness doesn't depend on our own efforts. God's sovereign, saving grace is what empowers the dead will of sinners and gives them a new heart too—a total spiritual rebirth. Will, mind and affections are renewed. With a heart aflame with the love *of* Christ, the will now desires to return this with love *for* Christ. Now enabled to choose right, the newly born spiritual baby does the work God requires, which is "to believe in the one [Jesus] he has sent" (Jn 6:29). God does for us what we cannot do for ourselves. "For what the law was powerless to do in that it was weakened by the sinful nature, *God* did by sending his own Son in the likeness of sinful man to be a sin offering. And so he condemned sin in sinful man, *in order that the righteous requirements of the law might be fully met in us"* (Rom 8:3-4). What God requires, he supplies.

In Bible terminology God's fulfillment for us of the requirements of the law is the new covenant, God's way of ensuring the success of his human reclamation spoken of by the prophet Ezekiel: "I will cleanse you from all your impurities and from all your idols. I will *give* you a new heart and *put* a new spirit in you; I will remove from you your heart of stone and give you a heart of flesh. And I will put my Spirit in you and *move you* to follow my decrees and be careful to keep my laws. . . . You will be my people, and I will be your God" (Ezek 36:25-28). Finally, a God-given empowerment for right living and faithful loving.

We see that grace is an active *power* (1 Cor 15:10; 2 Cor 12:9). Long ago, Augustine used the term "prevenient grace" to describe grace that enables the will to choose good. It is portrayed in a brief vignette during the ministry of Paul: "We sat down and began to speak to the women who had gathered there. One of those listening was a woman named Lydia. . . . The Lord opened her heart to respond to Paul's message" (Acts 16:13-14). This is the mystery of the new birth—the wind of God blowing where it wills (pleases) across cold hearts and warming them.

Years ago, during childbirth classes with my wife, I asked the instructor, "What initiates the moment of movement down the birth canal and out into the world?" Her nonchalant reply was, "It's unknown. The time comes. We're not in control." It's like that with the regenerating breath of God's Spirit—both at conception and birth. The apostle John said, "The wind blows where it wills" (Jn 3:8). It's not only the power, invisibility and mystery of air movement that's in view here but also the wind's independent, self-willed sovereignty. This quality of wind is evident in the many revisions needed by weather forecasters! The wind bringing birth from above is a symbol of God's purposeful and specific action which initiates movement. We are reborn not by human willpower but by God (Jn 1:12-13). Behind our believing reception of his Son is God's birthing Spirit, a divine granting of the *right* (authority) to become his child. Salvation is not a right we originally possess; it must be lovingly bestowed.

When a lonely college athlete entered a hotel in New York for a rowdy new-millennium celebration, he was not seeking God. But the wind was blowing that night—even during the music, laughter, foolishness, drinking and dazzling lights. Late that evening, one thought began to grip his mind: *I am not right with God. All this is vanity. God is the answer.* He couldn't shake this thought. It seemed such an obvious truth that he began to tell his friends, thinking he had just now found the secret that others must have already realized. Much to his surprise, they had no idea what he was talking about. Some humored him, as you would a naïve child. Others rebuked him, saying he was spoiling their fun with his God talk. Unswayed, he immediately joined a campus Bible study.

Now, over two years later, this student has lived out in the wild world of college sports the new life that the wind of God's Spirit brought to him that night. Startled by his "nonseeker, Damascus road" experience, I explored with him any trace of prior contact with the gospel. We have been able to pinpoint only three things. First, though dropping out of church in high school, he was taught truth through catechism and Scripture in his childhood as a Catholic. Second, there were people in his family who may have prayed for him. Third, a Christian classmate at college who did not know him chose to pray for him that fall. I had also been praying for the lacrosse players. He cannot recall anyone witnessing to him.

Prevailing grace does not operate in a vacuum. The Scriptures are always involved. Yet, God uses various means to accomplish his foreordained ends. The encounter with the living Word is inextricably connected with our enmeshment in the written Word. As Peter says, we have been born again "through the living and enduring word of God" (1 Pet 1:23). The Holy Spirit acts primarily in conjunction with the written Word. The Holy Spirit's role was to inspire men to accurately write down the words of the living Word and the Father's explanation of redemption. The Scriptures are what impart the wisdom of salvation to us.

For those who think in linear fashion, it could be put this way:

Grace to the Rescue

1. Human beings crash. We are "totaled" and "dis-abled."

2. Re-creation (new life) is needed.

3. Alien (from outside of ourselves) aid is needed.

4. Our Maker devises a salvation plan involving his Son and the Holy Spirit.

5. The Father, unobligated to save any, chooses to save many, not because of any quality in us but because it pleases him. He thus sends his Son.

6. Jesus, the God-Man, provides redemption via keeping perfectly the Father's law and through his death as our substitute sin-bearer and resurrection for those given to him (chosen) by the Father.

7. The Holy Spirit, following God's plan, regenerates those given to the Son, granting Christ's benefits to them.

8. Having spiritual new birth, they wholeheartedly respond in repentance and faith.

9. They willingly and freely love God because he first loved them, and they choose to do his will.

If you're visual, think of these images:

- The wind blowing so strongly it moves you
- A child being born—from conception to birth
- A brilliant light coming on in the dark
- Drinking water after being dehydrated
- Expressions of love operating as a catalyst to draw love out of someone
- Skeletons coming to life

There is a story about a young girl who passionately pursued her hobby of model making. Her delight was a detailed replica of a sailboat. Taking her prized possession to the lake, she gently pushed it out into the shallow water. Watching from a distance, she admired its bobbing motion. Unexpectedly a wind came up, and she realized her boat was moving rapidly away.

Unable to swim, she watched desperately as it disappeared, its sails torn and masts bent.

Months later, she was passing a store window and saw her boat on display. It was for sale. Breathless, she entered the store and asked the owner to give her back her boat. The owner, unsympathetic to her pleadings, simply said, "If you want it back, you must buy it back." The next day she returned with all of her other models and all the money she had. Impressed, the owner smiled and said, "It's yours." Now the child realized the boat was twice hers, first by right of ownership, then by right of redemption.

In this chapter we have seen God in action. He is grace-full. He is the God of the impossible. In spite of our "uncreation," he brings "re-creation." He is the Creator-Redeemer God.

Sovereign, Saving Grace

Love can be deserved, or at least evoked, by qualities in the person loved. Grace is a unique love, love for the undeserving; it is the unmerited love of God for those who deserve the opposite. We have forfeited any right to God's love and are living under a Damocles sword of impending judgment. Saving grace is what initiates and secures an individual's salvation.

Saving grace originates in God's gracious and giving nature, and is for people that are so incapacitated by love of themselves that they are unable to change. They are super-glued to their idols. When people elevate wordly things above God, they become enslaved to their petty desires and driven by their self-designed gods. Saving grace is the miracle cure for those who cannot save themselves and in no way merit their Maker's compassion. Grace only functions as grace when it comes to those who have absolutely nothing to recommend them as candidates for God's favor.

GRACE DISCRIMINATES

What does the concept of sovereign add to saving grace? The word *sovereign* has many synonyms: unequalled power, total control, highest authority, total superiority, ultimate. Christians give mental acknowledgment to these concepts when they revere God. They accept his control over the universe of stars, planets, wind and storms. They struggle with his supremacy over injustice, wars, health and death. In these hard things, by faith they eventually relinquish their supposed rights and questions, shutting their mouths before his inscrutable ways.

Yet when the question "How is it determined who will be saved and who will be lost?" is asked, we assert our challenge to God's ways and cling to the supposed sovereignty of our wills. Why are we so reluctant to surrender to the idea that God chooses whom he will save if no one deserves saving grace? Instead of asking why he doesn't save everyone, we should be asking why he should save anyone. Could it be that our distrust of God's sovereignty arises from a suspicion of his heart? A fear of being controlled, a loss of freedom or a prior commitment to a belief that we know what's best for us and that God doesn't have the best in mind for us? We begin, like Job, to doubt that God is a *good* God. We want to reserve for ourselves the option of evaluating God's purpose with our limited horizon and puny standard of whether God's sovereign acts fit our definition of love.

Think about the awesome loving results of believing that the Holy Spirit gives the new birth to people unable to respond (regeneration precedes faith, not vice versa). Could this mean that heaven might include millions whom God has chosen from among those aborted, infants and mentally incapacitated and also the confused elderly? This is the supremacy of grace!

At one point in Jesus' ministry a group of people became so furious with him that they tried to throw him off a rocky cliff to his death. What could Jesus have said to stir people to such bitter hatred? These were ordinary people, not the religious leaders who were constantly plotting his death. The writer, Luke, had just summed up their demeanor, saying, "All spoke well of him and were amazed at the gracious words that came from his lips" (Lk 4:22). They then requested to experience his grace, in the form of physical healing, for themselves. Being in his hometown and knowing his family, they felt deserving of his favors. Jesus saw through this. Their very familiarity with his human origins gave birth to contempt, and not to respect. In response, Christ says:

> I assure you that there were many widows in Israel in Elijah's time, when the sky was shut for three and a half years and there was a severe famine throughout the land. Yet Elijah was not sent to any of them, but to a widow in Zarephath in the region of Sidon. And there were many in Israel with leprosy in the time of Elisha the prophet, yet not one of them was cleansed—only Naaman the Syrian. (Lk 4:24-27)

Why did this statement create such incredible hostility toward Jesus? It is a bold statement of sovereignty over people's lives, a statement that God has his purposes. Jesus is following a divine principle seen in the ministry of the prophets: discrimination on the basis of God's plan as to who will receive his benefits. Two things about who was helped stirred up animosity. The first was the ethnicity of the people healed; they were both non-Jews. One was even a commander of an army of Israel's enemies. Uh-oh! The second was that people were bypassed. The withholding of God's grace is underscored by Jesus' reference to many widows and lepers. The implication that in their day God had *not sent* the prophet Jesus to heal them was intolerable. They couldn't control Jesus. They would not experience his benefits due to their unbelief—but also due to his not being sent to heal them. The doctrine of God's sovereignty is that God selects those on whom his favor will rest. God is self-determined. He has supreme independence; he is autonomous—a law unto himself. As each goes to their appointed destination in the afterlife, no one will shake their fist at God, saying, "I didn't get what I deserved." Except, of course, for the person in heaven!

Note how two theological students, Sarah and Jennifer, describe the blessing they experienced through the writings of Augustine and Luther, which convinced them of God's sovereignty and confronted them with an awesome God.

> If you asked me who was in control of the universe, I would have said God the Father Almighty. If you asked who had won my salvation, I would have said Jesus Christ. If you asked who had given faith to me, I would have said the Holy Spirit. Bur if you then asked me if I believed in predestination, I would have shaken my head vigorously and dismissed it as some theologian's arrogant presumption about who's going to the hot spot. . . .
>
> Yet it is part and parcel of human sin that we want to usurp God's right to be the Creator of everything, including love, and to stand in some neutral position in respect to God. . . .
>
> God is love. . . . All love has its source in him and cannot exist independently of him. So no standard of love exists outside God, because that would wrongly place love over and above God. . . .

This lack of neutrality offends free will. The human creature demands the right to make his own decisions. He follows in the footsteps of father Adam, who wanted to claim neutrality for himself (against the good decision of God to withhold the fruit) by gaining knowledge of good and evil. Adam thought this knowledge would allow him to make decisions as if he were God—without the input of God.

. . . Adam tried to use the free will granted him by his own good createdness in order to control a thing above him—the knowledge of good and evil—seeking "neutral" knowledge rather than knowledge of God.

But knowledge is never neutral. . . . We didn't have the power to resist evil once we came to know it. Now we are so bound by evil that we cannot even begin to have anything like neutral knowledge of it. . . . How prideful for the human being to think he can step away from his sins for a minute and make a good choice about God! . . . We are captives to our own lust for neutrality, which in fact kills neutrality utterly. The only way out is by the rescue of Christ's atoning death. . . .

Ironic as it sounds, accepting predestination into our lives was the most freeing thing that had ever happened to us spiritually. We were free to be creatures again! We no longer had the burden of trying to be the Creator. . . .

As a result, I became concretely interested in serving others, while before it had always seemed a necessary but burdensome obligation. Mission work became appealing. . . . Subconsciously I had viewed other people as a means to accomplishing good works. It was never as obvious as works-righteousness, because I knew I couldn't be saved by works. But I had lived the Christian life in service of my own ideas about being a Christian. . . .

Our gratitude overwhelms us, and that is the real motivation behind our actions. We aren't particularly trying to obey the law; this stuff just happens, wells up out of us like a spring. That's how we figured out that fear or moral laxity isn't a legitimate objection to the teaching of predestination. We don't get it all right—not by a long shot—but the idea of being indifferent to God's demands is simply unthinkable.

Our intellectual adjustment to predestination has completely transfigured everything in our lives. We have discovered our paradoxically bound freedom, and for us as creatures, it is the only real freedom.[1]

There is a verse in 1 John that sums it all up: "We love [God and others] because he *first* loved us" (4:19). God chose me first, and this triggered my choice of him. He loved me specifically from all eternity, and I, wooed by his prior love, freely love him back. I've come home into my Father's house. I love to be a mere human creature before my Creator. First grace, then respond-ability.

NOT FREE WILL BUT A FREED WILL

The Bible contains numerous verses indicating the activity of the human will in becoming a Christian. "The Spirit and the bride say, 'Come!' And let him who hears say, 'Come!' Whoever is thirsty, let him come; and whoever wishes [is willing], let him take the free gift of the water of life" (Rev 22:17). "For there is no difference between Jew and Gentile—the same Lord is Lord of all and richly blesses all who call on him, for, 'Everyone who calls on the name of the Lord will be saved'" (Rom 10:12-13). In both these verses we see the human will exhorted to break free from the power of sin and do something immensely good—come to Christ, call on God. In addition, we find many verses where people do this and find salvation. And these verses are addressed to "whoever" and "everyone." Many Christians read this and use the phrase "free will" to describe what they see in these verses. However, the phrase "human response" or "human responsibility" would be more accurate. Martin Luther, in *The Bondage of the Will*, attempts to put the nail in the coffin of this concept by questioning the use of *free*. He says many religious people describe the power of free will as small, and wholly ineffective apart from the grace of God. Agreed? But if God's grace is lacking, if it is taken away from that small power, what can the will do? It is ineffective and can do nothing good. Hence it follows that free will without God's grace is really not free will at all. For what is *ineffective* power but (in plain language) *no* power?

The Bible teaches that the Holy Spirit makes us willing; we do not do it ourselves. Here is a simple illustration that has been helpful to many.

John is a recluse. He lives in an old house with the windows boarded up and has his food supply delivered regularly. Avoiding contact with the world outside, he is comfortable in the only house he knows. From time to time he hears a voice outside, at first faint, then clearer. He can now distinguish the repeated words, "Come home."

Perturbed, he shouts through the boarded door, "Quiet! I am home."

The voice says, "No, you are deceived. This is not your real home. Open the door. Look out to the horizon. See the garden and the house awaiting you."

John replies, "Go away. There's nothing out there for me. I'm happy living life my way."

Days pass, and John hears the voice again. "Come home to me. Believe what I'm saying."

Angrily John stuffs in his earplugs, and shouts, "I don't want to be bothered. I don't want to change my ways."

That night he thinks of pictures he's seen of the world outside and recalls the sunlight seeping through cracks in the window boards. Then he hears noises in his basement. The temperature inside the house begins to rise. John realizes that someone has gotten in the house and has turned up the heat. At the same time, he hears the voice whispering at the door, "Come, come." Resisting this intrusion, he throws himself into moving the sofa, chairs, desk and even the large refrigerator in front of the door. Then he hides under the bed. But the heat is unbearable.

Unable to stand it any longer, he rushes to the door and rapidly claws away at the furniture. The voice is louder now, "Come to me. Come to me." He uncovers the long-unused peephole on the door and is stunned by a brilliant light and rainbow of colors. He thinks, *Could I have been wrong?* Drawn irresistibly, he unbolts the door and runs outside, heading for the house and garden in full bloom. Astonished neighbors hear him crying, "I'm coming. I'm coming. I'm willing to believe you. Please take me home."

So God, in Christ, calls to us in our complacency. We hear the outward call offering good news, but we are unwilling. Then the Holy Spirit enters the basement and turns up the heat of conviction. We now have an inner urge, a desire to get out of that house. That desire is fanned into a passionate flame by Christ's alluring beauty and his provision of a place of safety and love—at home with the Father and adopted into His family. I become willing and choose Christ because *what I desired in my mind was changed* by God's empowering, evocative grace! Sovereign saving grace gives power to obey, as well as grants a pardon for disobedience. My will is freed.

BECAUSE IT PLEASES HIM

As a young Christian I left home to attend a college that had its roots in a Protestant denomination. When I arrived I discovered I was unprepared for the unbelief that prevailed there. I wasn't at a public university, but I encountered something far worse than secularism: a humanistic and relativistic worldview overlaid with a religious veneer. I quickly discovered how deadly this was to my new, experience-centered faith.

As I wrestled with the trustworthiness of Scripture, I was forced to rigorously study the Bible. I had to make a crucial decision: Was I willing to follow Scripture (truth) wherever it led me, or would finite logic and human concepts of love and justice prevail? In particular, would I bow before the sovereignty of God in saving some people but not all, acknowledging that hell is deserved and that God's honor and justice are glorified there? Would I be willing to follow Scripture as it gave revelation, but leave those truths not yet revealed (hidden, incomplete) in God's hands? I had difficulty in acknowledging that God is God. I kept wondering, *Why does he do certain things?*

During that time a song came to mind. The song asked a question, but never gave the answer.

> Love sent my Savior to die in my stead,
> Why should He love me so?
> Meekly to Calvary's cross He was led,
> Why should He love me so?
> Why should He love me so? Why should He love me so?
> Why should my Savior to Calvary go?
> Why should He love me so?
> ANONYMOUS

The song does not answer why God should love us so, and Scripture gives no answer except to say, "Because he wanted to!"

In the Bible the reason God does anything is because *it pleases Him.*

> *"I am God, and there is no other:*
> *I am God and there is none like me. . . .*
> *I say: My purpose will stand,*
> *and I will do all that I please." (Is 46:9-10)*

"Our God is in heaven;
   he does whatever pleases him." (Ps 115:3)

"You are worthy, our Lord and God,
   to receive glory and honor and power,
for you created all things
    and by your will [for your pleasure] they were created
    and have their being." (Rev 4:11)

The apostle Paul is fond of using the phrase "according to his pleasure" when writing about God's plan of redemption. When God reveals that his plan began before the creation of the world, Paul twice attributes the reason for God's election of *specific people* in Christ (not a vague group) and predestination to the fact that it brought pleasure to him (Eph 1:5, 9). There is a huge number of persons for whom God planned salvation—simply because it is what he loves to do. You can't trace the reason for salvation back any further than this. Be humbled and give God all the honor. He is not a capricious God acting arbitrarily. Both his love and his wrath are purposeful outworkings of his character. God hides the truth from some people; he doesn't reveal himself or Jesus to them. Why (Lk 10:21-22)?

The Holy Spirit regenerates people because it *pleases* God (Gal 1:15). It is according to his good will or purpose. "God . . . has saved us and called us to a holy life—not because of anything we have done but *because of his own purpose and grace.* This grace was given us in Christ Jesus before the beginning of time" (2 Tim 1:9). Believers will share in individual salvation now, and also the entire future eternal kingdom of glory. Why? In tender words of encouragement Jesus says to his disciples, "Do not be afraid, little flock, for your Father has *been pleased* to give you the kingdom" (Lk 12:32). John Piper revels in God's motive of pleasure. "God is acting here in freedom . . . out of his deepest delight. This is what the word *[pleasure]* means: God's joy, His desire, His want and wish and hope and pleasure and gladness and delight is to give the Kingdom to His flock, . . . not his duty, necessity, obligation, but His pleasure. . . . That is the kind of God He is. That is the measure of the greatness of His heart."[2]

Are you in awe of these expressions of God's pleasure? There is another action that took place in the eternal purpose of God and became actual in history because it was pleasing to God: the torturous death of his Son.

> *"Surely he took up our infirmities*
>   *and carried our sorrows,*
> *yet we considered him stricken by God,*
>   *smitten by him, and afflicted. . . .*
> *Yet it was the LORD'S will [pleasure] to crush him and cause him to suffer."*
> (Is 53:4, 10)

Be amazed! We would not have dared to say such a thing unless Scripture had spoken it. "This man [Jesus] was handed over to you by God's set purpose and foreknowledge" (Acts 2:23). Why should he love me so? Because it brought him delight. Wonder at his willingness to run toward and embrace those who once hated him. Worship him for who he is in and of himself, not just for what he does and how we benefit. The crucifixion is a mind-boggling display of love and justice. God-centered evangelism includes both.

Worship
*The Whole-Souled Response
to the Gospel of Grace*

The greatest obstacle in personal evangelism is fear. Read any book on evangelism, take any training course—they all agree on this. We fear what others will think of us, that they might reject us. Proverbs tells us fear of man is a trap; it immobilizes us. We have all experienced this. So many helps are available, but what will dissolve fear and motivate and sustain evangelism?

Most people seem content to live a "good life," letting their light shine so others will hopefully figure out the source, rather than initiating conversations on spiritual matters. Being intricately involved in the lives/needs of those outside the kingdom and telling the gospel truth to them is an experience foreign to many. We seem to have bought into the idea that religion is a private affair and we shouldn't intrude on the beliefs of others. God talk in the public arena has been effectively "gagged." We may have our personal beliefs that Jesus is the only way, but we cringe at the thought of exposing them. We need to displace our fear of others with a "fear" of Someone else. Our kowtowing to the approval of others must be replaced by a strong desire for the approval of the awesome One and a confidence that I am loved.

MOTIVATION FOR EVANGELISM:
ENCOUNTERING A MACRO-GOD

When the shepherd boy David walked into the midst of God's army he found all of them trembling before the giant Goliath. Their reaction mystified David, who was not infected with their contagion of fear for a moment.

Day after day the very people who were to be God's warriors were dismayed and terrified. They even ran away with fright. But the boy David had a totally different reaction. He wondered who Goliath was that he should defy the armies of the *living* God—not just God of his fathers (past) but God of the present. Where did David get such conviction? The God who was "unable" to the Israelite soldiers was "able" to David. How could David be so sure? I'll let him tell the story: "I learned that God is alive while keeping sheep! It was there, when I had to fight off wild animals, that I experienced the reality of God. God enabled me to kill both lions and bears. God is with me. God is alive. God is real. He will not stand for someone defying him, robbing him of his honor. The Lord who delivered me from the paw of the lion and the paw of the bear will deliver me from Goliath! I know it" (paraphrase of 1 Sam 17:34-37).

David came into a situation where fear had paralyzed others. But he was not afraid. Why? He had personally experienced God's omnipotence. He had seen him work, even through him. Out of his vital sense of the reality of God, David spoke *and* acted. David had encountered God, and he could never be the same. The opinions of others made no difference to him: David knew a huge God, a God deserving of adoration and worship.

The Gospel of John tells the story of a Samaritan woman who went out at midday to draw water. She was used to doing things alone, for she was a social outcast. The other women shunned her and told stories about her. The men avoided her in public lest they be linked to her. (In private it was a different story.) She had a history of affairs—at least six—leaving behind her a landscape filled with broken relationships. The people avoided her, and she avoided them. Was she completely hardened to the opinions of others? No. None of us are. What turned this woman from an isolated person into an outgoing witness to others? As she dipped water from a well, she met Jesus and learned to worship. Being thirsty for spiritual water, she drank freely. Jesus was seeking worshipers that day, and he found one—and she ran and found others for him. "Many of the Samaritans from that town believed in him because of the woman's testimony" (Jn 4:39).

Both David and the Samaritan woman came to a point where what others thought of them was not primary. This change in perspective was not because

David was immature and the woman ostracized; rather, it was due to a personal encounter with the living God, an encounter leading to love and adoration—to worship. Powerful worship will energize you to witness. It changes the focus of attention from the opinions of self and others to the greatness of God and his intoxicating love. Throughout the ages, those who gave up their puny self-centeredness and were caught up in God's work impacted others in evangelism. An experience of worship mobilizes us to witness.

Many churches have diminished God by their traditions and by an abbreviated theology. Conforming him to their ideas and culture, they make him a comfortable God. As a result, the gospel is shirked by both novice evangelists and the unevangelized; it is no longer imperative. If evangelism is done at all, ideas about God are vague, fuzzy and often inaccurate. What may have begun as an attempt to relate to non-believers by being more loving, relational and personal ends up putting the person at the center, not God. Where is our confidence in the unique inspiration and divine authority of God's written Word? Do you cower before the contemporary mindset which questions the existence of any overarching, unifying truth (metanarrative)? Are you stymied by the deconstructionists' conclusion that all communication is meaningless? Who will tell the truth? Will you become someone who, gripped by grace, lives graciously and leaves an imprint of truth on your friend's heart and conscience?

God's language in his book is alive and full of power. Sharper than a two-edged sword, it cuts open the very thought life of people. It exposes and interprets what they think and feel. His words are a perfect correspondence with reality, achieving accurate transfer of information with the hearer/reader. Our macro-God's words are not restricted even though they are encased in human language. His word is powerful, bringing reality into being, as at creation when the words, "Let there be," resulted in, "And it was." When Jesus spoke two words to a dead man rotting in a tomb, "Come forth," the man did.

As Christians realize the grand scope of God's initiative in pouring out grace to nonbelievers, they become excited about God including them in his plan. Grace is active, enabling them to witness. Grace is empowering, enabling the nonbeliever to respond. We are not responsible for producing results. God is—and he will do it. When salvation is clearly seen as God's work of sovereign saving grace, grace is no longer emaciated, weakened, colorless. Dwelling on divine supremacy in salvation magnifies a grace-exalting God and humbles us. Saving grace means that God is neither coerced nor constrained by our value as humans. He is not obligated to save, but still he does! God is in debt to no one. For non-Christians, grace says their best efforts to be "good" are failures, for "if by grace, then it is no longer by works; if it were, *grace would no longer be grace*" (Rom 11:6). The apostle Paul, in writing to believers in Ephesus, was carried away with describing the theology of grace, and he wrote one of the longest sentences in the New Testament (Eph 1:3-14; translators of the Greek have to insert periods to help us read it). This passage of Scripture is stacked with deep theology—and it's these doctrines of grace that lead Paul into doxology! Exalting God provokes worship.

WORSHIP: THE PASSION FOR AND THE PURPOSE OF EVANGELISM

Chapter 15 of Luke's Gospel contains three stories, each involving a search, which reveal that God, by nature, is a seeker of the lost. Jesus' purpose in coming to earth was to seek and save the lost. The stories share a common climax—celebration, or worship, at finding what was lost. God doesn't just want workers dutifully doing their tasks. The people must celebrate! The finding of the lost evokes worship, in both the seeker and the one being found.

Jesus told a thirsty woman, "Yet a time is coming and has now come when the true worshipers will worship the Father in spirit and truth, for they are *the kind of worshipers the Father seeks*" (Jn 4:23). Changing worshipers of false gods into worshipers of the true God is the purpose of evangelism. We aren't seeking just "decisions for Jesus" but awe-inspired worshipers, people who have tasted and seen that the Lord is full of grace and who can't hold back their joy. Seeker and found, evangelist and new convert join in the dance.

Worship also creates the *passionate motive* for evangelism. It's the high-octane fuel that makes "liftoff" possible. Visualize how large the two fuel tanks are on the U.S. space shuttles. A lot of fuel is needed to break free from the downward pull of gravity. So what's holding you down? The white-hot, flaming fuel of worship will blast you out of your lethargy for the lost. Why? Because worship focuses us totally on a majestic, triumphant Creator-Redeemer, lifting us out of ourselves—our sins, inadequacies, whatever! Fear of people is displaced with fervor. We begin to overflow with concern and love for others, and we are compelled by the compassion of Christ. Worship is our response to his extreme grace.

By comparing worship to a celebration for the lost, I'm not saying worship is just emotion and fun. As in true conversion, the whole person is engaged in worship: mind, emotions, will. The mind fixates on truth, for we are to worship in "spirit and truth" Jesus said. The truth becomes experiential, not just mental. The core of our being, the heart, is moved upward. The will is moved to *desire* to submit and serve. We then move outward with the gospel, for we find our delight in the Lord High and Lifted Up.

Worship must be informed by revelation truth, which came to us in word form. God's word revelation both exalts and humbles the mind. The whole trajectory of Christian growth, according to the Bible, is to begin with doctrine and then experience it, rather than starting with our experience, codifying it into a doctrine and then teaching others to adhere to it. The highest use of our mind is to think God's thoughts. We do not worship an unknown God.

The written Word sets parameters for worship, just as a safety trench encircles a campfire. "Worship God acceptably with reverence and awe, for our 'God is a consuming fire'" (Heb 12:28-29). He is not safe; he cannot be approached just any old way in true worship. We no longer stand trembling as those under the old covenant stood before the fiery volcano of Mount Sinai. Rather, new-covenant worship involves the joyful assembly of saints and angels at Mount Zion (Heb 12:18-24). Still, when assembled in our churches on the Lord's day, we follow God's prescribed way of worship.

I hope you will excuse this small excursion on worship in a book on evangelism. I am compelled to put evangelism in its proper place: it's number *two* on God's agenda. Worship is number *one*. If churches kept this truth in perspective, a lot of them would be more honoring to God, and significantly more evangelism would be taking place. John Piper, an ambassador for God-centered worship, expresses it this way:

Missions is not the ultimate goal of the church. Worship is. Missions exists because worship doesn't. Worship is ultimate, not missions, because God is ultimate, not man. When this age is over, and the countless millions of the redeemed fall on their faces before the throne of God, missions will be no more. It is a temporary necessity. But worship abides forever.

Worship, therefore, is the fuel and goal in missions. It's the goal of missions because in missions we simply aim to bring the nations into the white-hot enjoyment of God's glory. The goal of missions is the gladness of the peoples in the greatness of God. "The Lord reigns; let the earth *rejoice*; let the many coastlands *be glad!*" (Psalm 97:1).

But worship is also the fuel of missions. Passion for God in worship precedes the offer of God in preaching. You can't commend what you don't cherish. Missionaries will never call out, "Let the nations *be glad!*", who cannot say from the heart, "*I rejoice* in the Lord. . . . I will be glad and exalt in thee, I will sing praise to thy name, O Most High*" (Psalm 104:34; 9:2). Missions begins and ends in worship. . . .

Compassion for the lost is a high and beautiful motive for missionary labor. Without it we lose the sweet humility of sharing a treasure we have freely received. But we have seen that compassion for people must not be detached from passion for the glory of God. John Dawson, a leader in Youth With a Mission, gives an additional reason why this is so. He points out that a strong feeling of love for "the lost" or "the world" is a very difficult experience to sustain and is not always recognizable when it comes.

> Don't wait for a feeling of love in order to share Christ with a stranger. You already love your heavenly Father, and you know that this stranger is created by Him, but separated from Him, so take those first steps in evangelism because you love God. It is not primarily out of a compassion for humanity that we share our faith or pray for the lost; it is first of all, love for God.

God is calling us above all else to be the kind of people whose theme and passion is the supremacy of God in all of life. No one will be able to rise to the magnificence of the missionary cause who does not feel the magnificence of Christ. There will be no big world vision without a big God. There will be no passion to draw others into our worship where there is no passion for worship.[1]

Meditate on these words from a hymn written in 1774 by a former captain of a slave tradeship.

Let us love, and sing, and wonder, Let us praise the Saviour's name!
He has hushed the law's loud thunder, He has quenched Mount Sinai's flame;
He has washed us with his blood, He has brought us nigh to God.

Let us love the Lord who bought us, Pitied us when enemies,
Called us by his grace, and taught us, Gave us ears and gave us eyes:
He has washed us with his blood, He presents our souls to God.

Let us wonder; grace and justice join, and point to mercy's store;
When through grace in Christ our trust is, Justice smiles, and asks no more:
He who washed us with his blood, Has secured our way to God.[2]

Perhaps this would be an appropriate point in your reading to enter into a time of personal worship.

REAL CONVERTS REALLY WORSHIP

Picture a woman scurrying through the graying dusk of a small village of rude brick homes. She's gingerly carrying a small exquisite flask. Heading toward the largest house in town, she sees the flickering candlelight on the large open portico. Many town and synagogue leaders are reclining on expensive mats, talking loudly and eating. A crowd of envious onlookers (the uninvited) hover close by, wanting to see what's happening. As she nears the house, the onlookers try to stop her, but she presses closer—and walks right into the midst of the dinner at the house of Simon the Pharisee. Her face reflects worry. Her eyes search through the crowd of men. Initially, the men are not aware of her. Another serving girl, they think.

Then an ominous silence spreads throughout the crowded courtyard. Men seemed to become uneasy. They look away from her, or down at the huge bowls of common food into which they dip their fingers. Worried looks appear on some of their faces. It is a different kind of worry from the woman's. This woman is well known, famous. The Scriptures state the reason for her fame euphemistically: "She was a woman who had lived a sinful life in that town." A few men quietly slip out. Others desperately hope she won't indicate that she knows them.

The woman's expression markedly changes to relief and joy. She sees the man she is looking for—Jesus. With unusual boldness and seemingly unaware of her impropriety, she goes to him. Standing behind him, she begins to weep. Her hands clutch a glazed alabaster jar that glistens in the candlelight. It is her most valuable possession, for it contains her savings in the form of very expensive perfume. Noticing that her profuse tears have begun to wet his feet, she kneels, and using her long, loose hair, which is the hallmark of her profession, she begins to wipe them. This progresses into kissing his feet. But no one can call these kisses sensuous. Rather, there is a childlike, adoring quality about them. Then, without hesitation, she takes the thin neck of the perfume jar and tilts it towards Jesus' feet. An aroma of lilies wafts across the room.

At this point, the men, though relieved she has avoided them, begin muttering louder and louder. Simon is appalled at her insolence. He is also drawing some conclusions about his guest, Jesus, who was the reason for the gathering. It might be more accurate to say Simon is drawing *more evidence* for a conclusion he has already reached about Jesus. But that's another part of the story. Jesus, reading Simon's thoughts—for he has not spoken anything—poses a riddle for him. Simon knows his catechism and quickly gives the correct answer.

> *Then he [Jesus] turned toward the woman and said to Simon, "Do you see this woman? I came into your house. You did not give me any water for my feet, but she wet my feet with her tears and wiped them with her hair. You did not give me a kiss, but this woman, from the time I entered, has not stopped kissing my feet. You did not put oil on my head, but she has poured perfume on my feet. Therefore, I tell you, her many sins have been forgiven—for she loved much. But he who has been forgiven little loves little."*
>
> *Then Jesus said to her, "Your sins are forgiven."*
>
> *The other guests began to say among themselves, "Who is this who even forgives sins?"*
>
> *Jesus said to the woman, "Your faith has saved you; go in peace."* (Lk 7:44-50)

The woman in this story illustrates worship as it's defined by Dr. Edmund Clowney:

Worship is what is evoked by the presence of God. It is a response, not a self-initiated, creative activity on our part. Worship is the only activity that can involve the totality of our personality without any residue. All other relationships are partial. Worship is always extravagant: Elders throw down their crowns, Mary pours out precious ointment, people prostrate themselves. We don't worship for what we can "get out of it."

Worship is the submission of all our nature to God:
The quickening of conscience by His holiness
The nourishment of mind with His truth
The purifying of imagination by His beauty
The opening of the heart to His love
The surrender of the will to His purpose.

All this is gathered up in *adoration,* the most selfless emotion of which our nature is capable, and therefore the chief remedy for that self-centeredness which is our original sin and the source of all actual sin.[2]

This woman *had* to get to Jesus. Why? Because she adored him in a way she had adored no other man. Why? Because He had forgiven her sins—and what a release that was for her! Freed, she became a worshiper. Regenerated, nothing could hold her back from taking this opportunity to honor him. He was nearby, and she wished to show her wonderfully new and pure love.

Some translations of this incident are misleading. Was this woman's love for Jesus what triggered (caused) the forgiveness of her sins? No, it was her love that gave *evidence* that she had been forgiven. Probably hearing Jesus' teaching at some other time, she has abandoned all other rivals for her love and placed all hope in him. Now Jesus speaks words confirming his forgiveness to her. When saving grace grants regeneration, change is inevitable. The recreated person desires to love and therefore wills to show that love. The faith that lays hold of Christ is an active faith. Worship is an intuitive response. I don't think she was aware of any hindrances that night. One objective was paramount—to honor Jesus and hope he would speak personally to her. Outrageous grace made her confident that she was loved.

Her act of worship was also an act of evangelism. She was a witness that Jesus was a Savior of sinners. "The other guests began to say among themselves, 'Who is this who even forgives sins?'" (Lk 7:49). Worship emboldens

Christians for witness. Sometimes, such as when unbelievers observe believers in worship, worship is witness. "But if an unbeliever or someone who does not understand comes in while everybody is prophesying, he will be convinced by all that he is a sinner and will be judged by all, and the secrets of his heart will be laid bare. So he will fall down and worship God, exclaiming, 'God is really among you!'" (1 Cor 14:24-25; cf. Lk 17:11-19).

GOD-CENTERED EVANGELISTS WORSHIP

What associations come to our mind when we think of the word *evangelist?* Many connotations are negative, like showperson or salesperson. Showperson evangelists will produce not converts but an audience of observers, taking up space in the pew, waiting to be entertained. Salesperson evangelists will produce not disciples but consumers, shopping haphazardly for the newest religious product. These evangelists and converts continue to be me-centered. But reverent evangelists have learned how to be patient and listen. They realize that God providentially rules in each detail of every day. Therefore the nonbelievers they meet are seen as divine appointments.

Attitudes and perspectives learned in worship can transfer into the way we evangelize. The doxological (worshiping) evangelist, therefore, is bold and not as concerned about the opinions of others. Delivered from worrying about others' opinions, they act for an audience of One. What an amazing witness they are, turning the simple gospel story into a melody of worship. What unbeliever would not be intrigued by such a combination of truth and beauty! From where have such powerful witnessing Christians arisen? They have warmed themselves at the fire of worship before a holy God. Theological conviction inspires and sustains evangelistic zeal.

Worship focuses and energizes us for witnessing. In the early church the Lord increased the numbers of new worshipers as they worshiped (Acts 2:46-47). Two Christians were singing and praising God. Overhearing truths of the gospel and seeing a demonstration of the Spirit's power, a man wanted to know how to be saved (Acts 16:25-31)! On another occasion, during worship at the church at Antioch, the Holy Spirit called two of the leaders to missions.

You cannot get close to the heart of God in worship without hearing his heartbeat for witnessing. When worshipers glimpse the glory of God, they become upset about situations where God is not glorified—and this moves them toward witnessing. "While Paul was waiting for them in Athens, he was greatly distressed to see that the city was full of idols" (Acts 17:16). The word for "distressed" means he had a "paroxysm." It was a mighty tremor to his heart; a trauma in his spirit. Christians, struck with a view of their high and mighty Lord, have heart attacks when he is defamed.

Fresh views of God's sovereignty in our times of individual and corporate worship sensitize us to the honoring of false gods and the dishonoring of the true God. Does it really upset you that in the various world power centers (governments, corporations, universities), God is omitted? My heart breaks as I see the total neglect of God when I walk through a university campus—teachers explaining the marvels of the universe and administrators managing the education of malleable minds with no credit given to God. I especially grieve for internationals, minorities, and others who have struggled to obtain the education ticket that claims to be their (and our society's) salvation. They find that the instruction has been disemboweled of God and any basis for morals and ethics.

As a Christian, when you see this disregard for God in world centers, does it stir you up to witness? When you see a family member or friend turn their back on Jesus, doesn't it hurt? God is being robbed of his glory. Will you recommit yourself to telling the truth? As you become intentional in witnessing, do you see how your worship times mold your attitude in and approach to evangelism? As a worshiper, you've learned to wait patiently and you've learned to love. As a worshiper you've been humbled, and you've grown to hate injustice. As a worshiper you've been in touch with a power beyond yourself. Perhaps you could sum up the worship experience by saying, "I've been in touch with Reality. Now I reenter my daily world with new eyes and new passion to bring others to the really Real."

Join with me in seeking fame for his Name, shouting to God, "You're number one." A passion for worship sustains a passion for evangelism.

"Will you not revive us again,
    that your people may rejoice in you?
Show us your unfailing love, O LORD,
    and grant us your salvation." (Ps 85:6-7)

PART FOUR

Offered by Whole People
Character and Communication in Witnessing

.

12

Ordinary Christians
Can Witness

When you begin to speak of Jesus as the way to God, it won't be long before someone will call you "intolerant." This label is what we all fear, and its use has become increasingly effective in not just muffling our witness but muzzling it. Like a muzzled dog, we find our gospel bark and bite restrained! Religious harassment has joined the list of crimes against humanity. At the outset of this section on learning to witness, we need to face this dilemma.

PLURALISM AND THE NEW DEFINITION OF TOLERANCE
When a student at the University of Delaware saw the sign outside the office of a Christian campus ministry, she immediately complained to university officials. Under the name of the ministry were the words, "Christ is Lord of the university." Feeling this was exclusivistic and intolerant language by

Christians, she asked for its removal. The university sympathized and felt sorry that she had suffered exposure to this offensive religious concept. "However," they replied, "although we'd like to protect you from such intolerance, there is nothing we can do, because the office is not on university property, but only adjacent to it."

Tolerance is the primary virtue these days. There is much good that has come from affirming diversity and multiculturalism. But in the process, the definition of tolerance has changed, even though the dictionaries don't yet record it. *Webster's Dictionary* defines *tolerance* as "a fair and objective attitude toward those whose opinions, practices, race, religion, nationality, etc., differ from one's own." *Toleration* is defined as "the act or an instance of tolerating, especially of what is not actually approved; forbearance."[1] The new meaning of *tolerance* has expanded to include the necessity to *approve* all beliefs, opinions, values, lifestyles. "To be truly tolerant . . . you must agree that another person's position is just as valid as your own. . . . You must give your approval, your endorsement, your sincere support to their beliefs and behaviors."[2]

The new definition of *tolerance* has made *evangelism* a negative word in the minds of many people. Now evangelizing is called proselytizing. Although the dictionary definition of this term is mild, meaning "to convert or change beliefs," it is now linked with actions that are manipulative, pressuring and bigoted.

A professor asked his students the question "Can a person's beliefs and values be criticized without being critical of the person—without attacking the person's integrity and character?" The vast majority say, "No," because, as some students went on to say, "what I believe can't be separated from who I am. To criticize what's important to someone is to criticize that person."[3] To question their values is to attack them personally. To disagree with an aspect of their culture or values is to judge them, and this is intolerance.

To begin to understand how to deal with this expanded view of tolerance, it's helpful to distinguish between three types of pluralism. Dr. Philip Ryken, pastor of historic Tenth Presbyterian Church in Philadelphia, summarizes Donald A. Carson's views about these three types of pluralism.

> The first he calls *empirical pluralism*, by which he means the fact that we live in a diverse society. America is a country of many languages, ethnicities, reli-

gions, world views. . . . A second kind of pluralism Carson terms *cherished pluralism*. Cherished pluralism goes beyond the empirical fact of pluralism to its value. To cherish pluralism is to appreciate it, welcome it, celebrate it, and approve of it. Carson goes on to explain that to celebrate divergent ethnic and cultural heritage is important. "A third kind of pluralism is *philosophical pluralism*. To review: empirical pluralism is a fact, and cherished pluralism values that fact. Philosophical pluralism goes one step further and demands it. . . . It takes the fact of pluralism and turns it into a mind set. It is the ideology that refuses to allow any single religion or worldview to claim an exclusive hold on truth. It denies that there are any absolutes. It insures that all religions and worldviews must be seen as equally valid. . . . Another name for philosophical pluralism is relativism.[4]

Christians have no dispute over the fact of empirical pluralism. Christians also agree with cherished pluralism. In fact, we celebrate it, finding prolific examples in the Bible for God's love for people of all cultures. The worldwide church is a rainbow of colors and cultures. The genuine friendship extended to international students studying in America is one example of Christians putting this belief into practice. As I have come into contact with hundreds of these students the primary comment that I hear is, "It is the Christian students and the church families that have reached out and cared about me." And this has come from non-Christians who, though not converted to Christianity, cannot deny this demonstration of nonmanipulative love.

But when it comes to endorsing religious diversity (pluralism), Christians cannot concur. As Dr. Ryken puts it:

To cherish *that* would mean the death of Christianity. A Christianity that loses its hold on the exclusive claims of Christ ceases to be Christianity at all. However, although Christians cannot cherish religious pluralism they must tolerate it. . . . Christianity insists on religious tolerance.

By tolerance I mean allowing other people to hold and to defend their own religious convictions. Tolerance does not mean that everyone has to agree with everyone else. That would not be tolerance at all. The word tolerance itself assumes disagreement, that there is something to be tolerated. Tolerance thus applies to persons, but not to their errors. . . . Pluralism, rightly understood, respects other people's convictions. It recognizes that there are important religious issues to be discussed and even argued about. Yet it carries out these arguments with humility and civility. . . .

Intolerant Christianity cannot be defended. It is not genuine Christianity at all. . . . Jesus said, "If someone strikes you on the right cheek, turn to him the other also. . . . Love your enemies and pray for those who persecute you" (Matt. 5:39, 44-45). If that is the kind of love Christians should have for violent enemies, they should have even more love for people who simply hold a different philosophy of life. Tolerance is a virtue, especially for Christians.

True Christianity thus preserves a powerful combination that is found nowhere else: tolerance *and* truth.

Some religions and most political philosophies claim to have the truth but are ruthlessly intolerant of those who disagree. They offer truth without tolerance.

Philosophical pluralism, on the other hand, is indifferent to the truth. It provides a pound of tolerance without an ounce of truth. . . . Philosophical pluralism idolizes tolerance while it eliminates the truth, although curiously it also tends to be intolerant of people—for example, Christians—who have strong religious convictions.

Ultimately Christians reject the demand of philosophical pluralism because they prize both tolerance and truth.[5]

Once again, speaking the truth in love (Eph 4:15) is the calling of Christians. We express truth and love by words like these: "We love you, but we think you are doing (or believing) what is wrong. We say this not because we are better, but because we think we have all been made by God for his purposes. He has revealed how to live in a way that brings honor to him and true freedom and love to us." Then we express these same words by actions springing from the Bible's definition of love found in 1 Corinthians 13: patience and not being easily angered; kindness and lack of rudeness; humility; refusing to keep a scorecard of wrongdoings, *yet not approving of evil*; refusing to be self-centered in any way, including envying others; seeking to be God-centered and caring for people by communicating hope and trust, enduring with them and protecting them by seeking God's best until they come to rejoice in the truth.

Think of a person to whom you wish to display Jesus Christ in the light of this description of love and truthfulness. As you pray over this, the Lord will show you the steps to take. Stop reacting to outlandish clothing, attitudes, bad language, sexual display and deviance. Ask for God's eyes to see beneath the outward behavior to the hurt and cry for love, meaning and real life. Weep for them and with them.

If you love a person, you will not act indifferently toward dangerous or destructive beliefs or behavior simply to avoid offending him or her. Yet the new
tolerance demands just that sort of indifference.

Tolerance says, "You must agree with me." Love responds, "I must do something harder; I will tell you the truth because I am convinced that 'the truth
will set you free.'"

Tolerance says, "You must approve of what I do." Love responds, "I must
do something harder; I will love you, even when your behavior offends me."

Tolerance says, "You must allow me to have my way." Love responds, "I
must do something harder; I will plead with you to follow the right way, because I believe you are worth the risk."

Tolerance seeks to be inoffensive; love takes risks. Tolerance is indifferent;
love is active. Tolerance costs nothing; love costs everything.

Once again, Jesus is the supreme example of true Christian love, which is
sometimes the antithesis of tolerance. His love drove Him to a cruel death on
the cross. Far from being indifferent to the "lifestyle choices" of others, he paid
the price of those choices with His own life, and lovingly paved the way for
everyone to "go, and sin no more" (John 8:11 KJV).[6]

When the Holy Spirit brings conviction of wrongdoing to a person, we can sometimes be blamed for "condemning them." We must then remind others that we are under the same condemnation; we are judged by the same standard. They must go to God about their guilt. We are not their accuser or judge. If our manner has been judgmental, we apologize. But truth wounds in order to heal—just like a surgeon. Be sure that a clear de-scription of the love and hope of God's forgiveness in Christ is coupled with reminding people of God's (not our) definition of sin. We're not say-ing we have figured out perfectly what's right and wrong and have a corner on the truth. The Bible is an open book, and it claims to accurately repre-sent what God says about our lives. Tell people to go to the book and to God directly. God, having made us, lovingly gives us instructions on the best way to live.

CHRIST, THE ONLY WAY TO GOD

Because of the prevalence of the new definition of tolerance, many Christians are fearful of speaking about the uniqueness of Jesus Christ. The near universal hostility to the "one way to God" teaching of Jesus and the hellish consequences for those who choose another way calls for renewed energy to help floundering Christians to respond in a godly way. We dare not play the victim card. Unless the relativists' anger is brought on by our pride or belligerence (we then confess our sin), we must remember the promise that persecution is part of our calling. We take the hit and rejoice! Here are some thoughts on getting people to *think*, not just emotionally react, to the *beauty* of the exclusivity of Christ.

The very exclusiveness of Christianity is what insures its inclusiveness of all types of people who otherwise would not have any hope for salvation. As many passages in the Bible insist, the biblical God is the One true God and his Son, Jesus Christ, the only true Savior. In the Old Testament God said:

> "Turn to me and be saved,
>   all you ends of the earth;
>   for I am God, and there is no other." (Is 45:22)

In the New Testament, Jesus says, "I am the way and the truth and the life. No one comes to the Father except through me" (Jn 14:6).

> On the one hand, Christianity is the most exclusive religion imaginable. It insists that belief in Jesus Christ is absolutely necessary for salvation. Jesus is the *only* way. You must go to Him to get eternal life.
>
> On the other hand, Christianity is the most inclusive religion possible because it makes salvation accessible to everyone. Salvation is offered for all people through one person. Whosoever believes in Him will not perish. Anyone who receives or believes in Jesus will live forever with God. There are no racial, social, intellectual, or economic criteria that prevent anyone from joining God's family.[7]

The story of three blind men touching an elephant is often used to make the point that no one religion has a view of the whole picture of truth. One, feeling the leg says, "It's like a tree." Another feeling the ear says, "It's like a large fan." The third, touching the trunk says, "I think it's a rope."

Ravi Zacharias, an expert on comparative religions, was raised in India to be a follower of one of the native religions but instead became a follower of Jesus Christ. Responding to the idea that each religion is a well meant but inadequate attempt to explain the mystery of God, he said this in an interview:

> The point is, . . . the parable has already given away the fact that this, indeed, is an elephant! The blind man may tell you it's a tree, but he's wrong. It is not a tree or a rope or a fan. The seeing man knows this is an elephant. He knows the truth; his sight has revealed it to him. And Jesus Christ has made it clear that the eternal truths of God may be known. Jesus Christ is the centerpiece of the gospel—in him, all of truth came together. So while there may be aspects of truth elsewhere, the sum total of truth is in Christ. . . .
>
> The problem with the parable is that it assumes the very thing it allegedly disproves—that all blind men are touching an elephant. Yet how do we know they are touching an elephant? Only because the story assumes it.[8]

All other paths to salvation require people to *do something*. But what if someone cannot perform the obligations necessary—either because of physical, psychological, mental or other handicaps, or because of moral disability? That person is excluded from salvation. Salvation through Christ is obtained not by trying to save yourself (doing) but by trusting what Someone else has done for you. It's not *doing*, but *done*. Jesus Christ grants new life not based on self-effort but as a gift. There is only one way to salvation because there is only one Person who has provided the one solution for humanity's one (main) problem.

If God exists, wouldn't he have the right to say how we should come to him? If God created us, is it reasonable that he would leave us on our own only to guess what he expects of us or how we are to worship him? These two questions carry in them certain assumptions about God that a nonbeliever has problems accepting, that is, that God has a claim on his creation. He has absolute rights; ours are only derived from his creation of us in his image. No person has inherent rights. God doesn't owe us anything. God does what he pleases (although not arbitrarily), and whatever he does is right. There is no "good" above God to which he must conform. He is sovereign.

God's sovereignty is the reason why there is no other way to God except through Christ. Not all roads (religions) lead to heaven. Different religions are not roads to the same God under various names. One religion is not as good as another. But to give the above explanation to a nonbeliever will almost guarantee you the label of "bigot." This question of whether all religions lead to God can never be answered to the nonbeliever's satisfaction, for the answer involves a submission to the biblical view of God, and that would be tantamount to conversion!

Acceptance of our answer of Christ as the only way would also involve the nonbeliever in acceptance of the biblical diagnosis of man's sickness and cure. The reason Christ is unique and necessary is that he is the *only* "religious leader" who has provided an answer to humanity's real problem. Only Christianity teaches that I can do nothing to save myself and that God takes the initiative in salvation. My need is forgiveness and confirmation in righteousness.

There are certain points and illustrations which can be of help in talking with people who are doubting whether Christ is the only way to God.

First, turn in Scripture to the story of Christ in Gethsemane (Mk 14:32-42). Reading together, explain that the cup was a symbol of his impending death: "Father, . . . everything is possible for you. Take this cup from me. Yet not what I will, but what you will" (Mk 14:36). Then ask, "What was the Father's answer to his Son's prayer?" There are only three possibilities: (1) He didn't give an answer. This would be a serious reflection on the character of God in ignoring the fervent need of His Son. (2) He answered, "Yes—there are other ways for me to accomplish my purpose in providing salvation for people," in which case the subsequent death and suffering of Christ on the cross was outside of God's control and *superfluous* in accomplishing God's will. (3) He answers, "No, there is no other way for sinners to be saved than by means of atonement. You must suffer and die in their stead. The wages of sin is death and someone must bear the penalty." This, I believe, was the way God answered his Son's prayer. Christ had already announced his mission of seeking and saving the lost. Even at the searching and fervent request of God's own Son, it is not possible for there to be any other way back to God. The answer to our original question "Is Christ the only way to God?" cannot be given in terms more forceful than this.

Second, an underlying assumption critics make of Christianity's uniqueness is that sincerity or intensity of belief can create truth. This is not so. I may be completely sincere when I go to the medicine cabinet at night and grope sleepily for the bottle that will alleviate my son's suffering. Yet if I grasp the wrong medicine and administer it to him, it could harm (or at least not help) him. Yet I sincerely believed what I gave him was the right medicine! Likewise, a person may be sincere in his religious beliefs, but they may be leading him away from the true God. It is a question of truth, and believing doesn't make something true, just as unbelief doesn't necessarily make something false. Faith is not an entity separate from its object; faith is always *in* something. The validity of faith is determined by its object. I can have all the confidence in the world that a certain chair will hold me up, but if I fail to notice its broken leg, I will go crashing to the floor! The point is, we did not make the rules for how the universe operates. God set up gravity, and whether we like it or not, what goes up will come down. So in the moral realm, to operate in harmony with God's ways puts us in harmony with him. Breaking these rules brings inevitable consequences. Non-Christians may reject this, but they have no right to redefine Christianity according to their likes. The biblical God is a "given." Christians are not being bigots on this point. We are not at liberty to change clear teachings of God's revelation.

Third, it is naive to say that all religions are alike. For instance, the Muslims' Qur'an says it is a sin to believe that Jesus is God or that the Trinity exists. This is diametrically opposed to the Bible. "Christianity teaches the existence of the individual believer eternally in fellowship with a personal God. Buddhism and Hinduism profess only to plot the path to final personal absorption into the all (extinction). Tribal religions are polytheistic. Hinduism is pantheistic. Buddhism is atheistic. Among monotheistic faiths, modern Judaism and Islam are as strongly unitarian as Christianity is trinitarian."[9] People have to choose. More than one can't be true.

This is not to deny that there may be an element of truth in other religions. Indeed, Christianity explains why this is so. All men, as creatures of God, know something inherently of the true God and adapt somewhat to live in his world (Rom 1:19-22; 2:14-15; Acts 17:28). Therefore, when they manufacture a religion, it will contain some borrowed capital from the biblical God and be ordered in such a way that it to some extent fits in with the real (God-created) world in which all men live. No matter how hard men work to suppress the knowledge of the true God, the works of their own hands will betray them. Therefore, we can learn from and appreciate many elements of other religions. Our problem is that they contradict one another and do not give the solution that is needed. Christianity's distinctive features can be summarized under three headings:

Ruin. Other faiths assume our ability to secure and retain God's favor by our action. A manual of instructions in "how to" is provided. Christ teaches that we are helpless and lost, wholly unable to save ourselves. A drowning person needs a rescuer to swim to him, not a book of swimming instructions.

Redemption. Other faiths direct us to follow the teaching of their deceased founders. Christ is *risen*, and we serve a living Savior who bore the Father's judgment on our sins.

Regeneration. There is no parallel to this in other religions. Christ recreates a new heart in us, and we live united with him in newness of life. Our nature is changed.[10]

Many people are attracted to a popular uncommitted attitude in which they profess to "study" religions in a detached, neutral way. However, there are some things in life which an observer can't learn or evaluate unless he does them. You'll never learn to swim by sitting on the pool's edge, even if you watch an Olympic champion! Here again, we can witness by pointing people to the true nature of faith as involvement in a commitment on their part.

REASONING WITH PEOPLE

Apologetics (the defense of the faith) has much value in witnessing and can be an effective tool to prepare the way for the gospel. All reality testifies to a Creator (Ps 19; Rom 1:20). The validity of Christianity is confirmed through archaeology, history and various sciences—but these are not proofs. For even if we are able to prove from archaeology that Christ died, we are still not able to scientifically prove it was for our sins. Thus, rational evidences (traditional or classical apologetics) are useful but only of limited value.

The most effective apologetic is to admit our presuppositions[11] and show how they make sense of both the real world and the creatures who live in it.

We ask unbelievers—we prod them—to look at life through our glasses. We expose their own assumptions to them (for many have unconscious beliefs about the world) and ask them to evaluate how consistently they live out those assumptions. We show them the dead-end and dehumanizing results of their positions. By reading some books on this topic we can get a feel for the trends in our culture and discern the non-Christian assumptions underlying them.[12] We each need to concentrate our study on one area of culture (such as art, science, philosophy or politics) or one trend (such as relativism or humanism). We need to learn how to lovingly take off the protective roof of a false worldview that people have built over their heads to keep God away. We can challenge the idol-manufacturing mind of twenty-first-century people, even those attracted to post-modernism.[13]

If we love people, we will desire to understand what they are thinking. Our apologetics will not be just to cross swords with them, but to help. The sharpness of our reasoning can be an ornament to our witness. It can also be a blight, for the danger is to become proud or to extensively "pre-evangelize," that is, spend all our time preparing a person to hear the gospel. We then feel good about how articulate we are but never get to the point of explaining the work of Christ and urging our listeners to repent and believe. God's chosen instrument in conversion is his Word, not our reasoning ability. So we must continue to study our culture but at the same time remember that books and films are only one means. We do not have to be intellectuals to analyze our culture. Not only can we become discerning by talking things over with our family and Christian friends, but we can put ourselves in crosscultural situations (spend time with international students, become ghetto-dwellers, visit other countries) and completely secular situations (university courses, activities, jobs) where we can learn firsthand.

SPEAKING TO THE CONSCIENCE

God has built into all of us a point of contact—a sense of the Deity and a sense of responsibility for our moral actions (Rom 2:14-15). This sense may be buried, denied or suppressed but it is there even in avowed atheists. The truth of the gospel fits with the way people are made. Our task is to remind them of what deep down they already know: God exists and has created them to act rightly. When I came to realize the implications of this truth for my personal witnessing, I was liberated almost as much as when I learned of God's sovereignty in salvation. I saw how much I had going for me every time I transmitted God's message, for he had put a built-in receptor inside each person. We are to reinforce, educate and illuminate the conscience of unbelievers.

As we touch the conscience, we bring truth alongside people's lives. Ultimately, the acceptance of the gospel is a moral problem, not an intellectual problem. When people tell me they are atheists, they are not just telling me about the way they think. They also tell me something about the way they live. Jesus accused people of not being willing to come to the light because of hatred in their hearts. The light of Christ exposes their evil deeds, and so they prefer darkness (Jn 3:19-20)—not because they have doubts, but because they love their sin and don't want to change. In showing people their moral guilt, we are not to leave them in despair nor tell them they are worthless. Hopefully, our witness will show them their guilt and need of forgiveness, not simply their despair and need for an answer. To elicit conviction (which is really a merciful work of the Holy Spirit) is not cruel, but kind. We can repent of guilt, but not of despair.

Conscience delivers messages (judgments) to us concerning whether an action or attitude of ours is right or wrong. It is like the thud of the judge's gavel in the courtroom of our conscience when the verdict of acquitted or guilty is rendered.

Jesus spoke to the conscience of his nonbelieving hearers. He put his finger on a sensitive spot in the Samaritan woman's heart when he told her to go and call her husband. He shamed Nicodemus when he indicated that as a teacher he should know of spiritual matters. There must have been a sting in the conscience of the moral young man when Jesus told him to stop coveting.

Peter's gospel sermon caused people to feel "cut to the heart," and they initiated a request for instructions on how to be saved (Acts 2:37). Paul, too, spoke powerfully to the conscience. We find him concluding his testimony to King Agrippa (Acts 26) by saying that he knows the king believes the prophets and by praying that he might be converted. Paul emphasizes that all he did, he did openly (not in a corner). All of Paul's hearers knew the way he had lived before and after his conversion. He could look straight at the Sanhedrin (Acts 23:1) because his own conscience was clear (Acts 24:16) commending him rather than condemning him. Paul witnessed before Felix about righteousness, self-control and the judgment to come (Acts 24:25—interesting content for evangelism) and his words struck fear in Felix's heart. In renouncing deception and distortion, Paul states his evangelistic goal: "to set forth the truth plainly we commend ourselves to every man's conscience in the sight of God. . . . Since, then, we know what it is to fear the Lord, we try to persuade men. What we are is plain to God, and I hope it is also plain to your conscience" (2 Cor 4:2; 5:11).

We realize that only the Holy Spirit can sensitize the conscience and bring conviction, but the Spirit has given us tools in the Ten Commandments, the Sermon on the Mount and other passages that explain true righteousness. It is not that we merely quote these Scriptures to others, but that we incorporate their emphasis into our conversation as we delve into the values of people. As we talk with people, we can move from one area where they feel guilt into all other aspects of their lives, showing them that the Bible's diagnosis of their need is that they have a sinful nature. Here are some questions to use in appealing to the conscience after we have discussed the gospel. We need to be careful not to use these to manipulate people while remembering that the *loving* thing is to show others their guilt.

- "Are there things in your life you are not willing to face and have God change?"

- "Isn't the real issue that you can't face your sin and guilt before God?"

- "If I were to answer all your questions about Christ satisfactorily, would you be willing to come to him? Why not?"

- "Assuming that God exists and has created you, don't you have a responsibility to him? Have you ever thanked him?"

- "If you had recorded in a notebook all your thoughts and judgments of others for the last day, and then lost it, how would you feel?"

- "How do you know what love is—and that you're not actually running away from it?"

In directing unbelievers in how to become Christians (closing with Christ as the Puritans termed it), nothing can be more succinct, theologically accurate and practical than the classic description given in *Pilgrim's Progress* by John Bunyan's character, Hopeful. Listen as Hopeful explains to Christian how he came to believe on the Lord Jesus Christ with Faithful's help.

> He [Faithful] said, "Why not go to Him and see?" I said that would be presumption. But he said, "No, for you are invited to come." Then he gave me a book of the very words of Jesus encouraging me to come; and he said that every dot and iota of that book stood firmer than heaven and earth. I asked him what I must do when I came to Christ. He said I must plead with all my heart and soul to the Father to reveal Him to me. Then I asked him what I must say in my pleading. He said, "You will find Him on a mercy seat, where He sits all the year long, granting pardons and forgiveness to them that come. You simply say (and mean it with all your heart): 'God be merciful to me a sinner. I acknowledge and confess my sinfulness and all my sins. Help me to know and believe in Jesus Christ, for I see that without His righteousness and mercy, and unless I believe in that righteousness and accept His offered mercy, I shall be lost forever. Lord, I have heard that you are a merciful God, and that You have ordained your Son Jesus Christ to be the Saviour of the world, and that You are willing to bestow His goodness and mercy upon a poor lost sinner like me—and I am a wretched, helpless sinner indeed. Lord, now take my sins and give me Your righteousness: magnify Your grace in the salvation of my soul. In Jesus' name, amen.'"[14]

Bunyan says that Christ did not reveal himself to Hopeful at first but only as he kept on praying, in the midst of increasing conviction of sin. (See appendix B for two resources that may be helpful in evangelism: a contrast of proud versus broken people and a paraphrase of the Ten Commandments.)

OUR FEARS

Evangelism is not just for the super-Christian; the Bible is clear that all real Christians have this privilege (Acts 8:1, 4; 2 Cor 5:18-20). I could have said *responsibility* instead of privilege, but our personal experience of sovereign and free grace turns duty into love, responsibility into privilege. Some may have gifts which especially suit them to this task—facility of speech, ease of meeting people and so on. Yet if we think we possess no "gift of evangelism," we could come to the false conclusion that we have no responsibility to witness. I am not sure what the gift of evangelism is, but I have a feeling that with God's help *many* people can be gifted in this area, since all are called to witness.

Much has been written and said to try to motivate Christians to witness. Later I will mention some reasons why our motivation is often weak. Actually, if people do not have the desire, there is no use trying to train them. We might try, instead, giving them a strong dose of teaching on justification by faith. Unmerited mercy softens cold hearts.

Even motivated Christians, however, will have misgivings as they witness. The basis of these apprehensions is fear. What kind of person has God called us to be as we seek to love and instruct others in the gospel? He wants us to be ourselves. People do not just hear syllables from our mouths; they pick up connotations from our lives. Even our body speaks. Body language (eye contact, stance, hand movements) indicates our interest or disinterest, our patience or impatience. If we are nervous, we will make others uncomfortable too.

Do you convey a proud I-have-it-and-you-don't spirit? Remind yourself that God's favor toward you is totally unmerited. Are you afraid of mentioning Christ? One of God's servants had to be reminded who had made his mouth (Ex 4: 11). Another was told not to be ashamed (2 Tim 1:8). You are no better nor worse than they—just a sinner saved by grace. How about your own ignorance and doubts? A sovereign God knows all this. Don't you realize he will give you the words and will teach you to trust?

We may feel insecure because we're not sure how people will respond to our message. But we need to face the fact that our gospel is unavoidably offensive to unbelievers. It is the gospel of a crucified Savior. As Paul points out in 1 Corinthians 1, it is a stumbling block and foolishness to others. It makes *exclusive* claims on its followers in our culture of religious syncretism. The modern mind is offended by concepts like a God who holds absolute sway over our destiny; a God who will hold us account able for our behavior; a God whose Son is the only person who can sign us up in the book of life; a God who says we must humble ourselves and base our hope on the righteousness of a substitute.

We can also overcome our insecurity by looking to Christ instead of others. I have not always been willing to admit this inherent offensiveness and thus bear the misunderstanding and mockery of others. I would either be silent about the faith, or I would try to paint it up so well that Christ couldn't help but be attractive. My reason was poor—I didn't want to look like a fool! My security and self-image desperately needed the acceptance of my peers. I was afraid of what they might think of me.

I remember returning home after my first year away at college, anxious to practice what I had learned about witnessing. A close friend of mine to whom I had never said anything about Christ had also just returned from his first year away. I carefully planned an afternoon of swimming so that Rick and I could be alone and talk. Here was the ideal situation for witnessing— and do you know what happened? I never brought up the subject! I felt so bad that night as I confessed my insecurities to God. Later I wrote a long letter to Rick at school. I was finding out the truth that "fear of man will prove to be a snare" (Prov 29:25).

Our weaknesses can become the means through which God works in evangelism. Both the Old and New Testaments describe how God's ministry was carried out by very ordinary people. God met them in their weakness. Jeremiah was young and fearful (Jer1:4-9), and Paul had to learn that his weakness was a plus factor (2 Cor 12:9-10). Turn your weakness into an asset by owning it in a way that produces humility. (See appendix A.I.)

God goes before us in each encounter with unbelievers. Knowing him, the God who initiates salvation, calms our fears and removes any reason for timidity or manipulation in a relationship. Along with humility, we can have the other necessary characteristic for witness: boldness. The New Testament evangelists are frequently described as bold (Acts 4:13, 29; 14:3; Eph 6:19-20; 1 Thess 1:5; 2:2). Boldness in prayer preceded boldness in witnessing. We discover we are not to confront people with ourselves but with the risen Christ, placing them in his presence.[15]

During spring break thousands of American college students flock to Florida for the "Four S" experience: sun, surf, sex and suds (foaming beer). A number of years back I was part of InterVarsity Christian Fellowship's beach evangelism team. After spending the daylight hours striking up conversations on the beach and preaching from under a large orange umbrella, I decided to scout out where the students went at night.

I soon discovered one old motel in the area that was crammed with beds. Arms and legs hung out the screenless windows. I asked the owner if he would mind if our group used the courtyard to play some guitars and try to talk to the students. As you can imagine, anything we wanted to do "to help these crazy kids" was all right with him. I began to make plans.

The next night at dusk I returned with my partners. I was filled with anticipation, since one of my helpers was Paul Little, experienced evangelist and author of many books on the subject. Then I found out he thought it would be a good idea for *me* to give the talk after we had drawn a crowd by some singing. Looking back on it now, I wonder at my eagerness.

It only took a few minutes for us to realize that things were not going to go our way that night. We were up against two factors we had not considered. First, I had not noticed there was no electric light in the courtyard. Second, since it had rained all day the students had not gone out to the beach but stayed in their rooms. As a result, their drinking had begun about noon. Unfortunately, it was only *after* I stood up on a picnic table to speak that I realized how dark it was and how drunk they were! I also noticed for the first time the high brick wall that I was backed up against.

Not five minutes into my talk, a heckler shouted a question. When I suggested he hold his question until the end, another voice in the crowd took it on himself to shout an answer. A loud argument ensued between two people whom I couldn't even see. I continued to try to finish my talk. Another question was shouted at me, and then another. Paul, sensing things were a little out of hand, whispered to me that I should walk over and talk to one of the questioners. He would take the other. This dispersed the crowd and all the curiosity seekers left. As one of the students was walking away I heard him ask another in a disgusted voice, "Hey, who are those two guys?" The reply that came was in slurred speech, "Oh, it's just Batman and Robin, the boy wonder," pointing a beer can at us.

It will take boldness to speak of Christ to strangers. Yet often more boldness will be needed to face friends and family than an unruly mob.

WHOLENESS IN ATTITUDES AND MOTIVATION

Following the command to make disciples will become the mechanical performance of a duty unless we have had an inward experience of Jesus discipling us. We can then talk about the things we have seen and heard (Acts 4:20).

Why then is lack of motivation often a problem? There can be many reasons. If there is unconfessed and unforsaken sin, it would be well to review Psalm 51. Be sure, however, to distinguish between true guilt (breaking God's standard) and false guilt (going against the customs of others, even the customs of evangelical Christians containing ideas of witnessing generated by humans). If we are waiting for that inner urge before we tell someone the gospel, it will probably never come. Our feelings were not meant to determine our actions. God calls us to obedience, not waiting for a feeling. Selfishness is often at the root of our nonwitness. We do not want to be troubled. Sometimes inexperience or perhaps a bad experience in witnessing can account for a lack of motivation. We can ask friends to share their witnessing experiences, and we can join together in some new attempts. A desire to witness is often caught from another.

We must be ourselves in our evangelism. We need to be honest and admit our hang-ups. How many times have nonbelievers not talked with Christians because they thought the believers were unreal? "You just couldn't understand because you never seem to have any problems." Honesty is often the opening to genuine witness. Why not? Are you afraid God's reputation will be tarnished? May God grant us a healthy self-forgetfulness at times. It's in the setting of our weakness that the gem of God's strength is reflected. We need to be real, be whole.

Do we love others? Translated into practical terms, "How much time do I give to others? Do I spend time only with people who are like me? What do I enjoy most? Would I forgo it to help someone? Am I constantly thinking only of my time, fun and interests?" Love is enterprising and has an inventive genius all its own. Gratitude for God's grace and a love for Christ spontaneously overflow to those around us. "Why is it that we who have assumed the name of the compassionate one are so lacking in compassion? . . . Without compassion, witness in all its varied forms is ineffective, flaccid, and at times obnoxious. . . . If you are going to involve yourself in the lives and problems of others, you will get your heart broken. You will have to suffer yourself—and not just a little bit! Involvement will mean real personal sacrifice."[16] Our heart must be set on the salvation of others. When this end is not reached, we will be deeply pained. Complacency is a sign of an indifference to even our own salvation. When have we been "moved with compassion" like our Lord or, like Paul, cried out with our hearts for the salvation of others (Mk 6:34; Rom 9:1-3)?

The glue for Christlike friendship is loyalty and faithfulness. With our culture becoming increasingly mobile (one out of every four people move each year) and fractured (the family, the last model of loyalty and security, is fading), most people end up being very self-centered and lonely. Opposed to this is the biblical picture of love (1 Cor 13). (See appendix A.VI.)

The supreme motive in witnessing is to glorify God, to see his perfections manifested through the joyous praises of his redeemed people. If in our heart of hearts this is not our driving force, if our witness is ruled by a lesser motive, we are out of harmony with the plan of salvation. The great aim of divine election is glorification of God (Rom 11:36; Eph 1:12). If we proclaim Christ without this master motive, we work at cross-purposes with both our message and with the Spirit.[17]

In speaking to the Thessalonians, Paul could point to himself and his companions as whole people (1 Thess 2:1-12). Their evangelistic methods were exemplary. Coming in weakness, suffering and at sacrifice to themselves, these evangelists spoke the Word of God boldly amid much opposition. They exhorted others with authority and could boast that their witness did not originate in error, impurity or deceit. Likewise, we are to be God-pleasers, not people-pleasers—for God examines our motivation. Let's not manipulate his Word to bring people to Christ. Let's not try to always look good. There should be no flattering speech, no pretext for greed, no seeking of fame. Rather, we are to have gentleness (like a nursing mother cares for her own) and a fond affection, and to impart the gospel (solid truth content) and our own lives (flesh-and-blood incarnation of the truth). Paul and his fellow evangelists fell in love with these people and supported themselves so as not to be a burden. They cared for them like a father for his children.[18]

PRAYER AND THE SPIRIT

Prayer for others is the supreme God-ordained method in evangelism. Unless God changes a person's heart, nothing lasting will be achieved. Prayer is a means of raising dead sinners to life! In the Old Testament, we read of the effect of prayer: God "remembered Abraham [his prayers], and he brought Lot out of the catastrophe that overthrew the cities where Lot had lived" (Gen 19:29). Until we see the incapacity of sinners and our helplessness to save them, we will not commit ourselves to pray; prayer is pleading our helplessness before God.

We should have a sense of expectancy in our prayers. God is willing and able to save a great number of people. We can reverently remind God of his promise and his purpose to build a kingdom. God will use us. Christ has promised to make us fishers of men.

We are to have a sense of longing as we pray. Paul said his heart's desire and prayer to God for Israel was that they might be saved. He had unceasing anguish and sorrow for unbelievers. Paul told Agrippa boldly of his longing for Agrippa's conversion. Do we really *desire* others to be saved?

> A hidden and deeply spiritual ministry of prayer is needed to back our evangelistic activity:
>
> > God will make us pray before He blesses our labors in order that we may constantly learn afresh that we depend on God for everything. And then, when God permits us to see conversions, we shall not be tempted to ascribe them to our own gifts, or skill or wisdom, or persuasiveness, but to His work alone, and so we shall know whom we ought to thank for them. . . . "Pray for us," writes Paul to the Thessalonians, "that the word of the Lord may run and be glorified." Paul was a great evangelist who had seen much fruit, but Paul knew that every particle of it had come from God. . . . This, to Paul, was an urgent request just because Paul sees so clearly that his preaching can save nobody unless God in sovereign mercy is pleased to bless it and use it to this end. . . . Evangelistic fruitfulness [will not come] unless God also reforms our praying, and pours out in us a new spirit of supplication for evangelistic work.[19]

C. John Miller, whom God used greatly in evangelism, missions and revival among Christians, points out two principles of evangelism and prayer. First, Christ is the one who reveals the Father through the outpouring of his

Spirit. "No one knows the Father except the Son and those to whom the Son chooses to reveal him" (Mt 11:27). Second, Christ works according to the prayerful obedience of his people. He gives his Spirit "to those who obey him" (Acts 5:32) so that they may proclaim the gospel with boldness (Acts 4:29; Eph 6:19-20).[20] (See appendix B.II.)

It is unfortunate that our mental image of an evangelist is often abnormal when compared with Scripture. Instead of our picture of a supersalesman who has stage presence and the gift of gab, we are to be merely humans at home with their Maker and themselves. God's evangelists are called to be whole (complete, real, balanced, integrated) people. God gives us his Spirit (the Comforter) not to make us comfortable but to make us comforters of others.

How to
Communicate Personally

Our age emphasizes the how-to, the do-it-yourself and the instant—the enthronement of the pragmatic and practical. This can be a healthy counterbalance to absorption in theoretical talk. We can become so concerned with understanding what to do that we never get around to doing it! We've talked about witnessing; the question now is, with what individuals are you involved? Will you "do it yourself"?

No Perfect Methods, but Help for Starting
In part one I set forth the need for a recovery of the gospel. Part two emphasized the need to reinstate the goal of complete conversion, and part three emphasized the importance of grace in evangelism. In this final part we explore the need to restore a connection between biblical knowledge about evangelism and the actions that result from and are compatible with that knowledge. Action should be the fruit of sound doctrine.

Why is it necessary to consider how we present the gospel? Martyn Lloyd-Jones contends that we cannot assume that those who believe the right way will necessarily present that belief in the right way.[1] Some Christians who are orthodox believers cannot point to a fruitful work. Others seem to get phenomenal results, but those results do not last. Lloyd-Jones explains that these two extremes both result from a gap between what a person believes and what he or she actually teaches. We all need to reexamine our evangelism to make sure that we do not simply talk around the gospel or that we are so interested in applying the gospel (getting results) that we slight the theological content.

There was a time when I would have avoided any mention of approaches or techniques to use to present the gospel. Now I see this was an overreaction to the abuses of method-centered evangelism. As I have labored both to be a more faithful witness myself, and to train others, I see an undeniable need for good training materials.

It is all well and good for Christians to speak of relational skills and say, "True witnessing is the overflow of a full life. You can't train someone to witness—it's out of character with the whole idea of witnessing." Yes, Jesus Christ should just spill over from our lives. But is witnessing only something we *are*? The Christians I see emphasizing this approach usually have great relational and verbal skills, while most of us do not.

Again and again as I meet Christians eager to witness, I find them asking for help: "How do I start? What do I say?" I agree that you can find no standard witnessing techniques in the ministry of our Lord. But we are not like him—yet. So we must start with would-be Christian evangelists where they are if we want to help them to witness. As we have seen, this involves instruction in gospel theology. They also need seed methods for how to relate this truth content to non-Christians. We must ask ourselves, What kind of evangelism training will lead to a natural and spontaneous communication of Jesus and ourselves? I believe our ability to witness begins with a big view of God and Jesus that will give young Christians a basis for being confident, expectant and comfortable with their humanity. Then we can show that the truth of the gospel frees people, for it has freed us to live differently and speak with conviction (Jn 8:32). As we speak God's Word we have the promise that our witness is not in vain (Is 55:11).

Relational evangelism, in spite of its good intentions, often does not emphasize hearing the word of truth as necessary kindling that the Holy Spirit ignites in regeneration (Rom 10:17). Relational evangelism's approach can neglect the theological content of the gospel by shifting the focus to the personality and experience of the evangelist. God intends us to be witnesses and has empowered us by the Holy Spirit (Acts 1:8). In our calling to be Exhibit A, not only are we to live our joy, but we are also to explain the ingredients of the gospel. Receiving the ingrafted word brings salvation (Jas 1:21).

As we follow Jesus' exhortation to fish for men, we not only need knowledge of the nature of the fish (the unbelievers) and the nature of our lure (the gospel), but we also need to understand how to use a fishing line! A fisherman selects a proper weight, line and hook according to what he is trying to catch. The novice must learn by rote certain methods and principles that sooner or later will become second nature. So too, we need help in choosing methods appropriate to our message and our audience. May we as fishers of men also find our fishing becoming second nature.

The problem of "dropout" from evangelism has been much debated.[2] We will never eliminate it. Yet we should not stop trying, for this is part of being faithful to our calling. The honor of our Savior demands as clear and balanced a witness as possible. Our high view of witnessing derives from our high view of God. Our witness should be consistent with our worship. Yet never are we to trust in the accuracy of our theological expression of the gospel.

What follows are some suggestions that have been helpful for me and others who desire to witness. Of course, they can be used in the wrong way. We need to pray that God will take away any timidity and give us a spirit of power, love and discernment. Nothing works automatically, but as we obey Jesus' command to speak of him to others, he will help us find a method that is compatible to our personality.[3]

DIFFERENT PEOPLE, DIFFERENT PLACES

What is appropriate in some situations and relationships is not appropriate in others. Usually we don't communicate in the same way to our parents as we do to a stranger. So also in expressing the gospel to parents and strangers we will normally see a difference in approach. Of course, the Holy Spirit will at times lead us differently.

I well remember the time I set up a display of Christian books for a fair at a large indoor shopping mall. I thought this would be a good time to catch up on my reading because I was sure nothing much would happen. A stranger came by and within fifteen minutes told me some of his most personal problems. "I don't know why I'm telling you these things. I haven't even told my wife," he said. God's Spirit opened the way for a very direct witness. Although he moved to a different city shortly thereafter, he followed my suggestion of reading the literature he bought and calling up a pastor. Now he and his family are in God's kingdom.

Normally, we proceed slowly with strangers and even more so with parents. We appreciate the zeal of a young convert who returns home to lecture to his parents on his newfound faith. Of course, what they *hear* him saying is, "You didn't raise me right. I reject you." We admire the zeal but can see it is ill suited to the situation.

Jesus provides us with many examples of the different relationships he had with people. He made friends with sinners and witnessed to them (Zaccheus). He confronted religious people (Nicodemus). Although little is said about it, he certainly carried on a witness in his own home, family and neighborhood. Jesus also spoke to strangers. The remarkable story in John 4 of Jesus' encounter with the Samaritan woman at the well gives instructive lessons in personal witness. Jesus breaks through several barriers that often stop us cold. He speaks to a woman (sex and cultural barriers of the day), who is a Samaritan (religious and ethnic barriers). He is never condescending but rather asks help of her. Moving from a common concern on the physical level (water, thirst), he develops a conversation about spiritual matters. He never manipulates her nor compromises the truth. He brings her back to the central issue again and again. He is patient, he exposes her unspoken needs, and he speaks to her conscience. He reveals himself to her as Messiah.

Our relationships with others can be broken down into these categories:

- Long-term intimate: family, close friends, roommate

- Long-term acquaintance: some relatives, neighbors, peers, people at school or work

- Short-term intimate: friends, business associates, classmates

- Short-term acquaintance: people met in passing: in a store, on a bus, at the beach

Our approach in evangelism is probably different according to the relationship. Surely we have a unique responsibility to those in long-term relationships. These people know our faults, and our deeds may well have to precede any words of witness we can speak.

Where most of us need to see our responsibility, however, is in the area of short-term relationships. We don't take the initiative, so these people are often on their way without hearing anything from us. I believe we have a responsibility to such people. Some of us use our personalities to excuse ourselves for lack of witness in these passing situations: "I'm not an outgoing person. I could never speak to a stranger!" However, *all* of us are responsible to step out in faith in *all* of our relationships with people. The point is not that we feel comfortable in witnessing but that we recognize God's sovereignty in bringing each person across our path. (see appendix A.III.)

If this sounds like theology, know that our theology is meant to prod us into new steps of obedience. How well I remember at college studying the book of Romans in my daily quiet time. I poured over the first nine chapters of that book for six months. I rewrote them in my own words. I memorized most of them. I took notes and wrote out questions and answers to each verse. The sovereignty of God and my response in grateful, holy obedience gripped me. I was not learning a system of doctrine and then imposing it on Scripture. I was following Scripture wherever it led and seeing how it all fit together in beautiful harmony. I was determined that my theology be shaped by all of Scripture—not just certain parts.

Long ago I had given up words like *luck, chance* and *accident.* But as I soaked myself in Scripture I saw that these non-Christian concepts had not been really uprooted. I would occasionally hitchhike home from college (you could do this in those days). Once I was boasting to a friend about God's goodness in supplying four timely rides so that I arrived home in record speed. It was seventy miles over back roads, and one person went out of his way to take me to my doorstep. It occurred to me that if God was truly in control of these rides, perhaps he wanted me to do more than sit in silence or talk about the weather. I cringed inside, but I couldn't escape this conclusion.

I began to think about how I could find out if these drivers were interested in Christ without forcing myself on them. So began a series of car rides back and forth during which I prayed and then opened my mouth about my beliefs. I bought large quantities of a well-written pamphlet that I would leave with the driver in exchange for his kindness to me. Time seemed so short on those trips, for I saw God use me. I learned how to live out my belief in a sovereign God.

In addition to our having a variety of relationships, we meet many different *types* of people. Various attempts have been made to categorize people needing to be evangelized.[4] Putting people into categories is dangerous if the result is to exclude certain types from evangelism or depersonalize someone. Yet to be able to uncover root attitudes a person holds in common with other unbelievers, and to be able to develop questions and answers accordingly is a great aid in presenting the gospel. Here is a partial list of spiritual classifications for people.

The ignorant and indifferent. This is the largest class of unbelievers. They need to be surprised and challenged to see their folly in throwing away their souls. We can tell them they are like people living in houses without fire insurance. Appropriate passages to present from Scripture would be the parable of the rich fool (Lk 12:13-21) and the woman at the well (Jn 4). We cannot just be gentle with the indifferent. Such people must be confronted and warned. They are to measure themselves by God's law. If their ignorance is real and not feigned, perhaps we can in meekness patiently instruct them—all the while prodding their conscience and ambushing them with our love.

The self-righteous. There are two types of self-righteous personalities: the nonreligious, who despise the idea of sin, and the nominally religious, whose hearts are like stone and, like the Pharisees, must be broken. Such people must be confronted with their self-righteousness (Mt 5:20; Lk 18:9), shown the difference between external righteousness and sins of the heart (Mt 23:25) and helped to understand that their supposed righteousness is only relative (Lk 18:9-14). We must hold a mirror up to these people to give them a glimpse of their pride.

The synthetic Christians. These people may think they are Christians, but they are not. They need to be shown the nature of regeneration and the evidences of saving faith in 1 John (also Jn 6:60-66; Lk 14:25-33).

The deliberate atheists. The vaunted intellectual problems these people express are often moral problems of the heart (Jn 3:14-20). If they do have real questions, however, these must be dealt with honestly and thoroughly. Jesus invites the skeptic, as he did Thomas, to examine more closely. "Honest answers to honest questions" should be our motto.

The seekers. The last group consists of those who have awakened to their need for spiritual solutions. They possess some conviction of sin and guilt. We point them to Christ and his promises and continue to speak to their conscience. Get them to read passages of Scripture such as Isaiah 53, Psalm 51 and John 3.

Many times we must be willing to confront and turn away those (such as cultists) hardened by distorted teaching (2 Jn 7-11; 2 Pet 2). If we can gain a hearing with them, however, we need to keep these points in mind: Be brief and to the point; these people can take up our time unnecessarily by arguing. Be firm and identify ourselves as Bible-believing Christians; they may want to end the conversation right there. Be sure to emphasize grace, as this is a great distinction between our faith and theirs. Every cult member is ultimately relying on his or her own efforts for salvation. Be concerned and share personal experiences of free forgiveness, inner peace and joy found in the love of Jesus. Be careful to not spend too much time alone with cult members; have a mature Christian along. Be ready to give them some literature.

If we were to encourage all Christians to be a light for Christ in the interest group(s) to which they already belong, we might find Christians with more non-Christian friends and more non-Christians seeing and hearing the gospel. The love of God can flow along the channel of our natural interests (e.g., quilting clubs, bowling groups, sports teams, musical groups, community service organizations or ski clubs). We don't need more evangelistic meetings. People simply need to pray and be intentional in these affinity groups. This also answers the problem of finding time for others since most people are already in some type of secular association. You like what this group does, so be yourself as a Christian. You can actually have *fun* witnessing.

GETTING STARTED

Any journey has to begin with the first step. Many of us never witness because we never start. We don't take the initiative. We are not assertive enough in bringing Christ into the conversation. Perhaps we worry about

what others will think of us. This is pride. Remember we can make others
nervous because we are nervous. We are also often negative in our tone,
adopting an unassertive stance: "You wouldn't be interested in God, would
you? You're not? (Phew.) I didn't think so." (For questions non-Christians
ask, see appendix A.X.)

If you are a gifted conversationalist, you may not have this problem of
getting started on sharing the gospel. Of course, you will need to be careful
not to rely only on your gifts instead of on the Lord. Most of us cringe inwardly and fumble in our attempts to convey the gospel, yet we should trust
God and speak. The only thing we have to lose is our pride! Keep in mind
some comments and questions that are natural and will help introduce your
subject. We can think through beforehand what we are going to say or ask.

Diagram 2 depicts three conversations. The circles represent the layers of
a person. The arrow shows different ways of conversing with him or her.

Most of us tend to talk only about safe, neutral, common things—the
weather, food prices and so on. We talk in the outside layer of our lives.

Perhaps a few go right to the heart of a person—their most personal
thoughts—with almost no introduction. They ask, "Are you saved?"
Many well-meaning people have used a hit-and-run approach to evangelism. By the grace of God, in spite of the method used, one in a thousand
has come to the Savior. However, we often overlook the nine hundred
ninety-nine who are infinitely harder to reach because of this abrasive
and blunt approach; and we fail to see that it is in spite of, rather than
because of, the method used that the one person has come to know the
Lord.[5] How often have you heard someone justify a large outlay of time
and money in some evangelistic endeavor by saying, "Well, it was all
worth it if one person came to the Lord." Was it? Maybe ten people would
have come to the Lord and many more softened rather than turned away
if another approach had been used. We must learn to become assertive
without being obnoxious.

A better conversation model is to begin with common interests and seek
to move deeper into values, attitudes and beliefs. We move gradually yet directly, and with a purpose in mind. Our goal is to touch the conscience. One
of the best ways to do this is by developing the art of questioning.

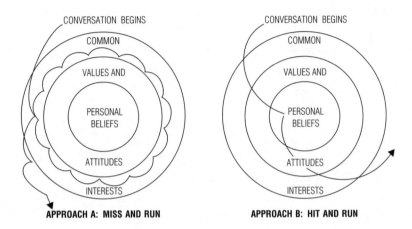

APPROACH A: MISS AND RUN   APPROACH B: HIT AND RUN

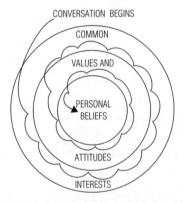

APPROACH C: RAISE QUESTIONS AND MAKE A POINT

Diagram 2. Three Ways to Converse About Christ

Some questions are better than others. God's answer will seem irrelevant if we ask questions like, "How may a person get fulfillment and purpose?" or "What about your joy and happiness?" To such me-centered questions, our theological answers that emphasize doctrines like justification will seem involved, academic and depressing. Evangelism is asking the right questions. It is leading them from secondary or misguided queries to the primary issues. We must meet and speak to people where they are, *and* we must know the gospel thoroughly—especially the focal point of justification by Christ through faith alone. The test of our evangelistic method is a simple question: does it make justification clear? The vital question is for people to know whether they are acquitted by God.[6]

CONVERSATION TURNERS

Enough for overall principles—here are examples of initiating sentences that might form a bridge into conversation about deeper issues. Some of these may seem awkward at first; nevertheless, we can prepare our own comments beforehand for many recurring circumstances. We don't need to pray for more opportunities, we just need to be ready to take advantage of the ones already there. Think of common situations you face, and develop your own response (see chart 2). The point of your remark is to help you find out if the Spirit is leading you to present more gospel content. Poor questions are ones that can be answered yes or no and don't lead into discussion. A good response leaves room for reaction and is open-ended. (See appendix A.V.)

In addition to conversation turners, there are also some general questions that open people up. Perhaps you've been talking with someone for a while. Why not attempt to move into more important things? Here are some questions I like:

"What is your religious background?"

"How have your ideas about God changed since . . . (coming to college, getting married, having children, being in this job, the death of your friend, traveling overseas, reading that book, being in the military)?"

Paul Little, an evangelist with InterVarsity Christian Fellowship for many years, suggested this progression:

Chart 2. Turning Conversations to Christ

Situation: Someone complains about developments in the world or among certain
                people.

Response: "Why do you think people do such terrible things? What do you think
                God thinks of that?"

Situation: Someone you have helped thanks you.

Response: "You're welcome. I want to help people. My perspective on life was really
                changed awhile back by Someone I met . . ."

Situation: Someone helps you.

Response: "I really appreciate your help. What made you that way? . . . I feel God has
                called me to be helpful to others too."

Situation: You receive a compliment for something you've done.

Response: "Why, thank you, I've gotten a new perspective on this since Jesus came
                into my life. I appreciate people/my work more knowing who made me
                and why. " (It is not improper just to say, "Thank you." It was you who did
                it. God uses you. Don't fall into an attitude of sickening self-abasement.)

Situation: Someone asks you what you do.

Response: (Scientist) "I'm involved in figuring out the structure of God's
                universe."(Give a descriptive or functional answer rather than where you
                work.)

Situation: A comment is made on the difficulty of raising children.

Response: "We're facing problems too. But we're encouraged by an interesting
                method that's quite helpful. We call it 'discipline with love,' and it's based
                on the Bible. Have you heard about it?"

Situation: Someone is telling of their good fortune or luck in a matter.

Response: "Do you think God has a reason for allowing you to experience this good
                thing? How do you account for the good things that have happened to
                you?"

Situation: You're given too much change after a purchase.

Response: "You know, at one time I would have kept the money, but Jesus Christ has
                turned my life around. Are you interested in spiritual things?"

"By the way, are you interested in spiritual things?" . . .

"What do you think a real Christian is?" . . .

"Have you ever personally trusted Christ, or are you still on the way?" . . .

"How far on the way are you?" or "Would you like to become a real Christian?"[7]

James Kennedy, pastor of a large church, recommends two questions to pinpoint basic issues for many:

"Have you come to a place in your spiritual life where you know for certain that if you were to die today you would go to heaven?"

"Suppose that you were to die tonight and stand before God and he were to say to you, 'Why should I let you into my heaven?' What would you say?"[8]

Sure, these questions may seem a little awkward and forced at times. But how else are we going to find out what the Holy Spirit is doing in someone's life, especially those we will know only on a short-term basis? I've been amazed at how many people are genuinely interested in spiritual things. In contacting some students at random during lunch at a university, many have thanked us for raising spiritual questions by saying, "You know, I wasn't aware there were people who could help me with my questions. Since most people don't talk about religion seriously, I thought I was alone in my search. Thanks for coming by."

Conversation with a Direction

Many committed Christians flounder in personal evangelism because sharing religious ideas in conversation seems unnatural or forced. In many cases this problem exists because of a compartmentalization in their thinking—a thought-world divided into compartments labeled "gospel," "art," "marriage" and so on. The contents of any one of these compartments is only superficially related to the contents of another. As a result, the gospel seems an intruder in a conversation instead of being an integral part of a dynamic, ongoing dialogue that encompasses the whole of life.

The solution to the problem is to eliminate the walls dividing the compartments and to relate religious ideas to ideas about art and marriage and other areas of everyday conversation. In other words, the solution is a unified, comprehensive thought life. Christians who have such a worldview can introduce religious ideas more naturally into a conversation. In a dialogue they can move more easily from the non-Christian's immediate interests to more abstract levels of thought and from there to issues of a theological nature. For example:

Non-Christian: Well, I've finally decided. I'm going to major in art.

Christian: Great! What made you finally decide on that?

NC: Well, I feel it's the best way to fulfill myself and to bring more beauty into the world.

C: That's interesting. Why do you suppose you have this desire to make beautiful things?

NC: That's hard to answer; but I know how much I enjoy the feeling I have when I make something new and beautiful.

C: Yeah, I feel that way sometimes. I'm sure that's why I write poetry. Do you ever wonder if this striving to make beautiful things means anything? I mean, that it might be an indication of some higher reality beyond the physical world?

NC: You mean like a God? I think about that sometimes, but I just don't know. I think somebody must have designed the beauty in nature.

C: That sure makes more sense than thinking everything is here by chance. You know, God didn't make much of a difference in my life until I understood he is a Creator who . . .

The basic beliefs behind the Christian's questions are (1) God is infinitely creative. (2) God is the source of beauty. (3) God created people in his image; therefore, we share God's creativity and yearn for beauty. These beliefs explain for the Christian why people strive to create beautiful things. So if the Christian can make the non-Christian consider the abstract question "Why do people strive to create beautiful things?" he or she can lead the unbeliever to consider Christian beliefs about the nature of God and the nature of humans.

Some non-Christians will immediately be able to discuss abstract questions; most will not. If we can begin with questions about the non-Christian's experience, we can help the person begin thinking about more abstract (less immediate) questions, and then about theological ones. In discussing theological truths, we can keep the discussion from becoming abstract by showing in our own lives how this truth is applied. Then we can attempt to speak to the non-Christian's conscience as to how he or she should be applying these truths. So in diagram 3 the movement of the dialogue is from the outer circle to the center. This is a specific example of how Approach C in diagram 2 might work.[9]

A Area of Interest: Art or Beauty

B Immediate Question: "Why do you feel a need to be creative?"

C Abstract Question: "Why is man creative?"

D Christian Explanations: "Man is created in God's image, reflecting his creativity and beauty."

E Applying Theological Truths: "God is the Creator of man and he wants us to acknowledge him as the source and fulfiller of our good desires."

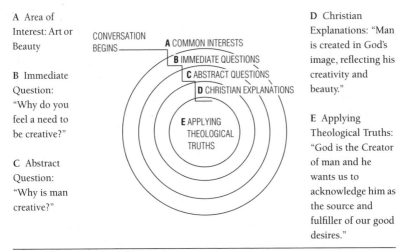

CONVERSATION BEGINS —— **A** COMMON INTERESTS
B IMMEDIATE QUESTIONS
C ABSTRACT QUESTIONS
D CHRISTIAN EXPLANATIONS
E APPLYING THEOLOGICAL TRUTHS

Diagram 3. Conversational Evangelism

Once again we see that witnessing begins with merely being friendly and taking a genuine interest in the concerns of others. Christians who see life as a whole, not as separate unrelated parts, begin to be free to enjoy and explore all aspects of God's world. These interests lead naturally to a discussion of meaning, values and God.

THE UNINTERESTED

What do we do if people just are not interested? We let them go their way, as Jesus did the moral young man (Lk 18:18-29). We should not feel guilty or embarrassed, even though we are disappointed. It is not failure to recognize and follow the Holy Spirit's leading. That young man would not bow to Christ's lordship. Jesus loved him and bore the pain of rejection. So must we.

Some me-centered evangelists, on hearing the young man ask about eternal life, would have been sure not to let him escape. After getting him to pray to receive Christ, they would likely ask him to give his testimony within the week. When his spiritual interest declined, he would be regarded as carnal, and earnest Christians would urge another level of Christian duty or a special experience on him. Such people are swept into a Christian group before the Spirit finishes his regenerative work. Thinking they are Christians, these "converts" move within the Christian community motivated by purely natural desires and remain parked immovably on the pew.

God's timing is always best. Remember my story of being in a childbirth clinic? The nurse said, "There isn't anything you can do to determine the moment of birth. When that baby's ready, nothing is going to stop him." God takes over, and the timing is all in his hands. That's also true in the timetable for the new spiritual birth.

Which is better, to push people hastily into the kingdom of God and give them a false basis for their supposed salvation, or to speak the truth and let them go until God's good timing is right? We will have both liberty and joy when our witnessing is controlled by faith in God's sovereignty.

We can picture ourselves as fishermen who throw out the net as often and as wide as possible. Our net is made up of questions and statements about the gospel. As the net entangles a fish (as a person shows an interest in spiritual things), we have an indication that God's Spirit has gone before us creating interest. We may find that even those who are at first hostile are really being worked on by the Spirit, but they struggle against him—often because they have a conscience that bothers them. A good question to ask is, "What has caused you to feel so negative about Christianity?" Then get ready to listen and learn.

Most people are not hostile; rather, they are indifferent. They seem happy and content. Does the gospel have anything to say to these people? Must they admit failure before we can relate Christ to them? No. Christ is the source of all our strength and happiness too. The seed idea to plant is, "God is to be thanked for his goodness to you, and the purpose of his goodness is to bring you to repentance" (see Rom 2:4). It is vital that we present God as holy and the law as absolute. People are never as indifferent as they seem.

We need to discover what they are concerned about and then move from this concern to the deepest issues of life.

I would say something like this: "You know there were people with just your attitude in Jesus' day. Did you know the Bible describes exactly your indifference and the consequences of it? Jesus himself dealt with this attitude on several occasions. Jesus said, 'It is not the healthy who need a doctor, but the sick. I have not come to call the righteous, but sinners to repentance' (Lk 5:31-32). Jesus did not come to help those who thought they were well; he would help those who knew they were not well. Jesus admitted that some people thought they had no need of him. 'Thanks, but no thanks,' they said. 'I can do perfectly well by myself (with perhaps a little help from my friends),' was their ingrained attitude. To these people Jesus had nothing to say.

"If a person refuses to admit serious needs or trace their felt needs (lonely, unloved, identity confusion, etc.) to consider a spiritual solution, why would they be interested in a Savior from sin? In this sense Jesus did not come for all—he came only for sinners. You assume you can heal (save) yourself. As long as you are unaware of your needs (either because you are blind to them or because you are too proud) you will be part of those people who in age after age have rejected Jesus as Savior and Lord. Yes, rejected. You can't be neutral in the presence of a physician who has come to tell you heart surgery is needed. Your rejection of Christ becomes a fact. It is as clear as if you wrote today's date on a card and the sentence, 'I have this day rejected Jesus Christ as my Savior and Lord,' and signed it."

Persistent indifference to Jesus and his claims is evidence of the completeness of Satan's bondage. Why? Because Satan's most effective work is done when he deceives people into thinking all is well. It is far more effective to lull people to sleep in indifference (they can even take pride in their self-sufficiency and open-mindedness) than to have them adopt an openly hostile attitude toward Christ. Their hostility might cause them to wonder at some point why they are so upset if there's really nothing to Christ. Satan could lose them, for they are awake and fighting! The sleep of complacency is much more effective.

I've met young men who have reacted to a friend's engagement with, "I'll never get married. Look at that fool! He's really caught now!" No matter how wonderful you tell them that love is, it makes no impression. Of course, the reason they see this exclusive lifetime commitment of marriage as frightful and limiting is that they aren't in love yet! They haven't admitted their need for such a love and begun to reach out by returning love. Of course they aren't ready to give themselves away to obtain another! Marriage (and religion) is conceived as a crutch for the weak. Our culture brainwashes us into thinking that independence is maturity and strength. Dependence—admission of weakness, failure, need of others—is often condemned. Of course, this is sheer pride.

In conclusion, there is very little that can be said to the self-complacent. We can pray for God to humble them. He does this in two ways: he woos us in our blessings and warns us in our tragedies. We can continue to hope that the constancy of our care for the indifferent unbelievers will prick their consciences.

One woman in my church, hearing that I was writing a book on evangelism and thinking that therefore I must be an expert on the topic, built up all her courage to ask me this burning question: "I was told that people were just waiting to hear the gospel and believe. You know, I've been trying for years to find all these people who are eagerly awaiting my gospel presentation. Can you tell me where they are?" She, along with many others, had become discouraged. When she was told that "the fields were white for harvest," she thought the grain would fall off easily with each evangelistic conversation. But is that what the Lord means when he speaks of the ripe fields?

USING A SUMMARY OF THE GOSPEL
We have already seen that evangelism is teaching. In addition, we saw that although the entire Scripture points to Christ and salvation, there are central truths to emphasize in witnessing. Examining 1 Corinthians 15, the speeches in Acts, the shape of Mark's Gospel and certain other passages in the New Testament, we can conclude that there was a fixed pattern in the evangelistic preaching of the early church. Of course the early evangelists were undoubtedly flexible and took into account the background and understanding of their listeners.[10]

Jesus' approach was constantly shaped not only by the truth he wished to convey but by the background of the unbeliever. He treated individuals as unique.[11] His approaches to a Jewish rabbi, Nicodemus (Jn 3), and a Samaritan woman with many love affairs (Jn 4) were different. Allowing this variety to stand, we can still see a definite table of contents to the gospel message.

In spite of the abuse to which a gospel outline can be subject, it is a very helpful tool, useful in training Christians about what constitutes the message and thus keeping them on the track when witnessing. A gospel summary is also helpful to a non-Christian who is often totally ignorant of what the Bible teaches. However, any outline that is used mechanically or in a way that doesn't provide for listening can be harmful. We are to listen, talk and question with a view to understanding a person's problem and applying the gospel at that point.

Running through a summary of the gospel does not evangelize a person, nor does the use of this tool guarantee your effectiveness, but it can help. For years, I reacted against any rote use of a method. I tried to be personal with others and let them lead the conversation where they wanted it to go. I would bring in Christian truth as I could. This is still a valid approach in some of our relationships. Later, however, I began where they were and kept bringing them back to one element of the gospel (such as the biblical view of God or the biblical definition of *sin*) in order to leave a message in their conscience. This approach also has its place and can result in a significant contribution to a person's understanding of the gospel. I did not always cover all the points in a gospel outline or follow their order. But I was sure to define and give synonyms for the Bible terms I used.

Many times, however, I have witnessed in a weak way simply because I have not clearly stated my main point—focusing on God as the Creator-Redeemer. The lack of a theistic framework in the minds of most people today makes a statement of our framework necessary for communication. Our ultimate confidence is in the power of God's Word—the naked gospel message. It is interesting to see that the creeds of the various churches that held to historic and biblical Christianity agree on many major doctrines. This solidarity is a tremendous testimony to the timelessness of the truths in the Bible and to the Bible's clarity in essential matters.

BLOOM WHERE YOU ARE PLANTED

The summer after my first year in college, I worked with my father in his tree-care business, which left my nights free. I wanted to use some of this time to share the joy of God's forgiveness with others. Through InterVarsity and a church near campus, I had grown tremendously in my faith during my freshman year and saw clearly that evangelism was not a spectator sport.

My first thought was of an inner-city mission in Baltimore, but a nightly foray would not do. Then I realized my hypocrisy in driving across town to help others when I had never reached out to those in my own suburban neighborhood. Fear and depression seized me. My conscience nagged me.

Reluctantly I came to a conclusion. I was to start where God had placed me! My home and my neighborhood were my Jerusalem that summer. I was young and inexperienced. I had never done house-to-house visitation before. I had no idea what to do. How I began to dread Tuesday nights, the time I had set aside to walk those long streets of our community. I clearly remember wishing for a rainstorm! Ours was a small community in which people settled for a good chunk of their lives. Our family was well known and had lived there for thirty years. I found it hardest to go to the doors of people I had known longest.

Gradually I learned to express myself. I was alone, afraid yet joyful by the end of each evening. I could honestly say I didn't want their money or church membership. I introduced myself as a neighbor and asked for a few minutes of their time. I learned that I needed to help them understand what was expected of them. So by the third week, I made my request more specific. I asked if I could take five minutes to read a passage from the New Testament (Acts 17:22-34) or the Old Testament (Is 53), since some were Jewish. If the answer was yes, I read the passage aloud. I explained I was doing this because I wanted others to consider Jesus, the God-man who had changed my life. Keeping to my time limit, I ended by asking, "Do you have any questions or comments?" Many did. I always left an appropriate pamphlet or a New Testament.

That experience of joy in witnessing has led me into a lifetime of sharing the gospel, sometimes with close friends and relatives, sometimes with strangers in faraway places—the boardwalk in Ocean City, Maryland; the beaches of Ft. Lauderdale, Florida; New York's Central Park, Greenwich Village, Washington Square. I've been in prisons, migrant camps and in swank resorts like Michigan's Mackinac Island and Colorado's town parks. I've seen people listen with intensity in Russia, Kazakhstan, Palestine, Israel, South Africa, England, Korea, Japan, Australia, Brazil, Trinidad, Haiti and many European countries. On every continent, truth implanted in the conscience by the power of the Holy Spirit through loving, humble Christians is leading to a spiritual awakening.

God leads Christians as they act. Nothing can substitute for *doing*. Too long have we followed an individualistic model rather than an apprentice-ship model in evangelism. We can get together with a Christian friend, pray together and study the content of the gospel. Then with some good literature we can go out together for one or two hours, door to door or to a place where people congregate. I think I know all the objections coming to your mind—I've used every one. But I know none of them hold water. The only thing we can lose is our pride—and that might be a good thing for all of us!

Some have made a fetish of this kind of witnessing, calling it "cold tur-key," "contact" or "one-on-one" evangelism. I prefer the name "personal wit-nessing," for it *is* possible to treat strangers as individuals and not be mechanical or impersonal. The value of sharing as much of the gospel as we can with as many people as we can is not measured in numbers of converts. I have not been privileged to be the last link in the chain of witness to very many people. The value is in knowing that we have obeyed our Lord and have been a reinforcer of his truths to many consciences. The value can be seen in how your experiences of witnessing change your Christian life. The value is in becoming an initiator of conversations about Christ with friends and family too. This is making God's name famous. (See appendix A.XI.)

What happened to me as I began witnessing? God quickened and deep-ened a conviction of his sovereignty, a joy that he uses me, a confidence that his Word is true, a desire to forsake my own sins and lead a holy life, a hunger to study the Bible, a fervency in prayer, and a concern and love for others.

The point is not to depend on a program of evangelism that becomes a narrow tradition (e.g., every Monday at 7 p.m. we do our witnessing for the week). Our aim is to use these methods to develop *an evangelistic way of life*. As I have continued to share the gospel, I am now more aware of people around me. I am friendlier, listen more carefully, ask more leading questions, give away more literature. I am bolder with close friends and relatives, taking advantage of our long-term relationship to help them understand the various points of the gospel, to show the difference Christ makes in my life and to stir their consciences over a period of time.

We can learn to expect and hope in God and not in ourselves. As we put ourselves in situations we cannot handle, we can watch God work! One reason God may not be real to us anymore is because we are no longer desperate. If the Holy Spirit were taken out of our lives today, what would change? What are we now depending on God to do for us that we could not carry on in our own strength?

PRACTICAL EFFECTS OF GRACE-CENTERED EVANGELISM

First and foremost we emphasize God's grace in our witnessing because it is scriptural. Truth needs no justification. We don't base our approach to witnessing on pragmatism, saying let's do it because "it works—just look at the results." Nevertheless, when the truth of God's sovereign grace shapes us, our evangelism will be different. Here is a partial list of the effects.

Grace-centered evangelists have a big view of God's role in salvation. Therefore they

- pray for God's will to be done, since his purposes are best
- are bold and less fearful of others
- are quietly confident, for God has promised to use them
- are humble, for they know God is taking the lead
- are filled with love, for it is God's love that motivates them
- speak to the conscience, knowing it is our point of contact
- are expectant, for God's purposes will come to pass
- are patient, trusting in God's timing to bring new life
- are persistent, realizing conversion is a process
- are honest, not hiding any of the hard parts of the gospel
- emphasize truth, not just subjective experiences

- lift up Jesus, knowing he will draw people to himself
- use the law of God to expose people's inability to save themselves
- wait for the Holy Spirit to give assurance of salvation

How does sovereign saving grace affect non-Christians? Primarily by humbling them. Do-it-yourself religion has been replaced by a call to a done-for-me faith.

- It shuts them in to the mercy of God.
- It undercuts any possibility of pride.
- It reminds them that God is not obligated to help them.
- It shows the wonderful nature of God's unmerited love.
- It clarifies that salvation has been done for them, they can only receive.
- It prevents them from turning faith into a work they must produce.

Key: It highlights regeneration as the solution rather than reformation by self-effort.

Our Goal: Disciples

Evangelizing is completed people presenting the complete gospel to the complete person. Our goal is not just decisions but disciples and a faithful witness that glorifies God. We do all we can to avoid premature birth and deformed children, trusting God to bring his "full-term" children into the kingdom. To clarify the difference between decisions and disciples, in chart 3 I have set up a series of contrasts between two evangelistic methodologies that have different goals and therefore conflict in approaches to witnessing.

In chart 3 we see again how imperative right theology is to our evangelistic methodology. Is this being overly precise? No. As one of the Puritans said when rebuked for his conscientiousness, "Sir, I serve a precise God!" And as one who follows in the good points of our Puritan heritage, J. I. Packer puts it this way:

> Evangelism and theology for the most part go separate ways, and the result is great loss for both. When theology is not held on course by the demands of evangelistic communication, it grows abstract and speculative, wayward in

method, theoretical in interest and irresponsible in stance. When evangelism is not fertilized, fed and controlled by theology, it becomes a stylized performance seeking its effect through manipulative skills rather than the power of vision and the force of truth. Both theology and evangelism are then, in one important sense, unreal, false to their own God-given nature; for all true theology has an evangelistic thrust, and all true evangelism is theology in action.[12]

In discipleship evangelism, we point non-Christians to Jesus Christ as Savior and Lord. We do not hide the demands of discipleship behind the benefits of salvation. Unbelievers will not, at the point of conversion, understand all the implications of Christ's lordship. Learning to be an obedient disciple develops through successive crisis experiences that call for repentance and faith throughout the Christian life. Nevertheless, we cannot divide Christ by presenting him as Savior and not as Lord.

The Lausanne Covenant, agreed on by evangelical leaders from over one hundred fifty different nations, says, "The results of evangelism include obedience to Christ, incorporation into his church and responsible service in the world."[13] Let's examine each of these in turn.

First, if people's response to the gospel is authentic, it will issue in sincere (not perfect) obedience. True sheep hear and follow the good shepherd (Jn 10:4). We can evaluate a profession of faith by its fruits. "When God prompts faith, He prompts it in such a way that the believer becomes hungry for Scripture. He wants to live by every word which proceeds from the mouth of God. He desires the pure spiritual milk."[14]

Second, an authentic conversion will lead to a love for the brethren (1 Jn 3:14-15). A Christian who desires to be a loner is inconceivable in terms of the New Testament. We have been placed in a body and must identify ourselves with the new humanity. We become part of a community of believers and can work out our new adherence to truth and love in our relationships with others. Being part of a local church is not optional.

Third, an authentic conversion results in a life of service. Obedience and holiness are not optional. Paul exhorts people to "prove their repentance by their deeds" (Acts 26:18-23). He is not teaching works as qualifications for salvation but as evidence of genuine repentance. Faith alone saves; but faith that is alone (unaccompanied by good works) is not saving faith.

Chart 3. The Goal in Witnessing Affects the Methods

Me-Centered Goals	God-Centered Goals
Decisions, mental assent, immediate responses by repeating a prayer	Disciples, conversion of the whole person, conscience moves them to call on God for mercy in their own words
Get them to agree mentally with certain facts or laws	Responsibly teach the gospel clearly, forcefully, patiently
Show as many advantages as possible	Balance the benefits of the gospel with the sacrificial demands of the gospel
Get them to pray a standardized prayer with you	Allow time for prayer in their own words—alone, or as you listen
Trigger their residual powers for freely choosing God	Face them with the impossibility of saving themselves or exercising faith on their own
Use an outward physical sign to confirm spiritual reality—signing a card, raising a hand, going forward, repeating a prayer	Emphasize baptism, partaking of the Lord's Supper to proclaim his death, changing sinful ways of life
Challenge their will with adventure, entice their emotions with excitement	Present truth to the mind, call on the will to obey, expect heartfelt emotions to follow
Give immediate assurance—don't allow them to doubt their own sincerity	Let the Holy Spirit give assurance via subjective inner witness and objective biblical evidence of changed life

If discipleship is our goal in God-centered evangelism, what do we need to witness? We need a knowledge of others and a knowledge of Scripture. We need to know how people think, rationalize, hurt, hope and desire. Any occasion is one in which we can show our interest in others. Be a friend, a listener, an observer, a questioner, a lover, a proclaimer!

D. Martyn Lloyd-Jones sums up our goal in knowing Scripture for evangelism with these wise words:

> If you want to be able to present the Gospel and the truth in the only right and
> true way, you must be constant students of the Word of God; you must read it
> without ceasing. . . . You must read what I call Biblical theology, the explanation of the great doctrines of the New Testament, so that you may come to understand them more and more clearly. . . . The work of this ministry does not
> consist merely in giving our own personal experience or talking about our own
> lives, or the lives of others—but in presenting the truth of God in as simple and
> clear a manner as possible. . . . We must make time to equip ourselves for the
> task, realizing the serious and terrible responsibility of the work.[15]

In the words of the Great Commission (Mt 28:19-20), we are to "go"—
not just talk but act; "make disciples"—not just superficial professors of faith
but possessors of the Son; "baptizing"—not just leaving them on their own
but incorporating them into a biblical church; "teaching"—not just offering
a few slickly packaged gospel facts but everything in Christ's commandments. In my opinion, this commission takes precedence over the cultural
mandate (Gen 1:28) since the resurrection of Christ.[16]

I think of how one student responded to God-centered evangelism. She
was part of a team of Christian students working at a large entertainment
park. These students had been asked to work at this park for a ten-week
period during the summer. There they would have what I had hoped
would be a life-changing influence on the other employees. During their
off hours we began to build a caring Christian community. We also learned
to see God as the Lord of our evangelism. We poured over Scripture passages, discussing God's role in salvation and our privilege to be his ambassadors. We repented of our shallow views of God, trust in techniques and
fear of others. This opened the door in a new way for this girl to witness.
In her words, "When I came, I thought you were going to teach technique
and force me to witness. All you did was open the Bible and give us a big
view of the majesty of God. Now that I see him, I want to witness. I feel
freed and confident."

A gospel that elevates humans and dethrones God is not the gospel. In
God-centered evangelism, there is a return to the royal gospel that exalts

God's grace at every point. The patient teaching of the theology of the gospel in a balanced and full way is greatly needed in our day. Do you want a snapshot of an evangelist in action? Then look at Ezekiel preaching in a cemetery to dry bones and commanding them to come alive (Ezek 37:1-10), or watch Jesus as he stands at the tomb of Lazarus and says, "Come out" (Jn 11:38-44). We are evangelists who trust in the sheer power of God's Word to raise the dead to life.

God-centered evangelism is a way of life. It does not advocate a method but encourages a knowledge of people and how to apply a macrogospel to the conscience and heart. Witness should be natural, educational and bold. It is something we are, not just something we do. "Personal witnessing" is the phrase that best describes the evangelistic life to which all of us are called. Will you tell the truth?

You are among those on whom the end of the ages has come. Will you wake up? It is said of David that "he served God's purposes in his own generation." Will you serve the Lord in your generation as David did in his? Will you pray for God to send regenerating grace? Will you proclaim the gospel with a holy longing for conversion? "After they prayed . . . they were all filled with the Holy Spirit and spoke the word of God boldly" (Acts 4:31).

Ask yourself these questions:

1. Do I know the saving grace of God in my own life? What is the evidence?

2. Am I daily drawing anew from the fountain of grace by gazing at Jesus?

3. Are there specific people for whose conversion I am praying, pleading, weeping?

4. Am I telling them the truths of the gospel? Can I articulate the gospel?

5. Is my attitude, "Lord, I want you to use me to point others to Jesus, so I will initiate the topic with people"?

6. How long has it been since I last explained Jesus to someone?

7. Have I ever been so entranced by the wonder of the gospel of enabling grace that my fear of rejection by others has disappeared?

O Breath of Life, come sweeping through us,
Revive Thy Church with life and power;
O Breath of Life, come, cleanse, renew us,
And fit Thy Church to meet this hour.

O Wind of God, come bend us, break us,
Till humbly we confess our need;
Then in Thy tenderness remake us,
Revive, restore; for this we plead.

O Breath of Love, come breathe within us,
Renewing thought and will and heart:
Come, Love of Christ, afresh to win us,
Revive Thy Church in every part.

Revive us, Lord! Is zeal abating
While harvest fields are vast and white?
Revive us, Lord, the world is waiting,
Equip Thy Church to spread the light.[17]

PLANS TO OBEY

By God's help, I plan in faith to respond to what I've learned about witnessing in the following ways (list what you are going to do, how you hope to do it and when you will begin):

Clearing My Conscience

What has the quiet voice of God been saying to me? Is there a sin to confess? Is there a relationship that needs to be put right? Anything else?

Goals Regarding Non-Christians

What is God calling me to do regarding non-Christians with whom I have a longterm relationship (such as family and friends)? What is God calling me to do regarding those with whom I have a short-term relationship (such as neighbors, classmates, business associates and people met in passing)?

Goals Regarding Christians

What is God calling me to do with one other Christian to encourage and practice witnessing? How can I encourage my church or fellowship group to respond to God in evangelism?

Goals Regarding Learning the Gospel

When will I begin to learn the gospel so well that I can explain it clearly? How can I make use of the "Come Home" diagram with someone now (see appendix B)?

Make me a captive, Lord, and then I shall be free;
Force me to render up my sword, and I shall conqueror be.
I sink in life's alarms when by myself I stand;
Imprison me within Thine arms, and strong shall be my hand.

My heart is weak and poor until it master find;
It has no spring of action sure; it varies with the wind;
It cannot freely move, till thou hast wrought its chain;
Enslave it with Thy matchless love, and deathless it shall reign.

My power is faint and low till I have learned to serve;
It wants the needed fire to glow, it wants the breeze to nerve;
It cannot drive the world, until itself be driv'n;
Its flag can only be unfurled when Thou shalt breathe from heaven.

My will is not my own till Thou hast made it Thine;
If it would reach a monarch's throne it must its crown resign;
It only stands unbent, amid the clashing strife,
When on Thy bosom it has leant and found in Thee its life.

GEORGE MATHESON
1842-1906

Appendix A
Training Materials for Learning God-Centered Evangelism

I. THE KIND OF PERSON GOD USES IN EVANGELISM

If you want to be the kind of person God uses in witnessing, study 2 Corinthians 4—5. Notice the characteristics of Paul and his ministry.

1. Christian service and witness is based on our *calling,* not just our gifts. We are a new person of character (4:1).

2. As Christians we don't lose heart in spite of the spiritual blindness of those we care about or temptations from failure in our personal lives. We don't resort to deception, pragmatism or water down God's Word (4:2).

3. We put the truth (Christ is Lord) up front and speak to the conscience, hoping to be both a mirror for others to see themselves and a window through which they can see Christ (4:3-4).

4. Our sight comes from the light that has changed us internally, a knowledge revealed, not figured out by us because we're smarter or better than others (4:5-6).

5. God uses us because we are weak, and therefore any "strength" that others see must come from outside us—from Christ. We have given up a self-centered life to pass on life to others (4:7-12).

6. Our newfound belief compels us to express it. Witness is not optional (4:13-15).

7. We have a different perspective and look at the present in light of the

future (transient vs. permanent). Paradoxically, this makes us more, not less, involved in this world. Also, we now see a reason for suffering (4:16-18).

8. We now have confidence and energy because of the resurrection of our body, which lies ahead. We don't put down roots in this world, for even our body is a tent. We're aliens and God has made us long for eternity. So we live by faith with our one goal of pleasing God. We love him and fear him. But this fear is the affectionate reverence by which children accommodate themselves to the Father's will (5:1-15).

9. We look at people differently—not with the world's standards but as Jesus saw them. We are *driven* to love because we have been loved by Christ. We've been re-created and given a mission! We are ambassadors representing our King and speaking what he tells us: "be reconciled to God" (5:16-20).

10. Christians not only know the gospel message, they *implore* people to respond (5:21).

Look at yourself in the light of these two chapters. Ask God to give you continuing encounters with his awesome love so you will have a stronger love for Christ and others. As you enjoy the love of Christ you will have a growing and genuine faith. An undeniably strong motivation for evangelism will also occur as you see God using you to move others closer to him. First feed on the bread of life yourself, then serve it to others.

II. PREPARING YOUR TESTIMONY

This is *your* spiritual autobiography. Many Christians do not always know the date when God brought them into his kingdom, but this does not mean you have nothing to testify about. Be winsome, honest and wholesome. Never go into detail about sins. After a person has heard your story, will they know basic truths about Christ or only know you better?

Use *some* of the phrases under each heading to help you focus on important things.

1. *What I Was Like:*

My family, friends, interest were . . .

My most important value was . . .

My religious background and attitude about Christ were . . .

2. *What God Used to Begin to Open My Eyes:*

I was awakened to my need by (people, books, circumstances) . . .

What I thought or noticed (about myself, God) at this point was . . .

3. *What I Saw/Understood:*

The aspects of the gospel that touched me were . . .

I came to understand that Christ . . .

I saw my need was . . .

4. *How Christ Has/Is Affecting My Life:*

What changed was . . .

My desires now are . . .

I'm now doing . . .

A difficult area of obedience is . . .

III. LEARNING TO SAY WHAT YOU MEAN

The Bible talks about boldness and says that our strength comes from the Lord and is manifested in quietness, confidence and love. Yet many Christians have communication traits which are indirect, self-effacing, subservient and obsequious. These qualities can be virtuous, but if they rule our relationships, they result in an unhealthy compliant personality. Nonassertiveness has been mistaken for a Christian virtue. Proper assertiveness is essential for loving, truthful relationships and for witnessing. An abundance of Christians develop a nonassertive character, confusing biblical teaching on submission, giving up our rights and putting others first with a total subordination of their legitimate needs. Women, especially, have been rewarded for being nonconfrontational, agreeable, quiet and servile. By not saying what they really think, feel or want, they hide their true selves and bury these things within until the day they explode in things like divorce, suicide, depression, codependency or addictions. To always conform to what others want of you is worldliness. To excuse yourself as "shy" may mean that you focus too much on what others think of you and are overly sensitive.

One of the ways to recognize nonassertive behavior is to ask youself:

1. Do I usually respond to what others say or do rather than initiating and being proactive?

2. Do I apologize or make excuses all the time and put myself down?

3. Do I avoid conflict with others, fearing their disapproval?

4. Do I refrain from expressing even my lowest-risk feelings, needs, opinions?

5. If I do express my ideas and needs, is it often in such an ingratiating way that others disregard me?

6. Am I inwardly angry, resentful, frustrated because I later wish I had said or done something?

7. Do I find myself often saying "yes" when I want to say "no"?

Indications of behaving nonassertively are continuing anxiety, dissatisfaction, anger, or discomfort after interaction with someone. Your important, legitimate needs are not being met. You've become a people-pleaser.

Aggressive behavior is not the solution. That would mean having your needs met by hurting others, clearly expressing your opinions, but humiliating and disregarding others. Some aggressive behavior is subtle: passive aggressors have needs met through silent resistance, stubbornness, sabo-tage, manipulation.

Assertiveness means knowing what you want, appropriately expressing it by communicating honestly and directly. You are able to express your needs, feelings, ideas. You stand up for your rights in ways that do not violate the rights and needs of others. In conflict you cooperate for a solution that will meet the needs of both persons.

At the end of the Bible in the midst of an awesome description of heaven, there is a graphic portrayal of those who will be in eternal hell. The unbe-lievers, vile, murderers, sexually immoral, occult, idolaters and liars (Rev 21:8). Do you know what heads this list? The cowardly. This stuns me. I think it means that people characterized by fear, not faith, are displeasing to God. Courage, rather than cowering or cringing before others, marks bibli-cal belief. The fear of others is a trap (Prov 29:25).

IV. BEING A GOOD LISTENER

Listening is hard work. It is active, not passive. Listening is not something to try to fake; it must come from within. It is the way to give quality attention to others and the way to love them.

Evaluate one or two conversations you have had recently in the light of the following ideas about listening.

POOR LISTENER	GOOD LISTENER
Assumes the subject is uninteresting	Finds something interesting in what is said and asks questions
Focuses on the person's manner of expression (word choice)	Finds the message more important than grammar, sentence structure or wording
Becomes overstimulated; makes snap judgments	Listens rationally; evaluates but suspends judgment
Listens only for the facts	Listens for the feelings too
Tries to outline the information	Notes patterns, traits, principles and basic ideas
Fakes attention to the person	Shows disciplined attention through brief comments, reactions

POOR LISTENER	GOOD LISTENER
Is distracted by surroundings	Concentrates by focusing eyes and mind
Evades grappling with difficult information	Welcomes expression of difficult ideas or problems
Satisfied with only hearing what is first said	Probes for the idea, assumption, problem behind the surface words
Lets emotional words or situations block information flow	Maintains emotional control and is unshockable
Thinks about own response to what is being said	Thinks about what is being said, and if advice is sought, uses biblical principles

1. Evaluation of Conversation 1:

2. Evaluation of Conversation 2:

V. HOW TO ASK GOOD QUESTIONS

Jesus was a master at asking questions (see Jn 3; 4; 9). Sometimes his questions are rhetorical; sometimes they are to expose the other person; sometimes they are to gain information; sometimes they are to give new insight.

Jesus also was constantly listening for the question behind the question. He didn't directly answer questions but looked for what was behind them. This is how he handled questions like Who's right when it comes to worshiping God (Jn 4:20)? What do I have to do to be assured of living forever (Mk 10: 17)? Why was this man born blind (Jn 9:2)? How can the new birth be true (Jn 3:9)? We need this same skill in listening. We need to ask ourselves if we have really heard what people are saying when they ask questions or make strong statements.

If we really wish to be friendly and helpful to people, whether we are thinking of group Bible study, personal counseling of Christians, witnessing or raising our children, we need to learn the art of questioning. Here are some principles to keep in mind:

1. Take every possible chance to ask a searching question, then keep quiet.

(When we're talking, we're not learning anything.)

2. One thoughtful question is worth a dozen interrogative ones. The prod-and-pry approach makes people clam up.

3. Questions that come close to people's true interests get the best answers, provided we are interested.

4. Be prepared to wait. Sometimes a long silence can be more rewarding than another question.

5. In every case, the quality of an answer depends on the quality of attention given by the questioner.

6. Questions must spring from honest inquiry, not from attempts at flattery or efforts to manipulate people's thinking.

7. Questions that deal with people's feelings are more provocative than those that deal with facts. Listen for and encourage all expressions of feeling.

8. What is our motive in asking questions? Are we just leading people on in order to argue or to trap them, or do we really care for them?

9. Ask questions to help people tell their story, not just about what interests you or things you want clarified.

Only a listening, loving heart can remove the mask we all wear.

Test Yourself
Some questions seem to close more doors than they open, while others lead to true dialogue. Check the good questions on the following list, and mark the poor ones with a zero.

1. What did you do today?

2. Would you explain that to me?

3. How was the game?

4. How do you feel about that?

5. Is something the matter?

6. What would you have done?

7. Do you love me?

8. Why did you say that?

9. Oh, really?

10. For instance?

The odd-numbered questions are poor because they are conversation stoppers, usually answerable in one or two words. The even-numbered questions are good because they call for thought-provoking answers that can send the conversational stone rolling and lead to more questions. They call for explanation and description and can lead to revealing a person's feelings and values.[1]

Helping People Think
Ask others to explain their values or view of life. Then be a good listener. Keep these four questions in mind, as developed by James Sire.

1. What do you mean?

2. How do you know?

3. What difference has this made in your relationships?

4. If you're wrong, what would be the consequences for you? for others?

VI. FRIENDSHIP EVANGELISM
1. What are characteristics of friendship?

2. Think of two non-Christian (a, b) and two Christian (c, d) friends. Answer the questions (last 3 do not apply to Christians) in reference to these people. How did you meet them? What is it about them that you appreciate? Have you told this to your friend?

   a)

   b)

   c)

   d)

3. What are two of their favorite interests?

    a)

    b)

    c)

    d)

4. How long have you known them?

    a)

    b)

    c)

    d)

5. Have you ever done anything of a nonreligious nature with them? What?

    a)

    b)

    c)

    d)

6. Have they ever talked with you about a personal problem they are having?

    a)

    b)

    c)

    d)

7. How have you honestly shared yourself and one of your problems with them?

    a)

    b)

    c)

    d)

8. How often during each week do you spend time with them? What do you do when you are together?

a)

b)

c)

d)

9. How often do you pray for them? Are your Christian friends praying for them?

a)

b)

10. Have you ever spoken specifically to them about the Lord Jesus Christ?

a)

b)

11. Identify an obstacle each of them has to becoming a Christian. What could you say or do about this?

a)

b)

12. What will it cost to be a friend (Phil 2:3-5, 20-21)? What barriers hinder you from giving yourself to others in friendship?

13. What is the relationship between friendship and witness (1 Thess 2:7-12)? What approach to people displays how truly concerned we are to meet their needs (Lk 24:17-19; Prov 18:13, 15)?

14. What was Jesus' attitude toward people? To what extent was he concerned for his own personal interests and prestige (Mt 9:36; 11:19; Mk 10:45; Jn 10:10-11)?

15. What have you learned about yourself as a friend through this exercise?

VII. LANGUAGE BARRIERS
Explain the following terms in your own words, as if you were talking with

someone who had no biblical background. Do not use any of the words listed in any of your explanations. Use synonyms where possible or a short
phrase; no long sentences.

1. lost—

2. saved—

3. born again—

4. repent—

5. justified—

6. atonement—

7. righteousness—

8. spiritual—

9. holy—

10. sin—

11. salvation—

12. saving faith—

13. redemption—

14. believe—

15. God—

16. gospel—

17. the finished work of Christ on the cross—

18. inviting Christ into your heart—

VIII. FOUR ROLE PLAYS FOR LEARNING TO WITNESS

1. Practicing the Gospel Diagram "Come Home" (Simplified Version)
Setting: Think of a non-Christian friend with whom you have had some opportunity to share certain aspects of Christian truth. This friend, by his or
her reactions (confusion, criticism, questions) obviously doesn't understand
what you're talking about.

Procedure: The first person assumes role of a Christian and begins with a statement similar to this: "You know, we've talked about Christianity a couple of times but I get the impression that I'm not communicating what I really mean. Can I give you an overview of where I'm coming from? Perhaps by giving you a framework for some of the pieces of Christianity you can see how it fits together. How about hearing me out—saving your questions till the end?"

The second person assumes role of a semi-interested non-Christian. He or she remains attentive for the presentation, not asking any questions, and concludes by saying, "Interesting. Let me think about this and then we'll talk." This person then gives feedback to the Christian on how well they did in expressing themselves.

Time: "Come Home" Simplified Version—20 minutes. Initially the diagram can be used. Evaluation of presentation—10 minutes. Evaluate content, illustrations, body language. Eventual goal is to be able to draw diagram and fill in five points from memory.

Additional ideas: You can switch roles if you add a half-hour. Or you can take another half-hour with the second person asking questions for clarification (not raising objections) instead of only remaining silent during the overview.

2. Answering Questions of Non-Christians

Setting: There are about a dozen recurring questions that non-Christians ask about the gospel. By beginning to get a handle on how to answer these, you can both help people and steer the conversation back to the real question, "What will you do with Christ?" While realizing that often these questions are a smokescreen hiding their real self and needs, nevertheless there are times when they are asked honestly. Pick one of the following questions:

1. Is the Bible trustworthy?

2. Is Christ the only way to God?

3. Why does a good God allow suffering and evil?

4. Isn't one person's opinion as good as another's in religion, since no one can really know what is true?

5. I try to do my best, so won't my good efforts get me to heaven?

Procedure: First person assumes role of non-Christian asking one of the questions. Ask additional questions to clarify as needed. Second person tries to answer them.

Time: Dialogue—15-minute minimum. Evaluation of answers—5 minutes.

Additional ideas: Switch roles for the next 20 minutes. This exercise could also be done in small groups, that is, with a number of others observing the dialogue between two people. Check appendix A.X.

3. Voicing the Objections of Your Non-Christian Friends

Setting: Think of a non-Christian friend or relative that you know well enough to know their objections to Christian beliefs.

Procedure: First person assumes role of their non-Christian friend, consistently reacting the way the friend would in the ensuing dialogue with a Christian. First person begins by saying, "Well, my problem with Christianity is . . ." Second person plays a Christian. The task is to listen and draw out the non-Christian and seek to answer.

Time: Dialogue—15-minute minimum. Evaluation of each other—10 minutes.

Additional ideas: Switch roles for the next 25 minutes. This is a good situation to include a third person who merely observes what the first two are saying and gives feedback to both.

4. Finding Out Someone's Level of Interest

Setting: Your non-Christian friend has been thinking about some of your talks together. He or she has actually started to become interested! But you don't know how much. How can you find out?

Procedure: First person plays role of one of their interested non-Christian friends. They pick one of four possible levels of interest without telling the other person what level is chosen: (1) intrigued enough to read a booklet; (2) interested enough to come to a Bible study; (3) would be willing to meet regularly to talk; (4) wants to find out how to become a Christian. Maintain that level throughout the dialogue. All questions and all statements should be made according to the appropriate level of interest. The goal of the second person is to find out how interested the other one is without immediately asking, for example, "Would you like to come to a Bible study?"

Time: Dialogue—15 minutes.

Additional ideas: Switch roles. Pray then and there for your non-Christian friends.

IX. EVALUATING THE CONTENT OF A GOSPEL PRESENTATION

Here are some questions to raise about the content of an evangelistic statement. As leaders we must develop a taste for weaknesses in a presentation that fails to offer the gospel in its fullness. Check first for some reference to God, man, Christ and response. Then move on to these specific questions.[2]

1. Was the nature of God defined, or was it assumed that the Christian view of God is understood? The increasing influence of Eastern concepts of deity and the idea of designing your own god require some careful explanation of the biblical God.

2. Is sin presented as primarily an offense against God or more as a psychological hunger (lack of fulfillment, etc.)? We must stress that God's law is broken by sin. That is, men not only feel guilty but they are objectively guilty before their Creator. Specific sins have been committed which must be forgiven.

3. Is sin presented in a way that goes beyond outward sins to the inward sin of idolatry? The average person thinks first of sexual immorality when the word *sin* is used. We must help them see that human sins arise from a sin nature of rebellion against God. Our independence of God expresses itself in ignoring God as well as in the breach of his commandments (see the great commandment—Matthew 22:34-40). Is sin explained as enslaving, addictive?

4. Is salvation clearly tied to one's relationship to the living Christ, or could one get the impression that a religious experience, loving thoughts, warm feelings, remorse, joining a church or trying to be good win God's favor?

5. Is salvation presented as the restoration of the human-God relationship for all of life or as something rather detached from life's primary concerns? The stress in the Bible is on serving, loving and being accepted

by a holy God now and forever. One must acknowledge God as Creator for life under God to be more than a religious hobby.

6. Is Jesus Christ presented as the bridge from humans to God or merely as the source of good advice, which if accepted, would improve our lives? Involved here is the way in which Jesus is the Savior. He gives us the legal right to come to a holy God (Jn 1:12; Heb 4:15-16; 1 Jn 2:1-2) because he has paid the penalty for our sin in his death. The teachings of Jesus would be merely an additional burden to us if he did nothing to solve our existing guilt before God and fulfill the obligations of God's law for us.

7. Is the biblical character of Jesus (the God-man) defined or assumed?

8. Is the necessity for a response to the gospel stressed or slighted? A decision is necessary once we understand the terms of the gospel. We dare not assume that people will know that they must consciously anchor their trust in Christ. Are they shown that no response is rejection and then lovingly urged to respond?

9. Is Christ as Lord made clear, or is future obedience to him obscured? It is easy to present the benefits of being a Christian without a clear understanding of life under the lordship of Christ and his Word. Salvation (acceptance with God) is free—we cannot earn it—yet it restores us to the proper place under God.

10. Are repentance (turning from sin) and faith in Christ made clear?

Another way to evaluate is by using the Amplified Version of "Come Home" as a standard, noting what was omitted under each point.

X. QUESTIONS NON-CHRISTIANS ASK

In speaking of Christ to others, the same questions are raised again and again. These recurring questions are often a smokescreen to put us on the defensive or throw us off track. Usually the questioner is not asking with a sincere desire for an answer. To determine how important a question really is to the poser, ask, "If I answered that question to your satisfaction, would you consider (then ask one of the following)—reading a booklet, reading the Gospel of Mark, coming to a Bible discussion, or listening to a summary of the Bible's themes?" Many will quickly answer, "No, it's just something I'm curious about," or "Not really; it's just a question I like to throw out to people." Depending on the background of the person, the amount of time you have and whether you perceive the question as crucial for the person, you can then adapt your answer. At times a short, biblical answer is best so you can get back to the really serious problems. For instance, when asked about the fate of the heathen, I will simply reply, "Will not the Judge of all the earth do right?" (Gen 18:25). God is fair, and everyone will be treated justly. It is unimaginable that there would be a scene in the afterlife in which a person shakes his fist at God, saying, "You didn't give me what I deserved!" The question is, "What have you done with the truth about God you have been privileged to hear?"

On the other hand, we should give honest and extended answers to honest questions, so we need to familiarize ourselves with the best in Christian apologetic literature. We must be willing to take time with people and bring them slowly along, if that is their need. Our confidence should never be in our ability to answer. It is better to say, "I don't know," than to try to give an uninformed answer. Even at best all our answers are partial. We cannot reason people into the kingdom even though ours is a reasonable faith. Even to use evidences to establish the probability of Christianity achieves little. Since the mind of natural, fallen people is at enmity with God, the answer we give will not be palatable. For instance, have you ever heard someone object to the concept of hell? I have, and after the lengthiest and most cogent explanation that I could muster, I've had the questioner stare at me and say, "Why, I'll never believe in a God like that!" That response shows she is not really interested in truth or she would be willing to follow truth wherever it leads her, even though it cuts against her grain and necessitates a change in thinking. Ultimately, the unresponsiveness of the questioners is not because of their intellectual misgivings but is due to their moral condition. People do not come to the light because their deeds are evil (Jn 3:19-21). To get below the surface objections, try this question: "I wonder if you would share with me one of your personal objections to Jesus?"

Here are common questions asked by non-Christians. Visit a Christian bookstore or contact InterVarsity Press for a catalog for help on where to find answers to these questions. If we are able to express introductory answers to these questions, we will be a help to many people. We will strengthen our own faith as we look more deeply into biblical teaching and develop stronger answers. It is important that we attempt to bring the answer to bear not only on the understanding of the questioners but also on their life and conscience as well.

1. Is the Bible trustworthy?
2. Is Christ the only way to God?
3. What about the people who have never heard?
4. Isn't one person's opinion as good as another's in religion, since no one can really know what is true?
5. I try to do my best, so won't my good efforts get me to heaven?
6. Is Jesus God?
7. Doesn't science contradict the Bible?
8. Why does a good God allow suffering and evil?
9. Life is meant to be meaningless; why bother trying to find answers?
10. Why do I need religion?
11. Why don't Christians do something about the needs of people in this world?
12. Why can't Christians agree among themselves?
13. Who am I?
14. Who can I trust?
15. Why am I so lonely? Is there a group that will accept me as is?
16. What will make a relationship work?
17. How is Jesus Christ real in your life?

XI. GUIDELINES FOR ORGANIZING CONTACT EVANGELISM

Introducing the Idea

As you invite people to join you in contact evangelism or as you train them, you will want to introduce a few basic concepts. Since we do not want to be only hearers of the Word, it is necessary to place ourselves in insecure situations in which we must lean hard on God. We are not saying that contact evangelism is the only way or that everyone will be equally gifted at it. But it is right to seek opportunities with strangers, and it is an important training experience for Christians in developing an ongoing life of evangelism. Jesus said, "I will make you fishers of men." Let's throw out our nets broadly, expecting God to respond. We do not need to manipulate or force people; we merely tie in with the work that God is already doing in the hearts of those we meet. He always goes before us. We never go alone. We need to learn how to be friendly, draw people out and confront them with the truth in a loving way.

Moving Out

Plan and announce details of where you are going, how to get there, and when to return for prayer and sharing. Explain that you will work in pairs and look for individuals or couples to approach (unless you are contacting people who have visited your church or fellowship group). Some possibilities are house visitation, beaches, parks, literature tables, or during lunch times at work or school. If it is a business or school, be sure you have asked the advice of any Christians who may already be ministering there. Distribute giveaway literature. Mention the importance of getting names or recording reactions for future follow-up. Pray and pair up.

The Encounter

A good opening question is essential. Here are a few possibilities:

1. "Here's some literature we're giving away. It's free. By the way, what's your religious background?"

2. "We're asking people for a few minutes of time so we can find out their opinions on some important matters. Could you spare a few minutes to answer some questions?"

3. "We're interested in finding out what people know about some of the main teachings of the Bible. Could you answer a few questions?"

4. "We're approaching people today to find out what they think about spir-

itual or religious matters. Most people are either hostile, indifferent or open to spiritual things. Could you tell us which you are? Why?"

The Spiritual Interest Questionnaire is very helpful to use (appendix A.XII).

After the initial exchange of questions, try one of the following for continuing the discussion:

1. "What you've said interests me. I've found that many people today have bits and pieces of religious knowledge but no clear and concise understanding of the theme of the Bible. Many people have found it helpful to hear a brief summary of this theme. I'm prepared to take fifteen minutes to go over it with you right now. Could we do that? I really think you'd find it helpful." Then present an outline of the gospel.

2. "What you've just said interests me. I'd like to know more about why you think that way. I wonder if you've ever considered this as an answer (or alternate view) to the point you just made." After picking up on a point they have made and really listening to them further, ask them if they would in turn give you fifteen minutes to try to give them a frame of reference for what you have been saying. Give them an overview of the gospel using your outline.

Ask them to consider these things seriously. Leave appropriate literature. Ask if you can come back again to bring them an answer to (or literature about) a question they raised. Set up a definite time. Get their names and phone number so you can call the day you are to meet them to make sure they are in.

Evaluation

1. What did you learn from this experience?

2. How will you apply what you learned?

XII. SPIRITUAL INTEREST QUESTIONNAIRE

Surveys are a common evangelistic technique, but I think most evangelicals use them improperly. Often Christians give people the impression that they are studying something, and the survey's answers will be tabulated, when in fact, the survey is a tool designed to engage people in conversation. It seems much more honest to forget the survey itself and simply approach people on a personal level, such as "Hello, I'm (your neighbor, fellow student, visiting for my church), and I'm interested in helping people with spiritual needs." You may have to add quickly, "We're not collecting money or interested in church membership," especially if the area you are visiting has been hit heavily by door-to-door religious sales reps.

You could then ask, "Do you have a few minutes to answer some questions?" Or you could just go right into a question like the ones mentioned earlier. If the interviewee is responsive, then you can ask for more time to talk, having said at the outset the questions would only take a few minutes. One good follow-up is, "I'm interested in what you have said. I used to think that way too. One thing that helped me was to get an overview of what Jesus taught. Could we take fifteen minutes more? I'm sure you'd find it helpful." Here is a way to be direct, yet respectful and honest with people.

A questionnaire can be helpful to, as it attempts to discover those people whom the Holy Spirit has prepared by allowing them to admit they have spiritual needs. Asking is the simplest way to find out if people will admit that some of their needs are spiritual. I have developed a spiritual needs questionnaire that could be used to find people who are open. The questions do not appeal to people's desires or attempt to manipulate them. By these questions we are asking, "Are you in any way interested in or aware that your needs are spiritual and there is a solution for such?" Their interest possibly indicates that they are seekers who have been awakened by God to their true needs.

You can hand the questionnaire to the person being questioned or merely use it as a prompter for the person learning to witness. After a while, Christians can dispense with the sheet and personalize the interview even more. I often begin by saying, "Wherever I go, I'm interested in meeting people. I especially like to find out if they have any sense of spiritual needs. I'd be interested in your response to nine questions that I've asked others. Are you interested in hearing them?"

If a person says they are interested in hearing a summary of the main theme of the Bible, I explain that it will take about fifteen minutes and ask if we could sit down. I give them a simplified copy of "Come Home" or sketch it as we talk.

Spiritual Interest Questionnaire

"We're asking people for five minutes to answer several brief questions about their spiritual interest and background. Can you give us five minutes?"

1. What is your religious background?

2. Do you think that various good things you've experienced might be due to God's love?

3. Do you think God might be a source of help for the problems you face?

4. Can you give one example of how your religion affects your behavior; that is, how it makes a practical difference in your life?

5. Do you think of yourself as a person created by God and therefore accountable to him for the way you live?

6. Do you ever think of yourself as in need of God's forgiveness for things you've thought, said or done?

7. In your opinion, who is Jesus Christ?

8. Summarize in one sentence what you think is the main theme of the Bible.

9. When it comes to spiritual matters, would you describe yourself as unconcerned or interested?

Unconcerned: "Thank you for your time. Perhaps as you reflect on these questions you might come to realize the Bible has a lot of practical help and meaning for our lives. Thanks."

Interested: "Thank you for your time. Your answers seem to indicate an interest in spiritual matters, and especially your response to the question about_____. Could we take a few more minutes to talk?"

"Many people have found it helpful to hear a brief outline summary of the main theme of the Bible. Could I do this for you now?"

If they answer no, thank them and offer free literature they can read when convenient. Sometimes you will not use this approach but say, "Your answer to question __ interested me. I'd like to know more about why you think that way if you have time." A natural conversation about the gospel often follows.

XIII. Schedule for a God-Centered Evangelism Training Seminar Weekend

The weekend format may be adjusted to be held at a church location. In this case the Sunday sessions would be altered to coincide with the Sunday school hour (session 9) and the worship service (session 10 in a sermon form). The leader/speaker will find invaluable help for preparing talks from the study guide (appendix C) and especially from the chapters in *Tell the Truth* cited for each session. Reproduction from appendixes A, B and C as well as charts and diagrams in the book is permitted.

No evangelism training is complete without field experience. Sometimes this can be built into the weekend itself. Otherwise, participants should sign up for visitation evangelism in the neighborhood or back on campus or make a commitment to speak to (write, phone) a friend or relative. Accountability is important.

Weekend Seminar

Preseminar Assignment: 1. Read part one and either two or three of *Tell the Truth*. 2. Write out your personal testimony (five minutes), using appendix A.II. 3. Study (two hours) the gospel outline in "Come Home: Amplified Version," then Simplified Version (appendix B, parts 1-3). 4. Pray that God would lead you to someone to witness to.

Friday Night

7:30   Session 1—Personal testimony(ies) on attempts at witnessing; personal witnessing defined (chap. 1)

8:30   Session 2—Talk: the gospel reduced (chap. 2); discussion

9:15   Prayer partners or prayer groups; hand out materials; overview of schedule

9:30   Conclude—hand in written personal testimony

Saturday

8:15   Quiet time—The nature of God and the nature of sin; read Acts 17:22-31, Mark 10:17-31

8:45   Session 3—Talk: the gospel recovered (chap. 3, Gospel Grammar, points 1, 2, 3); introduce "Come Home"

9:45	Break
10:00	Session 4—Small group Bible study: Jesus breaks the barriers to witness (Jn 4:1-42, questions developed by seminar leader)
11:15	Break
11:30	Session 5—Talk: the gospel recovered (chap. 3, Gospel Grammar points 4 and 5, overview of chaps. 4—6; allow for questions)
12:30	Lunch
2:45	Session 6—Talk: introduction to witnessing (chaps. 12—13, pick topics appropriate to your group); feedback from any lunchtime witnessing experiences
4:00	Individual study time: study "Come Home: Simplified Version"
4:30	Session 7—Meet in pairs to role-play a gospel presentation (use appendix A.VIII)
5:30	Dinner
7:00	Session 8—Feedback from any dinnertime witnessing experiences; questions non-Christians ask (a panel format with prepared people works well, use appendix A.X; may also use role-play format from A.XIII)
9:00	Prayer partners or prayer groups
9:30	Conclude

Sunday

8:15	Quiet time—Serving in weakness; our manner and methods; read 2 Corinthians 4—5
8:45	Session 9—Topic: personal witnessing. Talk on selected topics from chapters 12—13 or group Bible study on 2 Corinthians 4—5 using appendix A.I
9:45	Break
10:00	Session 10—Talk: worship—the passion and the purpose for evangelism (chap. 11), or Holy Spirit boldness and speaking to the conscience (chap. 12)
11:30	Plan to obey (in pairs, use format at end of chap. 13); these can be shared briefly with whole group; conclude with prayer and singing
12:30	Lunch

I. PROCEDURE FOR LEARNING THE "COME HOME" GOSPEL DIAGRAM

Introduction

People are looking for relationships where they can find love, meaning, security and joy. God designed families—both natural and spiritual—and homes for this purpose. As part of his plan he intends us to have a home on earth and a home after death.

Theme

God designed us for a relationship with him and others.

Learning the Content of the Gospel

It is essential to take two hours to carefully study the Amplified Version, including looking up the Bible passages.

Diagram

Draw the Road of Life line one inch from the top of the long side of an 8-1/2" x 11" paper two-thirds of the way across paper. Then draw the road going straight down to homelessness. Halfway down this line draw a short line intersected by a vertical line to form a cross. Next, extend the horizontal line up to the top of the paper and resume the Road of Life line. Put a triangle at each end to represent God and an H for *Hell* and another H for *Home* in appropriate places. Put a question mark on the left side of the cross where it intersects with the road downward. (This diagram is drawn on the cover of "Come Home.")

Practice

You are now ready to fill in the diagram with the five points of the gospel. You should fill in one point at a time, following the Simplified Version. Keep practicing this on different sheets of paper *until you can do it from memory.* As you fill in each point, you can also draw the two signs on the road and fill in the words on the bridge, which form a cross. You may add stick figures at the five points and a sign that says "My Way" over point 3 between the two crossed out signs.

Introducing the Diagram

Introduce the diagram by saying something like "Many people have found it helpful to see an overview of the main theme of the Bible. Can I show that to you, and then you can point out which part you don't understand or disagree with?"

Sharing How to "Come Home"

After reviewing the Amplified Version and again looking up the Bible passages, you are ready to share how to "come home" with a Christian friend, drawing the diagram and briefly mentioning the five points, main point, Bible verse and illustration under each of the five points. Be sure to *stop after point 3* and ask the big question and ascertain if they see the dilemma. Your partner can either say something like "I think a God of love would just overlook my failures" or "I'm pretty happy with my life right now; I don't see a need for religion." You have to decide how to answer this! (Hint: Point 1 is the basis for all we've said. God made you, and he is *not* only a love-giver; he has made road rules, and we are responsible to him—a personal God.) Then ask if you can continue the last two points, for this may clarify things. Reverse roles. Then give each other feedback on what was clear and what wasn't.

Objective

The objective of practicing the diagram is to help *you,* as a Christian, get a grip on the content of the good news (gospel). By so doing, you are able to listen to the person you are talking with and bring in various points of the gospel as appropriate. Many times simply communicating what God is like (point 1) is a successful conversation. By knowing the diagram, you can start at any point and move backward or forward as needed. However, it is best to *ask for the opportunity* to give this overview at some point.

This diagram is a *grid* on which to organize the truth that God says is so important for everyone to know. *Be sure you are thoroughly familiar with the Amplified Version* so you can draw on this background when in conversations. Most people are not convicted the first time they hear this story. Your job is to plant and water the seed of God's Word into the conscience and heart of people. The Holy Spirit uses truth joined with your friendliness and love to give them faith and a new birth according to *his* timetable. Sometimes people will find it helpful if you ask them, "What objections/problems do you have with Jesus Christ?" or "What do you think is keeping you from becoming a follower of Jesus?" These questions may allow you to clear up their misunderstandings, bad examples of other Christians or churches and so on—or just to listen to them! The danger is this may get you off on a tangent, so with the "Come Home" diagram in mind, keep coming back to it. What's really fun is to say, "Can I tell you a story?" Then tell them about Paul walking into Athens and talking to some university professors in Acts 17, or about the two lost sons in Luke 15 and so on. Practice reading these passages one paragraph at a time, explaining them to a Christian friend.

You may not get the opportunity to share the simplified version of "Come Home" very often. But knowing this diagram will help you realize when you are *not* talking about the gospel and only talking around the fringe—as in so many of our conversations. You can then be reminded, as you think back over a conversation, to next time bring in some of these truths. Most important, knowing "Come Home" prepares you for a lifetime of lifestyle witnessing.

The following pages (234-41) contain two versions of the "Come Home" diagram—an amplified version for study and a simplified version for sharing. Each set of pages, with a bit of ingenuity, can be photocopied and folded into handy $5\frac{1}{2}$" x $8\frac{1}{2}$" booklets. The simplified version is the easiest: just photocopy pages 240 and 241 back to back and fold in half with the diagram in the middle. The text of this version can be enlarged by about 33% and still fit ordinary paper size for easier reading. In each case you may want to cut pages from the book for easier photocopying.

COME HOME

Have you heard the story about the two roads in life?

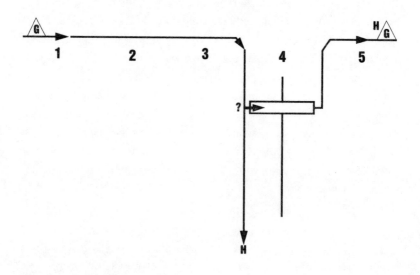

II. COME HOME: OVERVIEW FOR MEMORIZATION

1. Who Is God?
1. Maker (Owner)
2. Love-Giver (Father)
3. Law-Maker (Judge)
→ **Point:** God has rights over you; you are accountable.
Bible: Paul's sermon—Acts 17:22-34 (Rev 4:11)
Illustration: The inventor has patent rights and instruction book.

2. Life = God-Centered Living
1. One-way road home
2. Two rules
3. Perfect obedience required
→ **Point:** God's perfect rules measure all actions/attitudes.
Bible: Moral man—Mark 10:17-27 (Mk 12:30-31)
Illustration: Jumping over a pole 100-feet high.

3. Sin = Self-Centered Living
1. Disobedience is sin.
2. Sin separates you from God.
3. Sin must be punished for God is just.
→ **Point:** We are self-centered and separated from God.
Bible: Jesus and thirsty woman—John 4:4-30 (Rom 3:20)
Illustration: The Gap; failure of self-effort; heart disease; enslaved
Question: Do you admit you are a sinner?
Dilemma: How to get right with God

4. Jesus Christ: The Way Back to Life
1. God provides his Son as a bridge.
2. Jesus perfectly obeys God's rules.
3. Jesus is sin-bearer (takes our penalty).
4. Jesus lives and offers himself to us.
→ **Point:** Jesus is sinner's substitute/reconciler/liberator. He is the only Lord and Savior.
Bible: Crucifixion & resurrection—John 19:17—20:31 (Rom 5:6-8)
Illustration: The Bridge; no more doing—done by Jesus

5. Your Response: Coming Home to Jesus
1. Personal response commanded.
2. Turn from sin.
3. Trust in Christ.
Bible: Two lost sons—Luke 15:11-32 (Ps 51:1-4; Rom 10:9-10)
Illustration: A person is not received until welcomed in; only 3 possible responses (Lk 9:23-26; Acts 17:30-34)
→ **Point:** Receive Christ as your Savior and Lord.

Do You Know the Bible's Main Theme?

Are you able to express the main theme of the Bible, the most influential book of all literature? Most people, Christian or not, cannot! What is this theme called the "gospel"? This booklet is a tool to help you grasp the essentials of the gospel. Whether you are a seeker of Christ or secure in having found him, you need to get the facts straight.

Secure? If you are a true Christian but don't have a clear understanding of the gospel, your growth will be hindered in two ways. First, any vagueness about the basic truths might cause you to miss their implications for living the Christian life. You could be misled into looking for something more in addition to what you received when you became a Christian. Second, you won't be able to give a clear explanation of the gospel to others. Only when truth is kindled by the spark of the Holy Spirit are lives changed. But it's your responsibility to clearly express basic gospel truths! This booklet's five-point outline has many unique features: a clear theme (The Road of Life to Home) linking all the points; a starting point (God made you), which establishes that a person is responsible; inclusion of God's law to expose the need for a Savior; choice of brief verses or reference passages for "story telling" the gospel as Jesus did; illustrations in story and diagram form; emphasis on holiness, repentance and the lordship of Christ; a one-page summary for easy memorizing.

Having an outline of a God-centered gospel in your mind will free you to listen and be more natural as you tell the truth to others.

This Amplified Version of the gospel diagram "Come Home" is intended for detailed study by those who wish to have a thorough knowledge of the content of a God-centered gospel. Christianity is both something to be believed and Someone to be received. To impersonally present these truths would be to contradict the nature of the gospel. Prayer and a personal relationship showing love are all-important. You can follow a printed Simplified Version for sharing, although a conversation in which you draw the diagram is best. Live the gospel, but words are necessary, so use them.

Prayer for Others

"Father in heaven, I come to you humbly and yet boldly because of my salvation, which has united me with your Son. Your grace is reaching more and more people and calling them home. Therefore I pray for _____. Hear my prayer even as you heard the pleading of your friend Abraham and spared his nephew Lot from terrible judgment. Your Son invited the spiritually tired, burdened and thirsty to take of the free water of eternal life. Lord, will you please open still another heart as you did mine? You alone can break addictions to self-righteousness, unbelief and sinful desires. Would it please you to provide repentance and faith leading to a new birth? Magnify your glory by delivering _____ from spiritual death. Lord, bring fame to your name by once again showing mercy. My plea is not based on my own goodness but on the sovereign love of Jesus Christ. Lord, I desire that you use me in telling the gospel of grace to others. Nevertheless, not my will, but your will be done. Make your name famous. Amen."

These Scriptures provide incentive and direction for your prayers for others. If you're praying in a group, assign each person one or two passages as a basis for their prayer: Matthew 11:25-30; Luke 15; 16:19-31; John 4:1-42, 10:1-18; Acts 4:24-31; 5:27-32; 17:27-34; 26:19-29; Romans 10:1-4, 9-21; 1 Corinthians 1:18—2:16; 2 Corinthians 2:14-17; 4:1-18; 5:11-21; Ephesians 6:10-20; 1 Thessalonians 1:2—2:13; 2 Timothy 1:6-10; 4:1-5; Revelation 20:11—21:5; 22:17.

People for Whom I Will Pray:

1.   1.

2.   2.

3.   3.

Reprinted from *Tell the Truth* ©2002 by Will Metzger with permission from InterVarsity Press, Downers Grove, Illinois.
This helpful training manual for God-centered evangelism in book form is appropriate for individual or group study. It is available through Christian bookstores.

Come Home: Amplified Version (for learning)

Road Of Life To Your Real Home

Road Downward Away From Life & God

Road to Eternal Homelessness and Hell

G

| Love God Perfectly | Love Others Completely | | God's Law Broken | Others | | Sin Separates Us From God |

1. Who is God?

1. God made everyone.
Therefore He is your OWNER and you are accountable to put Him at the center of your life.

2. God is a love-giver.
Therefore He desires to be a FATHER and bring many home into His family as His adopted spiritual children.

3. God is a law-maker.
Therefore He is a morally perfect JUDGE whose instructions are to be obeyed as you travel His road of life.

→ **Point:** Since God made you, you belong to Him and are accountable to follow His instructions for a relationship of love centered on Him.

Bible Basis: Story - Paul's talk to the Athenians; Acts 17:22-34. Individual verses - Revelation 4:11.

Illustration: An inventor has patent rights (owns) and writes the operating instructions (biblical rules) for his creation.

Transition: Have you heard the story about the two roads in life?

2. Life = God-Centered Living

1. God designed a one way road.
Therefore all people are commanded to follow this road, enjoying friendship with Him now and later in His eternal home.

2. God has two rules for our journey.
These two rules do not destroy our freedom, but are for our safety and happiness, for we are made to live like this.

3. God's rules must be perfectly kept.
Obeying His rules perfectly keeps us on the road to real love and a home now and after we die.

God's Rules for Everyone

	Yes	No
1. I love God with everything that is in me, and more than anyone or anything else.	☐	☐
2. I love all people as I love myself, and always serve and do what is best for them.	☐	☐

→ **Point:** The two rules for God-centered living of perfect love for God and others, shows us that God's requirements measure all our actions and attitudes.

Bible Basis: Story - Jesus meets a young man enslaved to his desires; Mark 10:17-27. Individual verses - Mark 12:30-31; James 2:8-13. (A review of the Ten Commandments, Exodus 20:1-17 and sections from the Sermon on the Mount, Matthew 5:17-48 can be used to reinforce the extent of God's perfect standard.)

Illustration: A person may be able to jump over a pole if it is put one foot off the ground, but if this test begins with it at 100 feet, no one can jump over.

3. Sin = Self-Centered Living

1. Failing to obey and love God is sin.
Your failure to live by God's rules for life is disobedience to God who made the rules. This is called sin.

2. Sin separates you from God.
Your relationship with God is broken. Now there is a huge gap and you are unable to please God and change for the better. People try to please God by:

All attempts to "do" fail — Loving and doing good — Start doing religious things — Stop doing wrong things

3. Sin is punished by a God of justice.
God cannot just overlook evil; He must judge and punish sinners who have turned from their loving Father onto the road of death and hell.

→ **Point:** Having become self-centered, you are separated from God, unable to earn forgiveness, enslaved to your desires, experiencing guilt, and headed down the road to a hopeless eternity.

Bible Basis: Story - Jesus meets a self-centered and thirsty woman; John 4:4-30. Individual verses-Romans 3:20.

Illustration: Sin is like a wall separating (creating a gap) on the road between us and God. People try to cross this gap by doing good and earning favor with God. It is also enslaving and like having a heart disease.

CONCLUSIONS OF POINTS 1-3

SERIOUS QUESTIONS: Are you willing to admit that you are accountable for your sin and totally unable to keep God's rules? That you cannot save yourself by any attempts such as: good deeds, church membership, helping others, fighting injustice, etc.? Do you agree that the Bible teaches that you are spiritually helpless, for sin is like a deadly cancer in your life? Do you realize that the road you are on leads to self-centered living now and an eternity separated from God and others (hell)?

THE BIG DILEMMA: Therefore, you, and all humanity are in the dilemma of disobeying your Maker. The concern that should be yours is: "How can I, a guilty sinner, become acceptable (forgiven and righteous) before God my Maker?" Do you have this concern? (Admittedly, this is bad news—but unless you are convinced of your dilemma, the good news of a loving Savior and Father calling you to "Come Home" will seem irrelevant.) Take time now for serious reflection.

Come Home: Amplified Version (for learning)

A Home Now and In Heaven

G | H

4. Jesus Christ: The Way Back to Life

Adopted, Loved New Home and Family

5. Your Response: Coming Home To Jesus

1. God, your maker, calls you back to Him.

You are to do more than just intellectually acknowledge these historical facts—but to wholeheartedly respond to the force of these truths by:

2. Turning (repent).

From your sinful lifestyle and efforts at self-justification, and surrender to God's owner-ship of your life.

3. Trusting (faith).

In Jesus Christ as your forgiver (erases sin) who perfectly obeyed (giver of moral purity) enabling you to follow God's road plan for life.

Bible Basis: Story - Two lost sons, which are you?: Luke 15:11-32. Individual verses - Romans 10:9-10; Psalm 51:1-4.

Illustration: If a person stands at your door, until you open the door, you have rejected them.

→ **Point:** Which is your response? He is calling, "Come home."

☐ I receive Christ.

"Realizing my self-centeredness, I now want to *turn* from my sinful lifestyle. Unable to save myself, I now *trust* in the risen Jesus Christ for forgiveness of my many sins. I give you control of my life, and I desire to follow your instructions whatever it may cost me. I receive you as my Savior and Lord. I ask for Your Spirit to be merciful to and to enable me to respond to Your call home." (Your prayer for salvation.)

☐ I reject Christ.

"I do not want, as of this moment, to receive the love of Jesus Christ. I realize this means He will not represent me before God at the final judgment as my Savior and Lord. Therefore I reject Christ's offer of salvation."

☐ I want to investigate further.

"I commit myself to read, pray, and talk more with someone about the salvation that Jesus offers, so that I can find out if it is true."

Only three possible responses . . .

An invitation to believe is extended to you on the authority of the Word of Jesus Christ. A so-called "no interest" or "neutral" response to a person (Christ) standing before you is the same as rejection. (Luke 9:23-26; Acts 17:30-34)

JESUS CHRIST

SAVIOR AND LORD

3. Jesus Christ takes the punishment.

He submits to God's holy anger against sinners during His death on a cross. Bearing the sins of others, He dies as a substitute, taking the penalty we deserve, liberating us from sin's enslavement.

4. Jesus Christ rises from the dead.

His actions are approved by God the Father and now He offers true righteousness and forgiveness. This qualifies undeserving sinners to be adopted into His family and know they are on the road of life and have a real home.

Illustration: Jesus Christ is like a bridge which you trust to bring you across, instead of trying to get over to God by building a bridge of your own efforts. There is no more doing; Christ has done it all.

1. God provides a bridge back to Him.

He became the God-man Jesus Christ because He loves sinners.

2. Jesus Christ keeps the rules for life.

As our substitute during His lifetime here on earth, He perfectly meets all God's requirements for a moral life on our behalf.

Road to Eternal Homelessness and Hell

Bible Basis: Story - The crucifixion and resurrection: John 19:17—20:31. Individual verses - Romans 5:6-8; Mark 10:45; I Peter 3:18.

→ **Point:** God initiates a solution to sin's enslavement by offering His Son Jesus to give sinners a free gift of forgiveness and righteousness (integrity, blameless) thus bridging the gap. Instead of trying to earn our own righteousness, a substitute, Jesus, gives us His perfect goodness. There is a way back to the road of life and home.

H

COME HOME

Have you heard the story about the two roads in life?

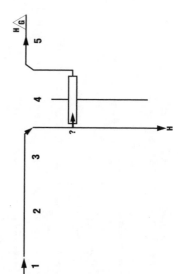

Being a Disciple of Jesus Christ

A New Confidence. If you have begun to seek a relationship with your Maker through praying to him, continue to read over these biblical passages, asking God to change you and make you a true Christian. You will know when God has answered your prayer when you begin to see a threefold change take place.

1. The Bible, especially the promises of God, will become personal to you. It will seem like God is speaking directly to you as you read it (Psalm 119:102-104; John 10:14-16).

2. You will have an inner sense of peace, forgiveness and being loved as a special, adopted child of God your Father. You will sense you've come home. The Holy Spirit has done this (Romans 8:14-17).

3. You will begin to see definite changes take place in your actions and attitudes. These are things such as a revulsion toward sin in your life, a willingness to acknowledge Christ before others, a love for other true Christians, progress in having victory over many sins in your life and so on. You should read the small letter 1 John in its entirety, for it was written so that you might have certainty that you now are joined to Jesus, God's Son (1 John 5:11-13).

A New Lifestyle

1. Tell a Christian what happened to you, and ask them to meet with you weekly to explain the basics of the Christian life.

2. Read your Bible, starting with the New Testament, for 20 minutes each day, praying about what you have read and for the people in your life.

3. Join with other Christians in a Bible-believing church and fellowship small group to learn to worship. Begin to use your time, talents and possessions for God.

4. Tell the truth of the gospel of Christ to others by your actions, attitudes and words.

Reprinted from *Tell the Truth* ©2002 by Will Metzger with permission from InterVarsity Press, Downers Grove, Illinois.
This helpful training manual for God-centered evangelism in book form is appropriate for individual or group study. It is available through Christian bookstores.

Come Home: Simplified Version (for sharing)

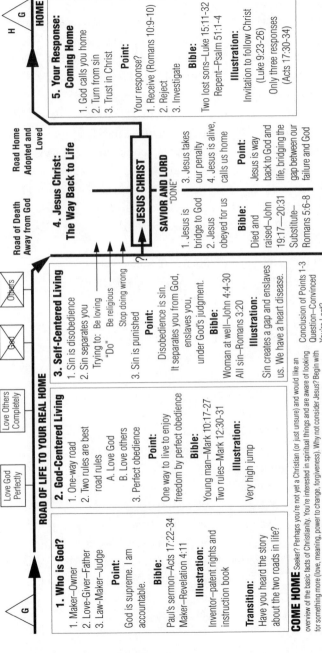

Love God Perfectly		Love Others Completely

ROAD OF LIFE TO YOUR REAL HOME

1. Who is God?
1. Maker—Owner
2. Love-Giver—Father
3. Law-Maker—Judge

Point:
God is supreme. I am accountable.

Bible:
Paul's sermon—Acts 17:22-34
Maker—Revelation 4:11

Illustration:
Inventor—patent rights and instruction book

Transition:
Have you heard the story about the two roads in life?

2. God-Centered Living
1. One-way road
2. Two rules are best road rules
   A. Love God
   B. Love others
3. Perfect obedience

Point:
One way to live to enjoy freedom by perfect obedience

Bible:
Young man—Mark 10:17-27
Two rules—Mark 12:30-31

Illustration:
Very high jump

3. Self-Centered Living
1. Sin is disobedience
2. Sin separates you
   Trying to: Be loving
   "Do" Be religious
   Stop doing wrong
3. Sin is punished

Point:
Disobedience is sin. It separates you from God, enslaves you, under God's judgment.

Bible:
Woman at well—John 4:4-30
All sin—Romans 3:20

Illustration:
Sin creates a gap and enslaves us. We have a heart disease.

Conclusion of Points 1-3
Question—Convinced You're Lost?
Dilemma—How to Get Right with God?

Road of Death Away from God

Road Home Adopted and Loved

4. Jesus Christ: The Way Back to Life

JESUS CHRIST

SAVIOR AND LORD
"DONE"

1. Jesus is bridge to God
2. Jesus obeyed for us
3. Jesus takes our penalty
4. Jesus is alive, calls us home

Point:
Jesus is way back to God and life, bridging the gap between our failure and God

Bible:
Died and raised—John 19:17—20:31
Substitute—Romans 5:6-8

Hell

HOME

5. Your Response: Coming Home
1. God calls you home
2. Turn from sin
3. Trust in Christ

Point:
Your response?
1. Receive (Romans 10:9-10)
2. Reject
3. Investigate

Bible:
Two lost sons—Luke 15:11-32
Repent—Psalm 51:1-4

Illustration:
Invitation to follow Christ (Luke 9:23-26)
Only three responses (Acts 17:30-34)

COME HOME Seeker? Perhaps you're not yet a Christian (or just unsure) and would like an overview of the basic facts of Christianity. You're interested in spiritual things and are aware of looking for something more (love, meaning, power to change, forgiveness). Why not consider Jesus? Begin with these basic concepts and get beyond myths, opinions and emotionalism. Examine something before you judge it. Don't be biblically illiterate or one who takes ideas out of their context. This booklet could be the means to introduce you to the biblical Jesus who is still fascinating and transforming people of all cultures into a new international family. By beginning with understanding these basic truths you will come to realize that Christianity is both something to be believed and someone to be received.

III. TELLING THE GOSPEL THROUGH STORIES

Here is a list of passages from the four Gospels that bring out parts of the gospel. After reading the story in the Bible and understanding the main point(s), decide which of the five points of the gospel is being described: (1) the character of God, (2) the high standard of God's law, (3) the breaking of God's law—sin and its consequences of separation, enslavement, diseased heart, (4) Jesus Christ as the achiever of salvation and the focus of faith, or (5) responding to God/Christ by turning and trusting. Next, retell the story to a friend in your own words either by using the biblical characters or by substituting an imaginary (or real) contemporary person. Ask the friend to give feedback about what they understood was your point. Repeat the story to others, saying, "Here's a good story . . ."

The five stories from the "Come Home" gospel diagram: Acts 17:22-34, Mark 10:17-27, John 4:4-30, John 19:17-20:31, Luke 15:11-32.

Other stories:

Matthew 11:25-30—Little Children and Burdened People

Matthew 13:1-9, 19-23—Four Kinds of Soil (Responses)

Matthew 14:13-21—Miracle of Multiplying Food

Matthew 14:16-20—Where Sin Originates

Matthew 14:21-28—Need for Humility

Matthew 16:13-17—Believing

Matthew 20:1-16—Grace, Not Obligation

Matthew 21:33-46—Murdering the King's Son

Mark 2:1-12—Forgiveness of Sins

Mark 2:13-17—We All Need a Doctor

Mark 5:1-20—Evil Power Is Overcome

Mark 6:1-6—Familiarity Breeds Contempt

Mark 8:31-38—Christ Calls Us to Come and Die

Mark 12:28-34—What Does God Require?

Mark 13:32-37—Warning: Christ Will Return

Luke 5:1-11—In the Presence of God, I Realize My Sin

Luke 7:36-50—The Result of Being Forgiven Is Great Love for Jesus

Luke 12:13-21—Our Possessions Can Be a Dangerous Distraction

Luke 12:32-34—God's Awesome Love

Luke 12:49-53—The Cost of Following Jesus

Luke 13:22-30—Salvation Is a Time-Limited Offer

Luke 15:1-7—God Is Seeking the Lost

Luke 16:19-31—Not a Miracle but the Bible Will Convict People

Luke 18:9-14—Pride Versus Humility

Luke 19:1-10—A Changed Life Is Evidence of a Changed Heart

Luke 24:13-49—A Dead Man Comes to Life

John 1:10-14—Reject or Receive?

John 3:1-21—Spiritual Rebirth Is Necessary

John 5:24-30—Crossing Over from Death to Life

John 8:31-36—Truth Sets You Free

John 9:1-34—Spiritual Blindness Is Worse Than Physical Blindness

John 20:24-31—A Doubter Believes

IV. GOD'S TEST FOR EVERYONE: MEASURE YOURSELF BY GOD'S LAW*

1. I have never put anything else before God in my life.
   I have always given God first place in my thinking, affections and actions.
   YES _____ NO _____

2. I have never had any wrong conceptions about God nor worshipped Him in a way not recommended by Him.
   I have always rejected any wrong imaginations or images of God that I've seen or thought and refused to remake God according to my liking.
   YES _____ NO _____

3. I have never slighted or abused the character of the true God by using His holy name as a swear word or using it in a thoughtless manner, such as by calling myself a follower of God yet not obeying.
   I have always held the name of God, which signifies His character, in highest respect, invoking it with thoughtfulness and reverence.
   YES _____ NO _____

4. I have never done less than a full week's work, and never done any of my normal work on the day set aside to worship God.
   I have always worked hard and willingly at whatever task is set before me, seeing it as a God-given service each day, and consistently remem-

bered to set apart one day weekly to worship God with others.
YES _____ NO _____

5. I have never disobeyed nor dishonored my parents or any others in authority over me.
I have always respected and been thankful for my parents and given them honor and willing obedience, as well as other authorities over me.
YES _____ NO _____

6. I have never murdered anyone nor had hateful thoughts or taken the slightest pleasure in seeing harm done to another human.
I have always thought more of others than I have of myself and practiced the highest regard for human life and justice.
YES _____ NO _____

7. I have never practiced any sexual impurity, either physically engaging in sex before marriage or mentally having impure thoughts about someone.
I have always treated others' sexuality with respect and dignity in both my physical actions and mental attitudes.
YES _____ NO _____

8. I have never taken anything that doesn't belong to me nor been deceitful in any attitudes or unwilling to work for my needs.
I have always respected the belongings, rights and creations of others and been completely truthful and fair.
YES _____ NO _____

9. I have never lied nor slandered another person or group of people.
I have always told the truth in every situation regarding every person I have known.
YES _____ NO _____

10. I have never been greedy for something that wasn't mine, nor jealous even of the abilities, looks, or status of others.
I have always shared and given of my possessions and myself to others and have been thankful in my heart for what they have and content with my possessions and situation.
YES _____ NO _____

*A paraphrase of the Ten Commandments in negative and positive form (Ex 20:1-17, cf. Mt 5:17-48; Mk 12:30-31).

V. DO YOU DARE LOOK INSIDE YOURSELF?

PROUD, UNBROKEN PEOPLE	BROKEN PEOPLE
focus on the failure of others	are overwhelmed with their own spiritual need
are self-righteous; have a critical, fault-finding spirit; look at own life/faults with a telescope but others with a microscope	are compassionate; have a forgiving spirit; look for best in others
look down on others	esteem all others better than self
are independent; have a self-sufficient spirit	have dependent spirit; recognize others' needs
maintain control; must have their way	surrender control
have to prove that they are right	are willing to yield the right to be right
claim rights	yield rights
have a demanding spirit	have a giving spirit
are self-protective of time, rights, reputation	are self-denying
desire to be served	are motivated to serve others
desire to be a success	desire to be faithful to make others a success
desire for self-advancement	desire to promote others
are driven to be recognized and appreciated	have a sense of unworthiness; are thrilled to be used at all; are eager for others to get the credit
are wounded when others are promoted and they are overlooked	rejoice when others are lifted up
think "The ministry is privileged to have me!"	think "I don't deserve to serve in this ministry!"
think of what they can do for God	know that they have nothing to offer God
feel confident in how much they know	are humbled by how much they have to learn
are self-conscious	have no concern with self at all
keep people at arm's length	risk getting close to others; are willing to take the risks of loving intimately

PROUD, UNBROKEN PEOPLE	BROKEN PEOPLE
are quick to blame others	accept personal responsibility; can see where they were wrong
are unapproachable	are easy to be entreated
are defensive when criticized	receive criticism with a humble, open heart
are concerned with being respectable	are concerned with being real
are concerned about what others think	know all that matters is what God knows
work to maintain image and protect reputation	die to own reputation
find it difficult to share their spiritual needs with others	are willing to be transparent with others
want to be sure no one finds out about their sin	are willing to be exposed; know once broken, there's nothing to lose
have a hard time saying, "I was wrong. Would you forgive me?"	are quick to admit fault and to seek forgiveness
deal in generalities when confessing sin	deal in specifics
are concerned about the consequences of their sin	are grieved over the root of their sin
are remorseful for being caught	are repentant over sin and forsake it
wait for the other party to come and ask for forgiveness in a conflict	take the initiative to be reconciled; gets there first
compare themselves with others and feel deserving of honor	compare themselves with the holiness of God and feel desperate for mercy
are blind to their true heart condition	walk in the light
don't think they have anything of which to repent	have a continual heart attitude toward repentance
don't think they need revival (think everybody else does)	continually sense their need for a fresh encounter with the filling of the Holy Spirit

Appendix C
Study Guide:
Twelve Sessions for
Individuals or Groups

(Assignments are for the *next* study. See leader's note at end.)

STUDY 1. GOD'S PART AND OUR PART IN EVANGELISM (PREFACE, INTRODUCTION, CHAPTER 1)

1. How might an emphasis on grace liberate and energize us for evangelism? (Preface, pp. 11, 22)

2. What does the author mean by "The gospel is for Christians"? (Preface, p. 13)

3. The author mentions two extremes in witnessing. What are they, and how have you struggled in witnessing (pp. 15-18)?

4. Explain the sentence, "Your methodology of evangelism flows from your theology of evangelism." Give an example (good or bad) of how a current practice in evangelism results from a theological reason (pp. 19, 36-37).

5. In what sense is the statement "I witness by the way I live" a good principle? In what ways is it not a good principle (pp. 24-25)?

6. From 1 Corinthians 3:5-9 explain what our role is and what God's role is in evangelism. How could this free us up in witnessing (pp. 28-30)?

7. Why don't you witness more? Write down three people you will pray for and speak to about Jesus.

Assignment: Read the preface, introduction and chapter one if you have not done so; then read chapter two.

STUDY 2. THE GOSPEL REDUCED (CHAPTER 2)

1. Justify the statement "Presenting the maximum amount of truth to the maximum number of people is the historical and biblical goal of evangelism" (pp. 33-38).

2. What are some ways that a me-centered gospel differs from a God-centered gospel (pp. 36-37)?

3. How can the truth "God loves sinners" become a half-truth and mislead people? What other parts of the gospel are often shrunken or neglected (pp. 39-41)?

4. What is method-centered evangelism? Why is this approach prone to manipulating people (pp. 41-42)?

5. What are three negative effects of me-centered evangelism (p. 44)?

6. Summarize Tim Keller's answer to the person who couldn't believe people are going to hell for not believing in Jesus (pp. 47-49).

7. Do you think the author has misstated his analysis of contemporary evangelism? Give examples for your view from the book or from your experiences (pp. 46-52).

Assignment: Read chapter 3, "Gospel Grammar." Read appendix B, and make copies of both versions of the "Come Home" gospel diagram, following the Learning Procedure.

STUDY 3. THE GOSPEL RECOVERED, PART ONE (CHAPTER 3, "GOSPEL GRAMMAR")

1. Contrast a secular definition of *God* and *sin* with a biblical definition. (pp. 53-55, 62-67

2. What three characteristics of God are important for the non-Christian to know, and why (pp. 54-58)?

3. Retell Paul's sermon on Mars Hill (Acts 17:22-34) as if you're talking to a non-Christian (pp. 56-57).

4. Why is reminding people of God's law an important part of evangelism (pp. 58-62)?

5. From Romans 7:7-13 and Philippians 3:4-11, explain what made Paul despair of self-sufficiency (self-generated righteousness) (p. 66).

6. Sin separates us from God and enslaves us. Give examples from Scripture and from your own experience (pp. 66-67).

7. What is the "dilemma" of which people must have some comprehension by the end of point 3? Why do we emphasize "bad news" when the gospel is "good news" (pp. 54, 67)?

8. What are some stories from Scripture and your life that exhibit the love of Christ (pp. 69-70)?

9. What is the significance for our salvation of Christ's keeping all of God's law (Rom 8:1-4) (pp. 72-74)?

10. Explain what Psalm 51 teaches about repentance and why it is a good indicator of whether a person might be ready to respond to Christ (p. 76).

11. What is justification by faith alone, and why is it central to evangelism and to living the Christian life (pp. 77-78)?

12. According to 1 John, what are the five marks of regeneration? The Bible also summarizes the basis for assurance of salvation by three indicators. What are these (pp. 79, 82)?

Assignment: Continue to use the "Procedure for Learning the 'Come Home' Diagram" in appendix B. Role-play this with someone. Read chapter 3. Use appendix A.VIII and A.IX.

STUDY 4. THE GOSPEL RECOVERED, PART TWO (CHAPTER 3, "GOSPEL TELLING")

1. Explain how the theme "come home" (and the images of a road of life and death, road rules, a separation, bridge, a Father, family and home) provides a biblical basis for linking the five points of the gospel (pp. 84-86).

2. What reasons are given for learning an extensive summary of the gospel, since God often uses a minimal amount of truth when regenerating people?

3. How can knowing a gospel summary hinder or help a person in evangelism (pp. 83-84)?

4. How would you feel about asking a person with whom you've already conversed about Christianity, "Could I take 20 minutes to give you an overview of the theme of the Bible? I think it would help to have a framework for what I'm saying. Afterward you can pinpoint which part you don't understand" (pp.196-97, 231-33)?

5. What contemporary illustrations have you found helpful in communicating particular aspects of the gospel?

6. What Bible stories/verses do you like to use? (Compare "Come Home" Bible references and appendix B.IV.)

7. Would you agree that most Christians have a poor grasp of the content of the gospel, and even less actually express much gospel content when they witness (appendix A.IX)?

8. If the gospel is the power of God for salvation (Rom 1:16), why aren't more of our friends becoming Christians? Review conversations you've had over the last six to twelve months; were they gospel-centered (pp.186-89)?

9. Why do you think we hesitate to ask people to *respond* to Christ (pp. 75-76)?

Assignment: Continue to learn "Come Home" and role-play, and ask two non-Christians, "Can you help me? I'm learning how to better communicate what I believe. Do you have 20 minutes?" Ask them for feedback. Read chapters 4—7.

STUDY 5. TRUE CONVERSION (CHAPTERS 4—7)

1. Many people use the term "carnal Christian" to describe someone who claims to be a Christian but whose life is characterized by disobedience. Is this what 1 Corinthians 3:1-4 is talking about, or is it referring to certain areas of sinful disobedience (pp 79-80, 87-88)?

2. What problem could occur if you misunderstand that conversion is a process (pp. 89-90)?

3. What are six scriptural examples of "partial" conversions (pp. 92-94)?

4. Describe how to help someone evaluate their profession of faith

(1 Cor 13:5) biblically (p. 94; review basis for assurance of salvation, pp. 78-82).

5. From chapter 5 or your own experience, give examples of evangelism that errs by being too intellectual or too neglectful of the mind (truth content) of the gospel.

6. From chapter 6, what problems arise from emotionalism in evangelism? How can we appropriately engage people's emotion with truth?

7. Discuss this quote by Dr. Martyn Lloyd-Jones from chapter 7: "The most serious of all dangers is that of seeking to produce decisions [for Christ] as a result of pressure brought to bear upon the listeners' will" (p. 105).

8. What is the labeling fallacy, and what negative effect does it have (pp. 107-8)?

9. At the end of chapter 7, the author says our evangelism must be directed to the whole person (mind, emotions, will) yet allow that their responses will vary according to each unique personality. Explain (pp. 109-10; see Rom 6:17).

10. The author says that as he grew in his understanding of Scripture, he reinterpreted when his conversion occurred. Do you wish to revise your testimony that you wrote earlier? Explain why or why not (pp. 91, 94, 261, notes 1, 2).

Assignment: Read chapter 8 and appendix D.

STUDY 6. GRACE IS ONLY FOR THE POWERLESS (CHAPTER 8)

1. To what extent has sin affected each aspect of human nature (mind, emotions, will)?

2. Read Luke 15:11-32 and Mark 10:17-27. Instead of obvious sinners, the author chose stories of two people who seemed to be morally good and candidates for God's favor. Explain how these stories show that self-generated salvation is unlikely.

3. Why are the entrance requirements (be holy, be perfect, etc.) into God's kingdom so high? What do you think of the statement, "There will be

no sinners in heaven, only righteous people" (Mt 5:20, 48) (p. 120)?

4. If reliance on good works to gain God's favor is ingrained in human nature, what will root it out (pp. 121-23, 28)?

5. Give examples from your life of how meriting God's favor creeps into the Christian life. What have you found helpful in nailing shut the lid on the coffin of good works?

6. Explain how trusting in good works (self-righteousness) undercuts grace (p. 123).

7. Which of the reasons for believing in free will are you attracted to (p. 125)?

8. Draw the diagram of God's method of salvation (a church with Christ as the door) and explain (p. 127).

10. If the picture of standing in a cemetery preaching to skeletons (Ezek 37:1-10) is an accurate portrayal of evangelism, where must our hope be? How does this affect our methods (p. 128)?

Assignment: Read chapters 9 and 10. Ask a non-Christian friend if you can practice expressing the Simplified Version of "Come Home."

STUDY 7. GOD'S SOVEREIGN GRACE BESTOWS SALVATION (CHAPTERS 9—10)

1. The turning point for the younger son in the parable of the prodigal son (Lk 15:11-24) is when he "comes to his senses." Was this brought about by a logical deduction in his own mind from his desperate situation, or was it by a Holy Spirit-induced admission of the providence of God in his circumstances and of his true guilt? How do his thoughts reveal the supernatural nature of his repentance and faith (pp. 130-32)?

2. Paul was secure in self-righteousness until he understood the implications of which commandment (Rom 7:7-13)? What phrase does he use (Gal 1:13-16) to describe what happened to him internally (cf. Phil 3:4-11 and pp. 133-34)?

3. The Old Testament reiterates the continuing failure of people to obey God from the heart and to keep their spiritual marriage commitment to

him. What new actions by God to solve this problem are promised in Ezekiel 36:25-28 and Hosea 2:14-23 (pp. 134-36)?

4. From the list "Grace to the Rescue" (p. 137), explain how the Trinity works in unity. (All persons of the Godhead have the same ultimate goal, not different ones. Compare chart 1 [view of God], pp. 36-37.) Is salvation only made possible or is it actually procured by the atonement?

5. Conclude this sentence from chapter 10, explaining what it means and how grace differs from love: "Grace only functions as grace when . . ." (p. 139; Rom 11:6).

6. Why do people resist teaching God's sovereignty in salvation (pp. 140-41)?

7. What do you find interesting in the account of two theological students whose conception of God's autonomy in salvation changed their whole orientation to the Christian life (pp. 141-42)?

8. Is it biblical to say, "I chose Jesus"? Why doesn't everyone respond to the gospel (Rom 9:1-25) (pp. 143-45)?

9. If you pursue the question "Why does God save anyone?" as far as you can in the Bible, what answer is given (pp. 145-47)?

Assignment: Read chapter 11. Spend time in personal worship using the passages from Scripture and hymns. Search your hearts with appendix B.V and B.VI.

STUDY 8. WORSHIP: THE WHOLE-SOULED RESPONSE TO THE GOSPEL OF GRACE (CHAPTER 11)

1. What do most people say is the greatest hindrance they face in witnessing (p. 148)? Give examples from past witnessing attempts.

2. How does a view of a macro-God (vs. micro-) motivate us in witnessing? What positive experiences in witnessing have encouraged you to continue witnessing (pp. 148-51)?

3. Can you identify with the idea that experiencing genuine worship has led you to be an initiator of evangelism and more intentional in witnessing (pp. 151-54, 157)? Explain.

4. How do the doctrines of God's grace in salvation stimulate worship (p. 158)?

5. Explain the following statement: "Worship is the fire (motivating power, fuel) for and the goal of evangelism" (pp. 151-54).

6. Do you agree that evangelism is not number one on God's agenda? What is? Justify your answer (pp. 152-53).

7. The closer we grow to God, the more conscious we become of our sinfulness. Do you identify with the woman who was forgiven much or with Simon who felt he had little to be forgiven? Discuss the story, Luke 7:36-50 (pp. 154-56).

8. The author makes the point that God is not just looking for decisions but is seeking worshipers (Jn 4:23-24). How does the story of the healing of the Samaritan leper illustrate this (Lk 17:11-19)? What has helped you to be a participant and not just a spectator in worship (pp. 154-57)?

9. Define *worship* in your own words. Now compare this with the definition on page 156.

Assignment: Read chapter 12 and appendix A.I. Write your testimony and be ready to give it at the next session (use guidelines in appendix A.II).

STUDY 9. ORDINARY CHRISTIANS CAN WITNESS (CHAPTER 12)

1. Discuss the dilemma that is created by the new definition of *tolerance*. Rehearse the answer you would give when challenged by, "You're intolerant to say that Jesus is the only way to God" (pp. 159-60, 165-67).

2. Philip Ryken posits three types of pluralism—empirical, cherished and philosophical. Explain each of them (pp. 160-63).

3. Can you clearly identify the weak point in the illustration of the three blind men examining an elephant (pp. 164-65)?

4. Define *apologetics*, and distinguish between classical apologetics and presuppositional apologetics (pp. 168-69).

5. The conscience is a key factor in evangelism (Rom 1:14-15). Review how Jesus and Paul reached into the consciences of nonbelievers (pp. 169-71).

6. What are your fears regarding witnessing (2 Cor 4:1-18; 5:11—6:10)? Discuss this passage and appendix A.I (pp. 172-75).

7. Role play your testimony in pairs, giving each other feedback.

Assignment: Take time to pray for two or three non-Christians using the prayer and Bible passages in appendix B, "Come Home: Amplified Version" section called "Prayer For Others." Make a plan to speak to someone about the Lord this week (over lunch? after class or a meeting?). Read chapter 13. Be prepared to participate in role play #3 and #4 in appendix A.VIII.

STUDY 10. HOW TO COMMUNICATE PERSONALLY (CHAPTER 13)

1. Make a list of at least two non-Christians in each of the four relationship categories. List some of their interests and other things you know about them (short-term acquaintances may be difficult). Ask God to give you insight into where they might be spiritually. Pray for them. Use appendix A.VI (pp. 182-86) to help you.

2. What are some phrases you could use to bring up the topic of Jesus with these people (pp. 186-93)? Pray, and plan to initiate the topic of Jesus with them.

3. In pairs or small groups do the role plays in A.VIII, numbers 3 and 4. Use A.IX to help give feedback to each other.

4. Go over your written personal testimony. Express it to two Christians or non-Christians.

5. Pray through the "Plans to Obey" list at the end of this chapter. You may fill it out now or wait till the final study (pp. 206-7).

Assignment: Read appendix A.III-VII and do the worksheets. Pray for others and tell God you are more than just available—you want him to use you in evangelism. Review and practice the "Come Home" diagram with someone. Memorize the "Simplified Version" for use in the next session. Ask a non-Christian friend to give you feedback on your testimony.

STUDY 11. TRAINING MATERIALS FOR LEARNING GOD-CENTERED EVANGELISM PART ONE (APPENDIX A.I-VIII)

1. Discuss "Learning to Say What You Mean," "Being a Good Listener" and

"How to Ask Good Questions" from appendix A.

2. Use the first role play in appendix A.VIII again to sharpen your ability to verbalize the gospel.

3. If you have not already done so, split into small groups and share your plans for witnessing to someone and willingness to be held accountable. Share prayer requests.

Assignment: Read appendix A.IX-XII. Choose two questions from A.X and write an outline of your answers, using the Bible and Christian books to help. Be prepared for all four of the role plays in A.VIII. Your "Plans to Obey" (end of ch. 13) should be ready to hand in.

STUDY 12. TRAINING MATERIALS FOR LEARNING GOD-CENTERED EVANGELISM PART TWO (APPENDIX A.IX-XII)

1. Use appendix A.X and practice in groups of three giving answers. See appendix A.VIII, role play 2. (One or more people should be assigned several questions to research beforehand. Class leader and participants may add additional insights.)

2. Conclude with prayer as a large group or in pairs. Hand in "Plans to Obey" to leader or accountability partner.

Assignment: Implement "Plans to Obey."

Leader: Allow one hour minimum for each session. While a Sunday school setting is possible, allowing $1\frac{1}{2}$ to 2 hours per session is ideal, as it will allow time for discussion and prayer. Build in assignments for practicing evangelism. If contact evangelism (see appendix A.XI) is not feasible, ask for commitments to pray for and speak to (write, phone) friends, relatives and people met during the course of the day.

Appendix D
Doctrine *Is Not an Obscene Word*

Perhaps some will say that "the gospel is a person, not a doctrine." This is a false dichotomy. The living Word and the written Word are not enemies but friends. As much as I agree with presenting the person of Christ, not just flinging concepts at people, Christ must be defined. A contentless Christ will not save anyone. Just as we found that the word *God* is used by people in various ways, similarly *Christ* is redefined to fit people's preconceptions. Biblical illiteracy abounds and the possibility of misleading people about Jesus is real. This means that the written Word is absolutely necessary to explain who Christ is. (In our explanation of who Christ is, we do not pit the Gospels against the apostolic letters. Both are equally inspired. Red-letter Bibles can be misleading—unless all the sentences [not just those of Jesus] are in red!)

Another popular tendency in evangelism is to embrace the results of the science of communication, which says, "People pay most attention to the nonverbal aspect of communication (55%) and then to the tone (38%). Only 7% of the words are remembered." This is a very helpful insight (although the percentages vary with the study), and we should help each other to communicate better. However, these studies cannot measure the powerful effect of words spoken by a person empowered by the Holy Spirit or the words of revelation spoken by writers who were uniquely inspired. This type of speech is "word impregnated with divine creative power" communication. At the risk of being misunderstood, I join with others[1] and say that even prayer can become too emphasized in evangelism to the neglect of the primary task of proclamation.

John Stott, an influential leader in the international Christian community since 1950, has emphasized sound, biblical teaching. In his essay "A Defense of Theological Definition" he writes that he aims

to argue that "evangelical" Christianity is authentic Christianity, true, original and pure, and to demonstrate it from the teaching of Jesus Christ Himself. . . .

Let me . . . try at once to anticipate, and perhaps to disarm, some of my readers' possible criticisms.

The spirit of our age is very unfriendly towards dogmatic people. Folk whose opinions are clearly formulated and strongly held are not popular. A person of conviction, however intelligent, sincere and humble he may be, will be fortunate if he escapes the charge of being a bigot. Nowadays the really great mind is thought to be both broad and open—broad enough to absorb every fresh idea which is presented to it, and open enough to go on doing so *ad infinitum*.

What are we to say to this? We must reply that historic Christianity is essentially dogmatic, because it purports to be a revealed faith. . . .

The second way in which the spirit of the age is unfriendly towards [my aim] . . . concerns the modern hatred of controversy. . . .

Perhaps the best way to insist that controversy is sometimes a painful necessity is to remember that our Lord Jesus Christ Himself was a controversialist. He was not "broad-minded" in the popular sense that He was prepared to countenance any views on any subject. On the contrary, as we are to see in the later chapters of this book, He engaged in continuous debate with the religious leaders of His day, the scribes and Pharisees, the Herodians and Sadducees. He said that He was the truth, that He had come to bear witness to the truth, and that the truth would set His followers free. As a result of His loyalty to the truth, He was not afraid to dissent publicly from official doctrines (if He knew them to be wrong), to expose error, and to warn His disciples of false teachers. He was also extremely outspoken in His language, calling them "blind guides," "wolves in sheep's clothing," "whitewashed tombs" and even a "brood of vipers."

The apostles also were controversialists, as is plain from the New Testament Epistles, and they appealed to their readers "to contend for the faith which was once for all delivered to the saints." Like their Lord and Master they found it necessary to warn the churches of false teachers and to urge them to stand firm in the truth. . . .

Revealed truth is thus likened to a building, and the church's calling is to be its "foundation" (holding it firm so that it is not moved) and its "pillar" (holding it aloft so that all may see it). However hostile the spirit of the age may be to an outspoken confession of the truth, the church has no liberty to reject its God-given task.[2]

Let's take one example of a controversial topic in Scripture: *election*—the truth of God's free, sovereign, unconditional choosing by grace of all who will be saved. Dr. John Piper believes in the importance of coming to a conclusion about this significant teaching of Christ and the apostles, and shares the following seven reasons for his view:

First, this truth [election] is biblical. It is biblical not only in being found once in Scripture, but in being found throughout Scripture. . . .

Second, this truth humbles sinners and exalts of the glory of God. This was the point of 1 Corinthians 1:26-31: "God *chose* . . . so that no human being might boast in the presence of God . . . [but] let him who boasts boast in the Lord.". . .

Third, this truth tends to preserve the church from slipping toward false philosophies of life. History seems to show that this is so [in the development of Unitarianism and universalism].

Fourth, this truth is the good news of a salvation that is not just offered but effected. Election is the guarantee that God not only invites people to be delivered, but also actually delivers them. "You call his name Jesus because *he shall save his people* from their sins" (Mt 1:21). . . .

Fifth, this truth enables us to own up to the demands for holiness in the Scripture and yet have assurance of salvation. . . .

Sixth, this truth opens us to the overwhelming experience of being loved personally with the unbreakable electing love of God. . . .

Seventh, this truth gives hope for effective evangelism and guarantees the triumph of Christ's mission in the end. Nothing I have said should be taken to imply that the urgency of evangelism is lessened. Evangelism and missions are not imperiled by the biblical truth of election, but empowered by it, and their triumph is secured by it.[3]

Notes

INTRODUCTION: THE WHOLE GOSPEL TO THE WHOLE PERSON WHOLLY BY
GRACE BY WHOLE PEOPLE

[1]Carl F. H. Henry, "The Purpose of God," in *The New Face of Evangelicalism,* ed. C. René Padilla (Downers Grove, Ill.: InterVarsity Press, 1976), p. 31.

[2]Kenneth S. Latourette, *A History of the Expansion of Christianity* (New York: Harper & Brothers, 1944), 1:230.

CHAPTER 1: PERSONAL WITNESS AS PLANTING AND WATERING

[1]Kenneth Prior, *The Gospel in a Pagan Society* (Downers Grove, Ill.: InterVarsity Press, 1975), p. 51.

[2]There are three primary words in the New Testament for proclaiming the Christian message: *euanggelizesthai* (tell good news), *keryssein* (proclaim) and *martyrein* (bear witness). The English words *evangelism* and *gospel* come from the same Greek word: *euanggelion.* This word is composed of two words meaning "good" and "news." Therefore, to evangelize is to set forth the good news. The context usually indicates that it includes a demonstration, or doing, as well as a proclamation, or saying. For a thorough study of the three words, see chapter three in Michael Green's *Evangelism in the Early Church* (Grand Rapids, Mich.: Eerdmans, 1970).

[3]J. I. Packer, *Evangelism and the Sovereignty of God* (Downers Grove, Ill.: InterVarsity Press, 1961), p. 56; see also pp. 37-45.

[4]D. Martyn Lloyd-Jones, *The Presentation of the Gospel* (London: Inter-Varsity Fellowship, 1949), pp. 6-7.

[5]C. S. Lewis, *The Lion, the Witch and the Wardrobe* (New York: Macmillan, 1953), pp. 149-51, my emphasis.

CHAPTER 2: THE GOSPEL REDUCED

[1]"Truly the essence of the apostolic method was not some all-consuming effort to reach as many different people as possible with the message, but rather, subject to both the leading and enablement of the Holy Spirit, the first-century Christians labored in a strategic center until a nucleus of believers was formed into a local church. Evangelization was not some truncated message of the plan of salvation, but a declaration of the whole counsel of God. It was then left to the local company of Christians to maintain continuing evangelism in their community" (C. Stacey Woods, "God's Initiative and Ours," *I.F.E.S. Journal* [1966]: 4).

[2]J. I. Packer, *Evangelism and the Sovereignty of God* (Downers Grove, Ill.: InterVarsity Press, 1961), pp. 47-49.

[3]Some roots are found in the techniques developed by the revivalist Charles Finney.

[4]This is not to say that we shouldn't rejoice whenever Christ is preached (even if the motives are wrong), as Paul did (Phil 1:15-18). But when there is a distortion of Christ and his salvation, we must object, as Paul also did (Gal 1:6-9).

[5]"Meet My Friend" (Westchester, Ill.: Good News Publishers, n.d.), n.p.

[6]A. W. Tozer, *The Old Cross and the New* (Harrisburg, Penn.: Christian Publications, n.d.), n.p.

[7]George Sweeting, *What Is Your Favorite Game?* (Chicago: Moody Press, n.d.), n.p.

[8]Tozer, *Old Cross*, n.p.

[9]David T. Smith, "You're a Beautiful Person" (Chicago: Moody Press, n.d.), n.p.

[10]John Blanchard, *Ultimate Questions* (Durham, England: Evangelical Press, 1987).

[11]Tim Keller, "Brimstone for the Broadminded," *Christianity Today*, July 13, 1998, p. 65.

[12]Mike Yaconelli, "The Safety of Fear," *The Door*, September/October 1993, n.p.

[13]Francis A. Schaeffer, *The God Who Is There* (Downers Grove, Ill.: InterVarsity Press, 1969), p. 169.

[14]It is interesting to note that within Pentecostal and Third World circles some of these same themes are being sounded. Juan Carlos Ortiz of Argentina contends for an evangelism that is not me-centered, calls for obedience to Christ as Lord and refuses to call people Christians who show none of the biblical distinctives. See his *Disciple* (Carol Stream, Ill.: Creation House, 1975), pp. 11-17.

[15]Walt Chantry, *Today's Gospel—Authentic or Synthetic?* (London: Banner of Truth, 1970), p. 17.

CHAPTER 3: THE GOSPEL RECOVERED

[1]See Michael Green, *Evangelism in the Early Church* (Grand Rapids, Mich.: Eerdmans, 1970), chaps. 2-5, and Kenneth Prior, *The Gospel in a Pagan Society* (Downers Grove, Ill.: InterVarsity Press, 1975).

[2]C. S. Lewis uses the powerful imagery of Aslan the lion to convey a biblical view of God. "But as for Aslan himself, the beavers and the children didn't know what to do or say when they saw him. People who have not been in Narnia sometimes think that a thing cannot be good and terrible at the same time" (C. S. Lewis, *The Lion, the Witch, and the Wardrobe* [New York: Collier, 1970], pp. 116-17).

[3]"The law is not to be rejected because a man has no power to keep it. When the rejection of the law is argued on this ground, it is often forgotten that, similarly, man has no power to obey the gospel. The command to believe is as impossible as the command to obey, and so the Gospel seems to speak just as impossible things as does the law. Absence of ability does not infer absence of obligation. . . . But it is an unreasonable thing to conceive of the law apart from the Spirit of God, and then to compare it with the Gospel for if the Gospel itself—even its promises of mercy and forgiveness—were to be thought of apart from the Spirit, it would achieve nothing: indeed, by itself it would be as much a dead letter as the law. But neither the law nor Gospel is a dead letter, for the Holy Spirit makes use of both in a saving manner" (Ernest Kevan, *Moral Law* [Grand Rapids, Mich.: Sovereign Grace, 1971], pp. 10-11).

[4]Rebecca Manley Pippert, *Out of the Saltshaker* (Downers Grove, Ill.: InterVarsity Press, 1999), chaps. 4-6.

[5]John Bunyan, *Pilgrim's Progress in Today's English* (Chicago: Moody Press, 1964), pp. 32-33.

[6]For an excellent and readable discussion of the relation of the Christian to the law, see Horatius Bonar, *God's Way of Holiness* (Chicago: Moody Press, n.d.) and Walt Chantry, *God's Right-*

eous Kingdom (Edinburgh: Banner of Truth, 1980).

[7]J. I. Packer, *Evangelism and the Sovereignty of God* (Downers Grove, Ill.: InterVarsity Press, 1961), pp. 60-61.

[8]Ibid., pp. 62-63.

[9]I owe these three points to an unpublished sermon on repentance by Rev. Al Martin of Trinity Baptist Church, Montville, New Jersey.

[10]Francis A. Schaeffer, *Death in the City* (Downers Grove, Ill.: InterVarsity Press, 1969), pp. 70-71.

[11]Lee Strobel, "How Can I Share My Faith with Others?" in *This We Believe*, ed. John N. Akers, John H. Armstrong and John D. Woodbridge (Grand Rapids, Mich.: Zondervan, 2000), p. 198.

[12]Packer, *Evangelism and the Sovereignty of God*, p. 71.

[13]Robert Horn, *Go Free* (Downers Grove, Ill.: InterVarsity Press, 1976), pp. 117-19. Compare Horatius Bonar, *God's Way of Peace* (Chicago: Moody Press, n.d.), John Owen, *Justification by Faith* (Grand Rapids, Mich.: Sovereign Grace, 1971) and R. C. Sproul, *Faith Alone* (Grand Rapids, Mich.: Baker, 1995).

[14]"True believers may have the assurance of their salvation diverse ways shaken, diminished, and intermitted; as by negligence in preserving of it; by failing into some special sin which woundeth the conscience and grieveth the Spirit; by some sudden or vehement temptation; by God's withdrawing the light of His countenance, and suffering even such as fear Him to walk in darkness and have no light" (Westminster Confession, chap. 28, sec. 4).

[15]A third type of person would be someone who lacks assurance simply because they do not believe in the doctrine of assurance. That is, they do not think Scripture teaches even the possibility of a person knowing with certainty they are redeemed and will be taken to heaven. They dismiss such ideas as conjecture and pride.

[16]G. I. Williamson, *The Westminster Confession of Faith: A Study Guide* (Philadelphia: Presbyterian & Reformed, 1964), p. 133.

[17]Ronald Wallace, *Calvin's Doctrine of the Christian Life* (Grand Rapids, Mich.: Eerdmans, 1962).

[18]John Donne, "Ravished by God," *Holy Sonnets*.

[19]Green, *Evangelism in the Early Church*, p. 70; see also p. 250.

CHAPTER 4: PROFESSORS BUT NOT POSSESSORS

[1] John Piper, "Letter to a Friend Concerning the So-Called 'Lordship Salvation,'" in *The Pleasures of God* (Portland: Multnomah Publishers, 1991), pp. 278-305. Cf. John F. MacArthur Jr., *The Gospel According to Jesus* (Grand Rapids, Mich: Zondervan, 1988), chap. 20 and appendixes 1 and 2.

[2]The term *conversion* is often defined as the individual's initial response of faith and repentance. Sometimes the Puritans used terms to describe the order of various aspects of the Spirit's work. A sinner went from awakening (a new sensitivity to God) to seeking (looking for answers) to conviction (felt guilt) to conversion (faith and repentance).

[3]Michael Green, *Evangelism in the Early Church* (Grand Rapids, Mich.: Eerdmans, 1970), pp. 159-61, 204-6.

[4]Joseph Hart, "Come, Ye Sinners, Poor and Wretched," 1759.

[5]These are adapted from Peter Masters, *Physician of Souls* (London: Wakeman, 1976), pp. 110-25.

CHAPTER 5: THE WHOLE GOSPEL TO THE MIND

[1]Even true Christians entering the secular campus have a rough time, especially if their religious background has emphasized only feelings and fellowship. Nevertheless, if God calls them to this situation, spectacular growth often follows.

²All doubt is not sinful. See Os Guinness, *In Two Minds* (Downers Grove, Ill.: InterVarsity Press, 1976).

³Bernard Ramm, *The Witness of the Spirit* (Grand Rapids, Mich.: Eerdmans, 1960), p. 89.

⁴John Stott, *Balanced Christianity* (Downers Grove, Ill.: InterVarsity Press, 1975), p. 13. See also John Stott's excellent book *Your Mind Matters* (Downers Grove, Ill.: InterVarsity Press, 1973).

⁵Calvin taught the priority of knowledge in faith but did not advocate spiritual intellectualism. He felt that the will could not act nor the emotions respond until both had been enlightened by the intellect (Abraham Kuyper, *The Work of the Holy Spirit* [Grand Rapids, Mich.: Eerdmans, 1975], p. 263).

Chapter 6: The Whole Gospel to the Emotions

¹John Stott, *Balanced Christianity* (Downers Grove, Ill.: InterVarsity Press, 1975), pp. 17-18. However, even in some of the most theologically orthodox groups there is a paucity of praise. Some of the Scripture turned into songs by the Jesus People and Pentecostals can help us learn how to weave emotion together with music, focusing on grace.

²For example, Edward T. Welch, *When People Are Big and God Is Small* (Phillipsburg, N.J.: Presbyterian & Reformed, 1997) and the writings of James Dobson, David Powlison and Paul David Tripp.

Chapter 7: The Whole Gospel to the Will

¹Andre Bustanoby, "An Open Letter to Jane Ordinary," *Christianity Today*, March 16, 1967, p. 14.

²"It is the citadel of the will which has to be stormed, and if he is wise, the evangelist will approach this fortress neither by the avenue of the mind alone, nor by the avenue of the heart alone, but by both" (John Stott, *Fundamentalism and Evangelism* [Grand Rapids, Mich.: Eerdmans, 1959], p. 58).

³D. Martyn Lloyd-Jones, *The Presentation of the Gospel* (London: Inter-Varsity Fellowship, 1949), p. 9. I owe many of the thoughts in this paragraph to this out-of-print, British IVF booklet.

⁴For a helpful discussion see J. I. Packer, *Evangelism and the Sovereignty of God* (Downers Grove, Ill.: InterVarsity Press, 1961).

⁵J. I. Packer, in the introduction to John Owen, *The Death of Death* (London: Banner of Truth, 1959), pp. 1-25.

⁶Compare D. Martyn Lloyd-Jones, *Spiritual Depression* (Grand Rapids, Mich.: Eerdmans, 1965), chap. 4, "Mind, Heart and Will," pp. 85-86.

⁷John Bunyan, *Pilgrim's Progress in Today's English* (Chicago: Moody Press, 1964), pp. 85-86. See also the conversations with Hopeful and Ignorance.

⁸Often the New Testament represents conversion in terms of our response not to a person but to the truth. Conversion is to obey the truth (Rom 2:8; 6:17; 1 Pet 1:22), to believe the truth (2 Thess 2:12-13) and to acknowledge or come to know the truth (Jn 8:32; 1 Tim 2:4; 4:3; 2 Tim 2:25; Tit 1:1; 1 Jn 2:21). Similarly, to preach the gospel is not to just proclaim Christ but to manifest the truth (2 Cor 4:2). See John Stott, *Your Mind Matters* (Downers Grove, Ill.: InterVarsity Press, 1973), pp. 49-50.

⁹C. John Miller, *Powerful Evangelism for the Powerless*, rev. ed. (Phillipsburg, N.J.: Presbyterian & Reformed, 1977), pp. 129-30.

Chapter 8: Grace Is Only for the Powerless

¹A fictitious name and composite story from several incidents.

²Henri Nouwen, *The Return of the Prodigal Son* (New York: Doubleday, 1994), pp. 72, 74, 76.

[3]Job—Job 1:21; 2:10; 40:8; 42:2-6. David—Psalm 115:3. Solomon—Proverbs 21:1. Jesus—John 5:21; 6:44-65. Paul—Romans 9:20-21; 11:35-36.

[4]James Montgomery Boice, Whatever Happened to the Gospel of Grace? (Wheaton, Ill.: Crossway, 2001), pp. 108, 121.

[5]Joseph M. Stowell, "The Evangelical Family: Its Blessings and Boundaries," in This We Believe, ed. John N. Akers, John H. Armstrong and John D. Woodbridge (Grand Rapids, Mich.: Zondervan, 2000), p. 215.

[6]"When Jonathan Edwards spoke of will as 'the mind of choosing,' he meant that we make choices according to what we deem preferable in terms of the options before us. Edwards concluded that we always choose according to the inclination that is strongest at the moment. This is a crucial insight into the will. It means that every choice we make has an antecedent cause. Our choices are not 'spontaneous,' arising out of nothing. There is a reason for every choice we make" (R. C. Sproul, Grace Unknown [Grand Rapids, Mich., Baker, 1997], p. 131). "Edwards' second major contribution was his discussion of what he called 'motives.' He pointed out that the mind is not neutral. It thinks some things are better than other things, and because it thinks some things are better than other things it always chooses the better things. If a person thought one course of action was better than another and yet chose the less desirable alternative, the person would be irrational. This means . . . that the will is always free. It is free to choose . . . what the mind thinks best.

"But what does the mind think best? Here we get to the heart of the matter. When confronted with God, the mind of a sinner never thinks that following or obeying God is a good choice. His will is free to choose God. Nothing is stopping him. But his mind does not regard submission to God as desirable. . . .

"Certainly, anyone who wants to come to Christ may come to him. That is why Edwards insisted that the will is not bound. But who is it who wills to come? The answer is: No one, except those in whom the Holy Spirit has already performed the entirely irresistible work of the new birth so that, as a result of this miracle the spiritually blind eyes of the natural man are opened to see God's truth, and the totally depraved mind of the sinner, which in itself has no spiritual understanding, is renewed to embrace the Lord Jesus Christ as Savior. This is teaching that very few professing Christians in our day, including the vast majority of evangelicals, believe or understand, which is another reason, perhaps the major reason, why they find grace boring" (Boice, Whatever Happened, pp. 115-16).

[7]For a fuller discussion of the human will and of how our moral inability does not release us from moral responsibility, see the appropriate chapters in Boice, Whatever Happened; Sproul, Grace Unknown; John Gerstner, A Primer on Free Will (Phillipsburg, N.J.: Presbyterian & Reformed, 1982); John Cheeseman, Saving Grace (Edinburgh: Banner of Truth, 1999); A. W. Pink, The Sovereignty of God (Edinburgh: Banner of Truth, 1961).

[8]Does sovereign grace dehumanize? No, it humanizes. A person who experiences the new creation that results from regeneration says, "I have become more myself than I ever thought possible. God, who has searched me and known me, has revealed to me who I really am (Ps 139). The admonition to 'know thyself' is futile without knowing God. At last, feeling at home with my Maker, I am at peace with myself." Contrast this with the identity confusion that prevails today and the promotion of a sovereign self that aims at self-mastery. Michael Horton describes one manifestation of this as the "therapeutic self." I see myself as good yet needy. Therefore I seek good advice with the goal of recovery, not redemption. The one thing I must not do is violate my true self. The long history of humanity's self-centeredness climaxes in a culture of narcissism. Felt needs mask real needs. When real needs are realized, this worldview has no

answers. Alister McGrath has gleaned from Scripture six images of human need: hunger, thirst, emptiness, loneliness, hopelessness, lostness. Powerful connections can be made when these are traced back to the staggering rupture in our relationship with our Maker.

CHAPTER 9: GOD IS GRACE-FULL

[1]Cornelius Plantinga Jr., quoted in J. I. Packer, "Doing It My Way: Are We Born Rebels?" in *This We Believe,* ed. John N. Akers, John H. Armstrong and John D. Woodbridge (Grand Rapids, Mich.: Zondervan, 2000), p. 44.

[2]John Murray, "Epistle to the Romans" in *New International Commentary on the New Testament,* ed. F. F. Bruce (Grand Rapids, Mich.: Eerdmans, 1968), p. 102.

[3]J. I. Packer, quoted in James Montgomery Boice, *Whatever Happened to the Gospel of Grace?* (Wheaton, Ill.: Crossway, 2001), p. 110.

CHAPTER 10: SOVEREIGN, SAVING GRACE

[1]Jennifer L. Bayne and Sarah E. Hinlicky, "Free to Be Creatures Again," *Christianity Today,* October 23, 2000, pp. 38-44.

[2]John Piper, *The Pleasures of God* (Portland, Ore.: Multnomah Publishers, 1991), p. 272.

CHAPTER 11: WORSHIP

[1]John Piper, *Let the Nations Be Glad* (Grand Rapids, Mich.: Baker, 1993), pp. 11, 38-40.

[2] John Newton, "Let Us Love, and Sing, and Wonder," 1774.

[3]Edmund Clowney, unpublished sermon.

CHAPTER 12: ORDINARY CHRISTIANS CAN WITNESS

[1]*Webster's Encyclopedic Unabridged Dictionary,* s.v. "tolerance." For an in-depth study of this topic, see Stan D. Gaede, *When Tolerance Is No Virtue* (Downers Grove, Ill.: InterVarsity Press, 1993).

[2]Josh McDowell and Bob Hostetler, *The New Tolerance* (Wheaton, Ill.: Tyndale House, 1998), p. 22.

[3]Ibid., p. 41. See also S. D. Gaede, *When Tolerance is No Virtue.*

[4]Philip Graham Ryken, *Is Jesus the Only Way?* (Wheaton, Ill.: Crossway, 1999), pp. 13-16.

[5]Ibid., pp. 30-32. Cf. Donald Carson, *The Gagging of God: Christianity Confronts Pluralism* (Grand Rapids, Mich.: Baker, 1996).

[6]McDowell and Hostetler, *New Tolerance,* p. 95.

[7]Ryken, *Is Jesus the Only Way?* pp. 29-31.

[8]Lee Strobel, *The Case for Faith* (Grand Rapids, Mich.: Zondervan, 2000), p. 217; Harold A. Netland and Keith E. Johnson, "Why Is Religious Pluralism Fun—and Dangerous?" in *Telling the Truth,* ed. D. A. Carson (Grand Rapids, Mich.: Zondervan, 2000), pp. 63-64.

[9]J. I. Packer, "Isn't One Religion as Good as Another?" in *Hard Questions,* ed. Frank Colquhoun (Downers Grove, Ill.: InterVarsity Press, 1977), p. 15.

[10]Packer, "Isn't One Religion," p. 16.

[11]All thought is based on assumptions that cannot be "proved." So as Christians, we begin with God, who reveals truth to us.

[12]Francis A. Schaeffer, *The God Who Is There* (Downers Grove, Ill.: InterVarsity Press, 1969), and Os Guinness, *The Dust of Death* (Downers Grove, Ill.: InterVarsity Press, 1973) are both good for an overview. The many writings of Francis and Edith Schaeffer taken together will beautifully illustrate the balance between taking the mind seriously and humbling it. They also

portray the connection between knowing truth and living out the truth.

[13]There is much handwringing among evangelicals about the need to reinvent evangelism to connect with postmoderns. Yet if there is a tendency to revise the gospel itself and not just the entry points or bridges, beware. Just because "Is it true?" is not the first question many are concerned about, doesn't mean that we compromise presenting objective truth lovingly and winsomely. Postmodernism is amply discussed with its implications for evangelism in D. A. Carson, ed. *Telling the Truth* (Grand Rapids, Mich.: Zondervan, 2000), chaps. 3-5, 9-10, 17, 28; and Douglas Groothuis, *Truth Decay* (Downers Grove, Ill.: InterVarsity Press, 2000) chaps. 3-7.

[14]John Bunyan, *Pilgrim's Progress in Today's English* (Chicago: Moody Press, 1964), pp. 134-35.

[15]C. John Miller, *Basic Guidelines for Witnessing* (Westminster Seminary, class syllabus), pp. 11, 13.

[16]Roger Barrett, "Motives for Witnessing—Good or Evil," *Christianity Today*, July 17, 1970, pp. 12-14.

[17]Miller, *Basic Guidelines*, p. 7.

[18]"We find it difficult to witness because we have not learned to be open. Being real means being free to express ourselves when it is appropriate to do so" (John White, *The Fight* [Downers Grove: InterVarsity Press, 1976], pp. 67-68).

[19]Packer, "Isn't One Religion," pp. 122-25.

[20]C. John Miller, "Evangelism and Prayer" (unpublished paper, no date).

CHAPTER 13: HOW TO COMMUNICATE PERSONALLY

[1]D. Martyn Lloyd-Jones, *The Presentation of the Gospel* (London: InterVarsity Fellowship, 1949), p, 3.

[2]For an evaluation of the results of contemporary mass evangelism, see *Eternity*, September 1977, including C. Peter Wagner, "Who Found It?" pp. 13-19; James F. Engel, "Great Commission or Great Commotion?" p. 14; Lynn Holman, "Here's Living Proof," p. 19.

[3]For a readable discussion on being yourself and emulating Jesus in evangelism, see Rebecca Manley Pippert, *Out of the Saltshaker* (Downers Grove, Ill.: InterVarsity Press, 1999).

[4]For example, E1 = evangelism among your own people (Jerusalem and Judea); E2 = evangelism among people different from you, yet still of your language and country (Samaria); E3 = evangelism among people who are different in language and race (uttermost parts of the earth) (Donald McGavern and Win Arn, *How to Grow a Church* [Glendale, Calif.: Regal, 1973], pp. 51-53).

[5]Paul Little, "How to Win Souls to Christ," *Presbyterian Journal*, January 13, 1965, p. 10.

[6]Robert Horn, *Go Free* (Downers Grove, Ill.: InterVarsity Press, 1976), pp. 120-21. Some questions leave a wrong impression. For example, "Why not try Jesus?" "Can you think of any reason to not become a Christian?"

[7]Paul Little, "How to Win Souls," p. 37.

[8]James Kennedy, *Evangelism Explosion* (Wheaton, Ill.: Tyndale House, 1970), p.21.

[9]I owe the material in this section to Donald C. Smith, "Conversational Evangelism," unpublished paper. It can also be found in Pippert, *Out of the Saltshaker*, pp. 145-48.

[10]C. H. Dodd, in Michael Green, *Evangelism in the Early Church* (Grand Rapids, Mich.: Eerdmans, 1970), pp. 60-64.

[11]"A Christian who perseveres with a stereotyped approach may meet with some success. Sooner or later he will presumably encounter someone to whom the way in which he presents the gospel applies. Furthermore, knowing what we do about the sovereign grace of God, we may

expect him to see that a dedicated evangelist will be rewarded by a contact that fits his approach" (Kenneth Prior, *The Gospel in a Pagan Society* [Downers Grove, Ill.: InterVarsity Press, 1975], p. 41).

[12]J. I. Packer, "What Is Evangelism?" in *Theological Perspectives on Church Growth,* ed. Harvie Conn (Philadelphia: Presbyterian & Reformed, 1976), p. 91.

[13]Lausanne Covenant, clause 4.

[14]Bernard Ramm, *The Witness of the Spirit* (Grand Rapids, Mich.: Eerdmans, 1960), p. 71.

[15]Lloyd-Jones, *The Presentation of the Gospel,* p. 15.

[16] I'm not reinstating the error of a secular/sacred worldview but promoting the priority in our daily lives of a verbal proclamation of the gospel by all believers. The goodness of God (common grace) which pervades the non-believers life enables us to deeply appreciate their contributions and links us together in many endeavors. Yet, the purpose of God's goodness is to lead them and us to repentance—that is, to Christ (Rom 2:4). We should be articulating this.

[17]Bessie Porter Head, "O Breath of Life," 1914.

APPENDIX A: TRAINING MATERIALS FOR LEARNING GOD-CENTERED EVANGELISM

[1]"Ask, Don't Tell," *Christian Herald,* August 1966.

[2]Allen Harris, unpublished paper.

APPENDIX D: *DOCTRINE* IS NOT AN OBSCENE WORD

[1]John Piper, *Let the Nations Be Glad* (Grand Rapids, Mich.: Baker, 1993), p. 62.

[2]John Stott, "A Defense of Theological Definition," in *Christ the Controversialist* (Downers Grove, Ill.: InterVarsity Press, 1972), pp. 13-26.

[3]John Piper, *The Pleasures of God* (Portland, Ore.: Multnomah Publishers, 1991), pp. 142-49.

Permissions